Asian Perspectives on Digital Culture

In Asia, amidst its varied levels of economic development, diverse cultural traditions, and political regimes, the internet and mobile communications are increasingly used in every aspect of life. Yet the analytical frames used to understand the impact of digital media on Asia predominantly originate from the Global North, neither rooted in Asia's rich philosophical traditions nor reflective of the sociocultural practices of this dynamic region. This volume examines digital phenomena and its impact on Asia by drawing on specifically Asian perspectives. Contributors apply a variety of Asian theoretical frameworks including *guanxi*, face, *qing*, *dharma*, and *karma*. With chapters focusing on emerging digital trends in Australia, China, Hong Kong, India, Japan, Malaysia, Korea, Philippines, Singapore, and Taiwan, the book presents compelling and diverse research on identity and selfhood, spirituality, social networking, corporate image, and national identity as shaped by and articulated through digital communication platforms.

Sun Sun Lim is an Associate Professor at the Department of Communications and New Media and Assistant Dean for Research at the Faculty of Arts and Social Sciences, National University of Singapore. She studies the social implications of technology domestication by young people and families, charting the ethnographies of their internet and mobile phone use, publishing more than 50 monographs, journal articles, and book chapters. She serves on the editorial boards of the *Journal of Computer Mediated Communication, Journal of Children and Media, Communication, Culture & Critique,* and *Mobile Media & Communication.*

Cheryll Ruth Soriano is an Associate Professor of Communication at the De La Salle University in the Philippines. She is interested in the social and political implications of new media, and she has published papers exploring the multiple intersections of cultural politics and activism, multiculturalism, ritual, and new media engagement in developing societies. Her recent works appear in international journals such as *Media, Culture & Society* and *Communication, Culture & Critique,* as well as edited volumes.

Routledge Advances in Internationalizing Media Studies

Edited by Daya Thussu, University of Westminster

Asian Perspectives on Digital Culture

Emerging Phenomena,
Enduring Concepts

Edited by
Sun Sun Lim and
Cheryll Ruth R. Soriano

Routledge
Taylor & Francis Group

NEW YORK AND LONDON

First published 2016
by Routledge
711 Third Avenue, New York, NY 10017

and by Routledge
2 Park Square, Milton Park, Abingdon, Oxon OX14 4RN

Routledge is an imprint of the Taylor & Francis Group, an informa business

Library of Congress Cataloging-in-Publication Data

Names: Lim, Sun Sun, 1972– editor. | Soriano, Cheryll Ruth R.,
1977– editor. | Lim, Sun Sun, 1972– Digital giant awakens.
Container of (work):
Title: Asian perspectives on digital culture: emerging phenomena, enduring
concepts / edited by Sun Sun Lim and Cheryll Ruth R. Soriano.
Description: New York: Routledge, 2016. | Series: Routledge advances in
internationalizing media studies; 15 | Includes bibliographical
references and index.
Identifiers: LCCN 2015046751
Subjects: LCSH: Information society—Asia. | Digital media—Social
aspects—Asia. | Social media—Asia.
Classification: LCC HN655.2.I56 A77 2016 | DDC 302.23/1095—dc23
LC record available at http://lccn.loc.gov/2015046751

ISBN: 978-1-138-84232-8 (hbk)
ISBN: 978-1-315-73165-0 (ebk)

Typeset in Sabon
by codeMantra

To our parents, who taught us about our Asian traditions, and to Kai Ryn, Kai Wyn, and Nicole, future custodians of our shared heritage.

Contents

Figures and Tables

Figures

Tables

Part I

Overview

1 A (Digital) Giant Awakens— Invigorating Media Studies with Asian Perspectives

Sun Sun Lim and Cheryll Ruth R. Soriano

The Emergence of Digital Asia

Digital, networked media have been embraced by countries around the globe, and Asia is at the very forefront of this trend. Amidst the region's diverse cultural traditions and political systems, internet and mobile communication are increasingly deployed in every aspect of life, instigating novel modes of interaction and collaboration and birthing technological breakthroughs and innovative applications (Lim & Goggin, 2014). The region's rapid economic growth and its youthful and increasingly well-educated populace have catalyzed the adoption, consumption, appropriation, and production of digital media content and new technology.

Indeed, Asia's internet users constitute just under half of the world's internet population at 45.6% (Internet World Statistics, 2015a). Chinese, Japanese, Arabic, and Korean are among the top ten most used languages on the web and Chinese speakers alone form almost a quarter (23.2%) of the world's internet population (Internet World Statistics, 2015b). Besides the sheer magnitude of Asia's online population, the relative youth and technophily of Asian consumers have contributed to an insatiable appetite for internet-related products and services (Lim, Sison, & Kim, 2008). The result is a boost in domestic innovation in information technology (IT), considerable growth in the quantity and quality of the region's IT clusters (Parthasarathy & Aoyama, 2006; Tseng, 2009; J. Wang, Cheng, & Ganapati, 2012), and a thriving start-up ecosystem (Anjum, 2014). Asian countries that first cut their teeth in electronics production are now making the most of technological leapfrogging (Rasiah, Xiao-Shan, & Chandran Govindaraju, 2014) to generate trend-setting innovations in social media (S. Chen, Zhang, Lin, & Lv, 2011), online games (Jin, 2010), mobile commerce (Zhang & Dodgson, 2007) and mobile health (Ganapathy & Ravindra, 2008), just to name a few.

Technology penetration is further bolstered in many Asian countries by concerted state support in educational initiatives and information and communication technology (ICT) infrastructure (Baskaran & Muchie, 2006; Franda, 2002; Wilson, 2004; Yue, 2006). Notably, though, the region is underscored by rising income inequalities, varying internet governance systems, and geographical diversity that translate into striking variations and experiences in internet and mobile access (Cortada, 2012). Widening rural-urban divides (Fan, Chen-Kang, & Mukherjee, 2005; Gugler, 2004) and migrant labor flows within and beyond Asia (Athukorala, 2006; Wickramasekera, 2002) have also generated new practices in person-to-person, business-to-business and state-citizenry communication, generating demands for novel services that ride on the enhanced online and mobile networks.

Underlying this bustling digital landscape is Asia's rich tapestry of history. The region is home to some of the world's oldest, most advanced civilizations, with lasting legacies of artistic, cultural, and scientific innovation of widespread influence. Asian philosophical traditions such as Indian, Chinese, Japanese, Buddhist and Islamic have also stood the test of time, serving as the foundational principles of governance, education, social interaction, and enterprise. The transformations in Asia's increasingly digitized sociotechnological landscape are as much shaping, as being shaped by, these enduring cultural and philosophical traditions. Yet the analytical frames used to understand the impact of digital media on Asia predominantly originate from the Global North, neither rooted in Asia's sophisticated intellectual heritage nor reflective of the sociocultural practices of this dynamic region. This edited volume seeks to remedy this imbalance by assembling the work of media scholars who use Asian concepts and precepts to understand, interpret, and explain media appropriation in the rapidly changing digital media landscape. In so doing, this volume aims to internationalize media studies by infusing critical research topics and established theoretical frames with Asian perspectives.

The Internationalization Imperative

This push toward the internationalization of media studies is by no means new. Many scholars have long called for more sedulous efforts to advance this cause. Thussu (2009a) traced the evolutionary trajectory of media studies and observed that three critical interventions have been undertaken to broaden the field: the first with perspectives from feminism, and the second from race and ethnicity. He argues that internationalization is the third key intervention as the globalization of media and higher education warrants enhancing media studies with global perspectives, "making it imperative to invest in new research angles, approaches and methodologies" (Thussu, 2009a, p. 3). Similarly, Curran and Park (2000) recognized the intensification of globalization as an impetus for 'de-Westernising' media studies, while Goggin and McLelland (2009) urged scholars to venture beyond Anglophone paradigms.

While such calls for greater diversity of intellectual perspectives have resonated, internationalization has been slow to gain momentum. Notably, significant impediments stand in the way of an Asia-centered and Asia-driven internationalization of media studies. Several issues need to be resolved, or acknowledged in the first instance, before a distinct shift from

Anglo-American domination of the discipline can be achieved. First, curricula, syllabi, and pedagogies have to be made far more inclusive and international (Thussu, 2009b). Presently, higher education and scholarship in media and communication worldwide, including in Asia, are predominantly framed by Western paradigms (Dissanayake, 1988, 2009a; Erni & Chua, 2005; Goggin & McLelland, 2009) that fail to accommodate historically- and culturally-specific imaginaries of technology (Goggin, 2011).

Second, a culture of knowledge and information sharing across nations needs to be developed and actively sustained in Asia. Unlike in the U.S. where reliable data on media use is made available by independent institutions such as Pew Research Center, or in Europe where EU-funded studies generate regional data, what little pan-Asian data available is neither particularly comprehensive nor objective, being often produced by market research companies with specific commercial agenda. Currently, different Asian countries fund research captured only in their native languages. Such nationally-defined and locally-focused research effectively resides in silos and fail to inform, influence or initiate meaningful comparative research. Instead, there should be a concerted effort to exploit digital communication platforms for intra-regional exchange of data and knowledge for greater cross-fertilization of ideas with a view towards more broadly grounded theorization. Failing which, Asian researchers will be unable to engage in cultural synthesis and chart new directions in thinking (G. Wang & Shen, 2000).

Third, a key obstacle to more active knowledge sharing within Asia is linguistic differences. While there is an active pool of media and communication scholars in Asia, those who publish in English form a significantly smaller group. The research conducted by these two groups remains quite discrete, resulting in very little mutual influence. By dint of their Anglophone bent, Asian scholars who write in English are likely to have been schooled in the West, thereby being more receptive towards Western theoretical concepts, more inclined to write in a manner that resonates with a Western audience, and seek international endorsement by publishing in high impact English journals. This inclination is exacerbated by the growing interest in global rankings of universities that assess research output on the basis of citation counts and impact factor indices (Hazelkorn, 2015). Conversely, scholars who publish in Asian languages may be more inclined to incorporate Asian concepts into their analytical endeavors, possibly developing new paradigms that will unfortunately fall outside the radar of the Anglophone academic world. Such trends contribute to more entrenched domination of Western concepts in research on media and communication in Asia. We propose that the Western domination of Asian communication research can be stemmed if more active attempts are made to translate work in Asian languages into English. When more resources are channelled into increasing the exposure of such works, Asian and international scholars alike will enjoy access to a wider body of research that incorporates a more encompassing range of theoretical, cultural and empirical insights, and media and communication research will be the richer for it.

Encouragingly, more scholars are steering Asian academics towards drawing inspiration from Asian cultures to develop theoretical concepts, expanding the geographical scope of research, actively juxtaposing and comparing different Asian cultures, infusing theoretical frames with historical dimensions and multiple perspectives and engaging with metatheoretical issues (G.-M. Chen, 2006; Miike & Chen, 2006). At the same time, the study of media and communication in Asia is intensifying, with tertiary programs being offered and students enrolled in unprecedented numbers (Cheung, 2009). Media and communication research in and around the region is also thriving, with a growing selection of communication journals and book series that adopt an explicitly Asian focus and the existence of more than 12 professional associations and research institutes that concentrate on Asian communication studies (G.-M. Chen & Miike, 2006). Asian representation at international communication and media studies conferences and communication publications by Asian scholars are also on the ascent.

Imaginaries of Asian Digital Cultures and Modernities

The concepts 'Asian' and 'Asian digital cultures' or a set of cultures forged from core beliefs and experiences unique to a geographically vast region has been the subject of active intellectual debate (Dissanayake, 2003, 2009a, 2009b; Massey & Chang, 2002; Miike, 2006, 2007; G. Wang & Kuo, 2010). Increasingly, the use of the internet and digital technologies accompanied by the rapid movement of people and ideas across physical and virtual spaces intensifies the overlapping of cultures and spaces for cultural articulation, production, and belonging. These continuing global flows of culture, technology, media, finance, and ideology, which Appadurai (1990) has earlier conceptualized as "scapes" are promoting ethnic, cultural, religious, and linguistic diversity even within national boundaries. These flows create "large and complex repertoires of images, narratives and *ethnoscapes*" that may alienate people from the direct experiences of geographically based metropolitan life and lead them to construct imagined worlds and communities (Appadurai, 1990, pp. 298–299). As the world becomes more enmeshed through global networks and imaginaries, the divisions between inside and outside, as well as between Asia and the West, appear to be more blurry and problematic. Further, as G. Wang and Kuo (2010) argued, with globalization and Western modernity driving transcultural adaptation, and many Asian nations bringing with them long histories of Western colonialism, even the concept of "Asia" itself may be construed as "Western." Here, the concept of Asia may be seen as a rhetorical strategy to construct Asia's "postcolonial relationship with the West" (Dissanayake, 2006; Naisbitt, 1995; Massey & Chang, 2002; see also Sreekumar, this volume).

However, amidst increasing globalization and media flows, many Asians would recognize that certain experiences of media use strongly resonate with locally entrenched and even regionally recognized rituals, histories, or values. Studies on media engagement behavior of migrant communities who are at the center of these rapid flows and "scapes" found that certain norms and values from the homeland continue to characterize their media usage or influence their "hybrid" identities (Durham, 2004, Komito, 2011; Mandaville, 2001). Further, despite the growth of global media products and markets, social, cultural, political and familial forces impinge upon Asian digital practices (Arora, 2010; Doron, 2012; Erni & Spires, 2005; Iwabuchi, 2005; Jin, 2010; Lim & Goggin, 2014). Past research has also shown the significant contribution of engaging indigenous Asian concepts of social capital (e.g., *'guanxi'* [Chinese]; *'sadharanikana'* [Indian]; or *'uchi-soto'* [Japanese]) as alternative frames by which to understand these modern media practices. Studies on regions beyond Asia have also argued that understanding cultural nuances can help facilitate a less normative theorization of internet engagement. For example, Slater's (2003) work has shown how our understanding of internet use for "freedom" or "unfreedom" needs to be understood within users' context of engagement and can be deepened by bringing in alternative (and less normative) notions of 'internet freedom' from non-American or European perspectives. Thus, while acknowledging that media systems and experiences are increasingly being shaped by global flows and exchanges rapidly fueled by the internet and mobile communication, language, history, tradition, local and regional economies and systems of politics and governance also continually shape our dynamic digital experiences. Locally grounded studies on technology mediation deepen the understanding of important aspects of human communication as these capture the level of complexity, detail, or ambiguity that are apparent in everyday Asian experiences of communication and technology engagement. The appreciation of such historically and culturally grounded relationships and experiences are what tend to be ignored through sweeping articulations about globalization and cultural insignificance.

It is not within the scope of this volume to reconcile this ensuing debate about Asian cultures, although the chapter by Sreekumar revisits these issues as it interrogates the concept of Asian modernity in the wake of new technologies. Rather, we aim to find windows for convergence that can lay the ground for the work that the book seeks to accomplish. The chapters in this volume present what Asia is from the perspective of diverse Asian people, hoping to provide a valuable input to this continuing dialogue of what makes Asian Asian. Moreover, the book's goal is not to replace Western communication theories, but to expand our theoretical options so that we can forge fresh analytical frames and facilitate more dynamic conversations across these frames and the scholars who explore them.

Seminal works on Asian communication have been emphasizing the importance of generating communication concepts that are inscribed in traditional Asian religious and intellectual traditions (Dissanayake, 2009a, 2009b; Miike, 2006, 2007). Given the long history and cultural tradition of countries in the region, it is reasonable to examine how such rich cultural heritage that fueled complex civilizations over the millennia can help explain individual and collective media experiences and uses. Efforts in this direction include examining classical Asian texts to distill ideas about human communication; extrapolating concepts from classical traditions of thought and current cultural practices; focusing on the dimensions of rituals, ceremonies, and performances salient in Asian culture; and probing into how everyday communicative actions are informed by traditional systems of thought. As we build on these previous works, the volume is also cognizant of the warning on the threats of *cultural essentialism* (or the tendency to regard objects, events, and spaces as unchanging) and *binarism* (seeing only in terms of distinct East-West spheres as if they were two well-defined entities) (Dissanayake, 2009a, 2009b). This collection of "Asian perspectives on digital culture" presents diverse local and regional experiences and perspectives while noting colonial histories and the dynamic influences of the forces of globalization and cultural exchange.

For this book, we refer both to concepts emerging from the region, as a geographical space, and those developed by scholars from the region. The assertion of Asian concepts represents an attempt to recognize Asia's cultural distinctiveness amidst media and communication theories that dominate the intellectual tradition of our field. In looking back at indigenous concepts, classic texts, and cultural histories associated with Asian traditions, our contributors present new tools for analysis that we envision expanding and enriching the broader field of media and communication studies. The contributors of this book engage local concepts to explain digital practices while simultaneously recognizing their possible global applications. In the process of forging ties between past and present, the book also hopes to surface new explanations, inquiries, and directions into communication research.

Organization of the Volume

The internationalization of media studies implies not only the inclusion of geographically diverse experiences of media use, but also the exploration of alternative frameworks from our intricate global landscape for understanding notions of the self, collective imaginaries, and rethinking mainstream discourses and conceptual constructions of communicative phenomena.

Self and Identity

The "self" has been an important focus of past and present literature on communication and media, and the digital environment has been distinguished for rapid transformations in the construction of the "self" and of the "self in relation to the other" (Baym, 2010; Papacharissi, 2010). The three papers in this section explore the salience of Asian concepts and practices in grasping new digital developments that challenge and enrich traditional understandings of the self. The concept of face is at the forefront of understanding the digital self, for it serves as the foundation for more complex concepts such as identity, pride, and dignity. The opening chapter by Lim and Basnyat reflects on the diverse Asian conceptions of face in the context of social media interactions. In emphasizing the sociality of the self, the chapter argues that expressions and practices of gaining, saving, losing, and giving face apparent in Asian cultures can sharpen dominant analytical threads for studying the self in the context of social networking. As our digital experiences expand, cultural practices traditionally understood as 'sacred' have also been imported into the digital realm. In this process of 'mediatization' of religious practices (Hjarvard, 2006), the chapter by Sapitula and Soriano explores translocal piety and understandings of the self in relation to the divine, as religious authorities utilize the internet to extend devotional practice beyond geographical space and toward virtual space. Like Lim and Basnyat, Sapitula and Soriano argue that local notions of interiority of the self (*loob*) in mediated piety heavily intersects with notions of shared identity. The paper by Prieler analyzes "face-ism" indices (a measurement of facial prominence associated with gender stereotyping) in people's self-representations in online dating site profiles in Japan, South Korea, Sweden, and the United States. The paper finds that *Confucianism,* which posits the family as the fundamental unit influencing the understanding of social roles, appears to lend greater nuance for explaining gender distinctions in digital self-representations. These three papers show that a conception of the self as culturally nuanced and socially shaped is crucial in understanding digital cultures within this region.

Group Processes and Collective Imaginaries

Mediated spaces have been host to various expressions of collective imaginaries. At the same time, processes of group and collective identity formation have been radically transformed by the changes accompanying the increasing complexity and global nature of our media environment. In this section, Asian concepts of *guanxi*, *jeong*, and *kapwa* are featured in the understanding of symbolic and embodied practices of the construction of collective imaginaries. The chapter by Liu draws our attention to the concept of *guanxi* in understanding the relevance of mobile communication for protest mobilization in China. Liu proposes that *guanxi* acts as a key driver for protest recruitment and participation as it engenders a sense of simultaneous credibility, reliability, and reciprocity that enhances feelings of solidarity crucial for organizing protests in this specific context. The next chapter by Yoon examines how mobile communication has altered the social interaction of young South Koreans, but also that their communicative practices are ultimately anchored in *jeong*, a traditional framework of sociality. The paper in this section by Soriano and Lim explores how television advertising of mobile services articulates rituals that mobilize the various dimensions of social and collective identity underscored by the Filipino notion of *kapwa*. In turn, such mode of advertising entrenches social arrangements as well the centrality of mobile communication in this particular social organization.

Discourses and Discursive Constructions of Meaning

Exploring diverse communicative phenomena such as corporate social responsibility (CSR), newsworthiness, or memorializing, the three papers in this section engage indigenous concepts and Asian cultural practices to provide important (re)constructions of the meaning of old practices and concepts. Dhanesh's chapter assesses the discursive constructions of the meaning of CSR through the analysis of websites and annual reports of Indian corporations. This study highlights the importance of ancient cultural texts and traditions such as *sarva loka hitam* and *lokah samastah sukhino bhavanthu* in making sense of the CSR discourses in India and proposes a rethinking of traditional concepts of CSR to encompass the narrative of coexistence and collective welfare. The paper by Lee examines culture-specific discourses that frame the notion of "newsworthiness" in Korea. Lee's paper analyzes the tweets picked up by the Korean mass media and advances the argument that Korean values significantly account for the determination of newsworthiness in this specific locale. Finally, the paper by Liew examines the contemporary process of 'remembering' and 'resurrection' by analyzing recent innovations in stereoscopic holography that 're-witness' departed Chinese pop celebrities. Engaging the Asian concepts of *ying* (shadow) and *hun* (soul), the paper features interesting case studies that juxtapose the temporal-spatial dynamics in this holographic re-imaging of celebrities to provide an alternative framing of the communication of affect in this cyber-digital landscape.

   The chapters in this volume do not confine their discussions to explanations of how Asian concepts apply to Asian digital cultures alone, but inspire the engagement of such concepts for explaining other similar or related phenomena in other parts of the world. Further, the contributions juxtapose these concepts with other modes of theoretical inquiry. As each chapter historicizes and contextualizes each concept, contributors also present a critical interrogation of indigenous concepts with other established concepts in media studies, such as Putnam's bridging and bonding social capital, Hofstede's cultural dimensions, or Bourdieu's habitus. A glossary that introduces and explains the Asian concepts used in the different chapters serves as a useful guide for future scholarship.

Examining Digital Cultures Through Asian Precepts:
Conclusions and Ruminations

The final two papers offer valuable take-off points for dynamic conversations about contemporary Asian digital cultures and chart future directions and challenges in the internationalization of Asian media studies. In the quest to move away from the dominance of Western rationality and consideration of the multiplicity of modernities in Asia, the complex project of arriving at a notion of 'Asian modernity' is problematized by Sreekumar's paper, which presents the emergence of the concept of Asian modernity and the complex dynamics and contestations of the concept, as foregrounded by the politics of technology as well as the role of technology in the uneven developments in the region. Goggin's concluding chapter on re-Orienting global digital cultures serves as a useful capstone to this volume by reflecting on the different chapters' contributions in the broader context of digital cultures and the "Asian" turn in theorizing and researching the same. He argues that the implications of the studies are significant for our understanding of Asian communication and impel us to rethink global communication in a general sense.

Reflection and Acknowledgments

None of the contributors to this volume would lay claim to considerable breadth or depth of expertise in the internationalization of media studies. However, we are unified in our perception of the inadequacies of existing media theories in relation to our experiences, as media consumers who engage and as media scholars who theorize. Our proclivity to draw inspiration from indigenous Asian concepts stems from our instinctive grasp of these concepts and appreciation of their ability to illuminate nuances in values, attitudes, and behaviors that resonate with our lived experience. These concepts quietly but inexorably mold the epistemological and ontological frames that shape how we as academics contemplate, apprehend, and interpret the socio-technical relationships that are emerging from Asia's increasingly digitized media landscape. The analytical profit we derived from applying these concepts in our research motivated us to pool together our collective experience. In doing so, we hope to encourage dynamic conversations on Asian digital phenomena, as well as inspire greater exploration of indigenous concepts for understanding media use in other contexts.

In editing this volume, we have benefited from the support of a community of scholars whose generosity and wisdom have fortified us in our push for greater diversity in media studies. We thank our respective departments, colleagues, past and present collaborators, and the broader community of scholars whose work has been such a source of guidance and intellectual stimulation. As we follow the lead of these scholars who have passionately advanced the internationalization of media studies, we also hope that this volume will ignite more global efforts to examine global digital cultures through alternative lenses and locally grounded conceptual frameworks.

References

Anjum, Z. (2014). *Startup capitals: Discovering the global hotspots of innovation.* Guargaon, India: Random House India.

Appadurai, A. (1990). Disjuncture and difference in the global cultural economy. *Theory, culture and society*, 7(2), 295–310.

Arora, P. (2010). *Dot com mantra: Social computing in the Central Himalayas.* Burlington, VT: Ashgate.

Athukorala, P.-C. (2006). International labour migration in East Asia: Trends, patterns and policy issues. *Asian-Pacific Economic Literature*, 20(1): 18–39. doi: 10.1111/j.1467-8411.2006.00176.x.

Baskaran, A., & Muchie, M. (2006). *Bridging the digital divide: Innovation systems for ICT in Brazil, China, India, Thailand and Southern Africa.* London, UK: Adonis & Abbey Publishers Ltd.

Baym, N. K. (2010). *Personal connections in the digital age.* London: Polity.

Chen, G.-M. (2006). Asian communication studies: What and where to now. *The Review of Communication*, 6(4): 295–311.

Chen, G.-M., & Miike, Y. (2006). The ferment and future of communication studies in Asia: Chinese and Japanese perspectives. *China Media Research*, 2(1): 1–12.

Chen, S., Zhang, H., Lin, M., & Lv, S. (2011). *Comparison of microblogging service between Sina Weibo and Twitter.* Paper presented at the Computer Science and Network Technology (ICCSNT), 2011 International Conference on.

Cheung, C.-K. (Ed.). (2009). *Media education in Asia.* Dordrecht: Springer.

Cortada, J. (2012). *The digital flood: The diffusion of information technology across the U.S., Europe, and Asia.* New York, NY: Oxford University Press.

Curran, J & Park, M.-J. (2000). Beyond globalisation theory. In J. Curran & M.J. Park (Eds.), *De-Westernising media studies* (pp. 3–18). London: Routledge.

Dissanayake, W. (Ed.). (1988). *Communication theory: the Asian perspective.* Asian Mass Communication Research and Information Centre.

Dissanayake, W. (2003). Asian approaches to human communication: Retrospect and prospect. *Intercultural Communication Studies*, 12(4): 17–38.

Dissanayake, W. (2006). Postcolonial theory and Asian communication theory: Toward a creative dialogue. *China Media Research*, 2(4): 1–8.

Dissanayake, W. (2009a). The production of Asian theories of communication: Contexts and challenges. *Asian Journal of Communication*, 19(4): 453–468.

Dissanayake, W. (2009b). The desire to excavate Asian theories of communication: One strand of the history. *Journal of Multicultural Discourses*, 4(1): 7–27.

Doron, A. (2012). Mobile persons: Cell phones, gender and the self in North India. *The Asia Pacific Journal of Anthropology*, 13(5): 414–433.

Durham, M. (2004). Constructing the "new ethnicities": Media, sexuality, and diaspora identity in the lives of South Asian immigrant girls. *Critical Studies in Media Communication*, 21(2): 140–161.

Erni, J. N., & Chua, S. K. (2005). Introduction: Our Asian media studies? In J. N. Erni & S. K. Chua (Eds.), *Asia media studies: Politics of subjectivities* (pp. 1–15). Malden, MA: Blackwell.

Erni, J.N. & Spires, A. (2005). The formation of a queer-imagined community in post-martial law Taiwan. In J. N. Erni & S. K. Chua (Eds.), *Asia media studies: Politics of subjectivities* (pp. 225–252). Malden, MA: Blackwell.

Fan, S., Chen-Kang, C., & Mukherjee, A. (2005). *Rural and urban dynamics and poverty: Evidence from China and India*. Washington, DC: International Food Policy Research Institute (IFPRI).

Franda, M. F. (2002). *Launching into cyberspace: Internet development and politics in five world regions*. New York City, NY: Lynne Rienner Pub.

Ganapathy, K., & Ravindra, A. (2008). *mHealth: A potential tool for health care delivery in India*. Rockefeller Foundation.

Goggin, G. (2011). *Global mobile media*. New York, NY: Routledge.

Goggin, G., & McLelland, M. (2009). Internationalizing internet studies: Beyond Anglophone paradigms. In G. Goggin & M. McLelland (Eds.), *Internationalizing internet studies: Beyond Anglophone paradigms* (pp. 3–17). New York, NY: Routledge.

Gugler, J. (2004). *World cities beyond the west: globalization, development and inequality*: New York, NY: Cambridge University Press.

Hazelkorn, E. (2015). *Rankings and the reshaping of higher education: The battle for world-class excellence*. London, UK: Palgrave Macmillan.

Hjarvard, S. (2006). *The mediatization of religion. A theory of media as an agent of religious change*. Paper presented to the 5th International Conference on Media, Religion and Culture: Mediating Religion in the Context of Multicultural Tension The Sigtuna Foundation, Stockholm/Sigtuna/Uppsala, Sweden, 6–9 July.

Internet World Stats (2015a, June 14). Internet Users in the world: Distribution by region. Retrieved from http://www.internetworldstats.com/stats7.htm.

Internet World Stats (2015b, June 14). Internet world users by language: Top 10 languages. Retrieved from http://www.internetworldstats.com/stats7.htm.

Iwabuchi, K. (2005). Discrepant intimacy: Popular culture flows in East Asia. In J. N. Erni & S. K. Chua (Eds.), *Asia media studies: Politics of subjectivities* (pp. 19–36). Malden, MA: Blackwell.

Jin, D. Y. (2010). *Korea's online gaming empire*. Cambridge, MA: The MIT Press.

Komito, L. (2011). Social media and migration: Virtual community 2.0. *Journal of the American Society for Information Science and Technology*, 62(6): 1075–1086.

Lim, S. S., & Goggin, G. (2014). Mobile communication in Asia: Issues and imperatives. *Journal of Computer-Mediated Communication*, 19(3): 663–666.

Lim, S. S., Sison, R. C., & Kim, D.-Y. (Eds.) (2008). *The promise of ICTs in Asia: Key trends and issues*. Seoul, Korea: Jimoondang.

Mandaville, P. (2001). Reimagining Islam in diaspora. The politics of mediated community. *International Communication Gazette*, 63(2–3): 169–186.

Massey, B. L., & Chang, L. J. A. (2002). Locating Asian values in Asian journalism: A content analysis of web newspapers. *Journal of Communication*, 52(4): 987–1003.

Miike, Y. (2006). Non-Western theory in Western research? An Asiacentric agenda for Asian communication studies. *Review of Communication,* 6(1/2): 4–31.

Miike, Y. (2007). An Asiacentric reflection on Eurocentric bias in communication theory. *Communication Monographs*, 74(2): 272–278.

Miike, Y., & Chen, G.-M. (2006). Perspectives on Asian cultures and communication: An updated bibliography. *China Media Research*, 2(1): 98–106.

Naisbitt, J. (1995). *Megatrends Asia: The eight Asian megatrends that are changing the world*. London: Nicolas Brealey Publishing.

Papacharissi, Z. (Ed.). (2010). *A networked self: Identity, community and culture on social network sites*. New York, NY: Routledge.

Parthasarathy, B., & Aoyama, Y. (2006). From software services to R&D services: Local entrepreneurship in the software industry in Bangalore, India. *Environment and Planning, 38*(7): 1269.

Rasiah, R., Xiao-Shan, Y., & Chandran Govindaraju, V. G. R. (2014). Crisis effects on the electronics industry in Southeast Asia. *Journal of Contemporary Asia, 44*(4): 645–663.

Slater, D. (2003). Modernity under construction. Building the internet in Trinidad, In. Misa, T., Brey, P. & Feenberg, A. (Eds.), *Modernity and technology* (pp. 139–160). Cambridge, MA: MIT Press.

Sreekumar, T. T. (2015). Asian modernity and the posthuman future: Some reflections. In S. S. Lim & C. R. Soriano (Eds.), *Asian perspectives on digital cultures: Emerging phenomena, enduring concepts.* London & New York, NY: Routledge.

Thussu, D. K. (2009a). Introduction. In D. K. Thussu (Ed.), *Internationalizing media studies* (pp. 1–10). London & New York, NY: Routledge.

Thussu, D. K. (2009b). Why internationalise media studies and how? In D. K. Thussu (Ed.), *Internationalizing media studies* (pp. 13–31). London & New York, NY: Routledge.

Tseng, C.-Y. (2009). Technological innovation and knowledge network in Asia: Evidence from comparison of information and communication technologies among six countries. *Technological Forecasting and Social Change, 76*(5): 654–663. doi: http://dx.doi.org/10.1016/j.techfore.2008.03.007.

Wang, G., and Kuo, E.C.Y. (2010). The Asian communication debate: Culture-specificity, culture-generality, and beyond. *Asian Journal of Communication, 20*(2): 152–165.

Wang, G., & Shen, V. (2000). East, west, communication, and theory: Searching for the meaning of searching for Asian communication theories. *Asian Journal of Communication, 10*(2): 14–32. doi: 10.1080/01292980009364782.

Wang, J., Cheng, S., & Ganapati, S. (2012). Path dependence in regional ICT innovation: Differential evolution of Zhongguancun and Bangalore. *Regional Science Policy & Practice, 4*(3): 231–245. doi: 10.1111/j.1757–7802.2012.01070.x.

Wickramasekera, P. (2002). *Asian labour migration: Issues and challenges in an era of globalization.* Genève, Switzerland: International Migration Programme, International Labour Office.

Wilson, E. J. (2004). *The information revolution and developing countries.* Cambridge, MA: MIT Press.

Yue, A. (2006). Cultural governance and creative industries in Singapore. *International Journal of Cultural Policy, 12*(1): 17–33.

Zhang, M. Y., & Dodgson, M. (2007). *High-tech entrepreneurship in Asia: Innovation, industry and institutional dynamics in mobile payments.* Northhampton, MA: Edward Elgar Publishing.

Part II
Self and Identity

2 Face and Online Social Networking

Sun Sun Lim and Iccha Basnyat

What is Face?

The term "face" is commonly used in everyday parlance to refer to acts of deference, for example, *"I gave face to her on account of her experience."* Face is also often used to describe efforts to maintain one's pride and dignity, for example, *"to save face, I agreed on a compromise."* Face is therefore both a means and an end: one gives face to another person to attain something; one also strives to maintain face in order to sustain one's position within one's social circle. Face therefore bears a distinct personal dimension but is also vested with a palpable social dimension.

Even as "face" seems to be a commonsensical notion that people instinctively understand, practice and articulate in daily social interactions, it is fundamentally steeped in cultural norms and social customs. Indeed, it is expressed, interpreted, and experienced through a plethora of complex verbal and non-verbal codes, even (and perhaps especially) in the online realm. This chapter explores how face can be applied to our understanding of interpersonal interactions via social networking sites such as Twitter, Facebook, and Instagram. Although much of self-presentation research has been on Facebook, we extend our argument to other social networking sites (SNS) that share similar dynamics of social interaction and publicness. We will first discuss the origins of the concept of face, and probe into whether it is an Asian or a universal phenomenon, while also reviewing the variety of Asian conceptions of face. We then canvass previous research on online social networks to consider how 'face' has and has not been utilized as a lens for understanding such interactions. Finally, we ruminate on the utility of "face" as a construct for interpreting and assessing online social network interactions compared to other typical analytical frames.

Face—Asian or Universal?

The concept of face is commonly attributed to the Chinese, but its origins can be traced to many cultural and philosophical traditions within Asia. Analogues of the term face can be found in many different Asian societies—*mian/lian* (China), *izzat* (India/Pakistan), *taimen/mentsu* (Japan), *Chemyon* (Korea), Nâa (Thailand), and *mặt* (Vietnam).

The Chinese notion of face can be discussed as *Mianzi* (*mien-tzu*) and *Lian* (*lien*) (Liang & Walker, 2011). *Mianzi* refers to a person's honor and standing within his/her social circle or the social perception of the person's prestige. *Mianzi* thus represents a positive social value that one successfully earns from others in and through specific social interactions (Lin, 2011), essentially the reputation or prestige a person attains through personal effort and/or being supported by the encompassing society (Hu, 2004 in Liang & Walker, 2011). On the other hand, *Lian* represents a person's social morality achieved by behaving properly, in accordance with social norms and standards (Hu, 2004 in Liang & Walker, 2011). It refers primarily to a person's integrity and moral character and is usually expressed in its negative form *bu yao lian* (i.e., shameless) when seeking to condemn immoral behavior (Liang & Walker, 2011). While *Mianzi* is viewed through the positive lens of gaining face, *Lian* tends to be used in the context of loss of face. However, the two terms are often used interchangeably in the real world (Gao, 1998 in Liang & Walker, 2011). A related term is *guanxi*, the Chinese term for one's personalized networks among whom one seeks to maintain face. The Chinese emphasize individuals' social capital within their group of friends, relatives, and close associates (Huang & Wang, 2011). Therefore, *guanxi* refers to the web of social connections between people that lubricates and even cements relationships. Consequently, *Mianzi* is integral to one's position in a *guanxi* network because it is difficult to achieve effective *guanxi* without *Mianzi* (Huang & Wang, 2011). The Chinese notion of face thus encompasses: gaining face, maintaining face, saving face, and losing face. The fact that face can be gained or lost in the Chinese conception is worthy of note.

The Japanese conception of face, *Mentsu,* is understood to mean a person's honor as derived from the external judgments of others and adjustments to others so as to maintain harmonious relationships within one's social network (Boiger, Güngör, Karasawa, & Mesquita, 2014). Indeed, harmony is the foremost priority. Relatedly, "social identity" is then the principal motivation in interpersonal dealings, taking precedence over individual wants. Matsumoto (1988) explains that the "[a]cknowledgement and maintenance of the relative position of others, rather than preservation of an individual's proper territory, governs all social interaction" (p. 405). So when Japanese people strive to be courteous, they must be cognizant of their position within the social group and must openly articulate their reliance on other people. The distinctions between the positions and roles of interacting parties are used to reflect hierarchical interdependence. Individuals must be acutely aware of their social standing, especially in superior-subordinate relationships (Haugh & Watanabe, 2009). This pronounced performative dimension of *Mentsu* serves to therefore underline individual status and highlight interdependent relationships, all in the pursuit of harmony. Notably, too, the negative aspects of face (i.e., face-threatening behavior that leads another person to lose face due to individuals' natural desire to be free from impositions (Brown & Levinson, 1978, 1987) are less pronounced in the Japanese conception. Hierarchical interdependence is thus a common thread that runs through Chinese and Japanese concepts of face, and both are orientated toward an ideal social identity (Pham, 2014).

Whereas the Chinese and Japanese notions of face greatly privilege the social dimension, the personal aspect is also highlighted in *Chemyon*, the Korean equivalent. *Chemyon* guides how someone in a social position or status should behave so that one's character is positively demonstrated. Not unlike the Chinese *Mianzi* and the Japanese *Mentsu*, social *Chemyon* refers to the social representation of self (Yang, 2015). It is closely related to hierarchical status that reinforces *Chemyon*-related behaviors (Yang, 2015) and therefore fulfils an important role in maintaining good social relationships (Kim & Yang, 2010), where saving one's and others' face is crucial in gaining others' approval/acceptance (Kim & Yang, 2010). Therefore, social *Chemyon* places value on external evaluation, and people with high social *Chemyon* feel pressured to meet the expectations of others in order not to lose *Chemyon* (Jung 2011 in Yang, 2015). Social *Chemyon* is thus concerned with others' evaluation while personal *Chemyon* is related to self-evaluation and individual autonomy (Lim & Choi, 1996, cited in Yang, 2015).

Face in the Thai conception, *Nâa*, is considered the "representation of ego," and the underlying rule of all Thai interaction is preserving one another's ego or face (Ukosakul, 2003, 2005). The importance of face in Thai society cannot be underestimated considering that no less than 180 idioms are based on the Thai word *Nâa* (Ukosakul, 2003). *Nâa* centers around ego, self-identity, dignity, and pride (Ukosakul, 2003). Essentially, it involves both the self and the other in gaining face, as well as not making others lose face and is therefore intimately linked to honor and shame (Ukosakul, 2009). Preserving one's honor or self-esteem, as well as recognizing one's status in society implies maintaining one another's "face" (Ukosakul, 2005). In other words, the notion of face relates to giving face to others, through which one also maintains face. One's face thus exists in relation to not making others lose face and in turn saving one's own face. This ego-orientation underlies other cultural values such as "face saving," where if one gains face, *dâj nâa*, more honor is earned, thereby engendering feelings of social acceptance. In contrast, losing face, *sĭa nâa,* resulting in the loss of one's honor, causes embarrassment (Ukosakul, 2003).

Similarly, the Vietnamese concept of face is made up of social roles and role-driven characteristics such that it revolves around individuals' desire to be approved of, and appreciated by, other people (Pham, 2014). *Mặt* (from *Mianzi*), and *thể diện* (from *Lian*) are the two equivalent concepts of face in Vietnam and has variations such as "*mất mặt* and *mất thể diện* (face loss); *vắng/mất mặt*—being absent (literally: absent face), *vác mặt/mò mặt*— showing/turning up (literally: bringing face), *cách mặt*—being out of sight (literally: separating face), *từ mặt*—giving up associating with (literally: abandoning face), and *tránh mặt*—avoiding meeting someone (literally:

avoiding face)" (Pham, 2014, p. 225). The Vietnamese conception of face bears close resemblance to the Chinese understanding of *Mianzi* and *Lian* but extends it further into many idioms of face similar to those of the Thai conception. However, the Vietnamese concept of face is a person's image in social evaluations and seems to have a more salient negative quality, being attached to a sense of shame, i.e., the loss of face (Pham, 2014).

Although most of the discussion around face is orientated around East Asia, a loosely related term *izzat* is found in South Asia. *Izzat* refers to respect, honor, reputation, or prestige that guides social relationships through a set of societal and personal conduct rules in order to protect the family honor and one's position within the community (Baig, Ting-Toomey, & Dorjee, 2014). *Izzat* is described as a learnt set of rules to adhere to in order to protect the family honor and sustain one's position in the community (Gilbert, Gilbert, & Sanghera, 2004). *Izzat* is derived from the Arabic noun *izzah*, meaning glory, and upholding *izzat* is a driving motivation for vast numbers of people who believe in it, including Hindus, Muslims, and Sikhs (Baig et al., 2014). *Izzat* is therefore a shared notion in India and Pakistan (Gilbert et al., 2004). To lose honor by the actions of another or to bring dishonor (i.e., *be-zzat*) is to be externally shamed (i.e., *sharam*—bringing shame upon oneself or one's family) and consequently to lose status in the eyes of others (Gilbert et al., 2004). Avoidance of shame and loss of honor to one's family is about conserving face vis-à-vis others. *Izzat* then is maintaining the face of one's family according to personal and social rules, thereby gaining and preserving the family's honor within the community. The individual's obligation to shoring up the family's standing and the family as the key unit by which an individual interacts with broader society and from which an individual derives personal status are the distinctive aspects of this particular instantiation of face.

As the preceding discussion shows, the concept of face has considerable currency in Asia and is deeply rooted in many societies. While each of these aforementioned iterations of face bears particular cultural specificities, nuances, and inflections, commonalities can clearly be discerned that point to an "Asian" conception of face. Public judgment is a necessary condition in the understanding of face in different Asian cultures because face exists in relation to social relationships. Indeed, face in the Asian conception has pronounced personal and social dimensions. Society is not meant to be atomized or individualistic, and the mutual interdependence of its members serves as its bedrock. Members must be conscious of their relative social standing, recognize their reliance on others, and behave in accordance with shared norms. In doing so, members earn for themselves pride and dignity, as well honor for the family. Face management is the manifestation of these principles, as well as the mechanism by which such social order is maintained, influencing both individual and group activities in these societies.

Broadly therefore, the Asian concept of face is observed to encompass three dimensions: self-face, or the concern for one's own image; other-face, or the concern for another individual's image; and mutual face, or concern for the images of both parties and the image of their relationship (Ting-Toomey & Oetzel, 2002). In self-face, a person gains face by attaining status that is conferred by one's social group or by earning the status through competition and individual effort (Ho, 1976). Individuals who lose face acquire a bad reputation, loss of respect or prestige and suffer embarrassment or humiliation among the peer group (Ting-Toomey & Oetzel, 2002). Loss of face also occurs when people expect group members to respond to them or their requests in particular ways but do not find these expectations realized (Ho, 1976). In concerns about other-face, the impetus to uphold other people's image motivates individuals to give face to others by displaying affirmation and acquiescent behavior. Mutual face is attained in reciprocal relationships where interested parties collectively give face to one another, such that every member of the social group is subjected to mutual restrictions and possibly coercion. Instantiations of face in different Asian cultures accord with these broad conceptions of self-face, other-face, and mutual face.

Despite its Asian origins, the concept of face has also influenced Western understandings of interpersonal communication and social interaction, although scholars have sought to identify the distinctions between Asian and Western conceptions of face. The point of departure for much extant research on Western notions of face has been Goffman's (1972) work on ritual elements in social interaction, where face is a positive social value framed in largely prosocial terms: "Face is an image of self delineated in terms of approved social attributes—albeit an image that others may share, as when a person makes a good showing for his profession or region by making a good showing for himself" (p. 5). Notably, Goffman acknowledged that his treatise on face was inspired by that of the Chinese. Building on Goffman's work, Brown and Levinson (1978) developed a model of politeness that hinged on face: "Face is something that is emotionally invested, and that can be lost, maintained, or enhanced, and must be constantly attended to in interaction" (p. 61).

Face has therefore extended beyond its Asian origins to inform and influence understandings of interpersonal interactions. However, the universality of face is not a given considering how cultural norms and contexts determine the specific ways in which face is asserted, practiced, experienced, and upheld. Ho (1976) acknowledged that "the conceptualization of what constitutes face and the rules governing face behaviour vary considerably across cultures," but nevertheless argues that "the concern for face is invariant. Defined at a high level of generality, the concept of face is (a) universal" (p. 882). Similarly, Ting-Toomey (1994) asserts that face has dimensions that are both "cultural-universal" and "cultural-specific" and attributes the principal differences between Asian and Western societies' conceptions and practices of face to the collectivism characterizing the former and the individualism marking the latter (Ting-Toomey et al., 1991). In individualistic Western cultures, therefore, individual behavior is regulated by an in-built sense of self, but in contrast the behavior of people in collectivistic Asian cultures is influenced by a sense of self as perceived by others. As earlier mentioned, a central trope across the different Asian conceptions of face is "social face," which reflects this relational dimension of self that is stronger than in the Western conception.

Another distinct characteristic of face management in most Asian societies is the importance of maintaining prevailing role relationships and sustaining interpersonal harmony (Gao, Ting-Toomey, & Gudykunst, 1996), where face is not just the means but the veritable purpose of social interaction (Qi, 2011). For example, facework in Chinese culture involves observing status differences between individuals in a group, managing conflicts in a non-confrontational manner (through the use of intermediaries if necessary), and opting for compliant and non-assertive communication. One other distinction between the Western notion of face and the Asian conception is a broader definition of socially acceptable behavior. Whereas Goffman stressed that face management behavior had to be positively and socially approved, Qi (2011) argues that as long as actions are socially shared or approved for one instance in a particular social situation by a specific social group, face is gained, even if those actions violate wider societal norms. Despite these distinctions, however, there is sufficient evidence from research in Asian and Western settings to suggest that "the presentation of self vis-à-vis others is a basic problem that no one, in any society, can avoid" (Ho, 1976, p. 881).

Face Management in Online Social Networking

Indeed, with the emergence of online social networks, individuals have unprecedented opportunities for self-presentation and by implication, face management. Online social networks with an international reach such as Facebook, Google+, Instagram, LinkedIn, and Twitter, as well as regional favorites such as Weibo (China), Mixi (Japan), Me2Day and KakaoStory (Korea), and LINE (Thailand), have opened up new realms for people to maintain their relationships with friends and acquaintances. With their unique architectural characteristics, these online social networks facilitate social connections that can be deep yet expansive, allowing for close interactions with significant others while facilitating superficial contact with a web of weak ties. Prior research on the motivations and gratifications of individuals' use of online social networks have not explicitly referenced face as understood in the Asian context. Yet these studies have been dominated by two salient analytical threads that are analogous to the concept of face—self-presentation and impression management. While these two terms are often used interchangeably in extant literature, we would like to draw a finer distinction between them. We consider self-presentation as discrete everyday acts that individuals use to create and present themselves to others in their social networks and impression management as a more sustained, long-term endeavor of shaping and maintaining a certain public image and reputation. In other words, impression management is what one hopes to achieve in the long term through discrete short-term acts of self-presentation. For instance, acts of self-presentation involve an active usage of social networking sites through acts that require liking, sharing, tweeting, re-tweeting, posting, commenting, and uploading to create and maintain a certain impression of oneself within a social network. We will proceed to review how these two terms have been used in previous research on online social networking before considering how their application and analysis are complicated and perhaps enhanced by the concept of face.

Self-Presentation

Individuals engage in self-presentation to make others accept the images they claim for themselves (Goffman, p. 959 in Rui & Stefanone, 2013). Self-presentation thus refers to social situations where individuals attempt to control images of, or information about, themselves or that are self-related (Schlenker, 1980 in Stritzke, Nguyen, & Durkin, 2004). With the advent of online social networks, self-images and identities are no longer private but become social and visible. These online identities are self-generated and self-curated within a particular social network in a bid to make others accept the image. In some ways, the mediated online environment makes it easier for individuals to do so more comfortably and confidently. For instance, Stritzke, Nguyen, and Durkin (2004) found that for shy individuals the online environment results in lower levels of rejection sensitivity and a greater interest in initiating relationships and ease of self-disclosure. Online social networking sites offer powerful tools for self-presentation such as customizing pages, updating one's status, writing comments, sharing images, disclosing selected personal details, and so on (Hogan, 2010; Rui & Stefanone, 2013). All of these acts serve as a way to present the self, even an idealized self, to one's online social network. In such a setting, self-presentations can be carefully constructed and managed (Utz, 2010). Rosenberg and Egbert (2011) note that before engaging in self-presentation tactics, individuals first have to establish what their desired impression is. This desired impression can then be created and managed through strategized self-presentation. Self-presentation thus comprises online practices of creating, controlling, and managing online identities to maintain the long-term desired impression in the online social network.

What about the audience to whom such efforts at self-presentation are directed? Invariably, people do make social judgments about one another in an online social network based on each individual's self-presentation (Tong, Van Der Heide, Langwell, & Walther, 2008). For instance, Hall, Pennington, and Lueders (2013) found that those without personal photographs were judged by strangers to be less agreeable, and those with attractive photographs as more agreeable. In fact, Bakhshi, Shamma, and Gilbert (2014) found that on Instagram, profiles with faces were 38% more likely to receive likes and 32% more likely to receive comments. Face, here is represented by one's personal photograph that is in turn judged by both friends and strangers. Similarly, Utz (2010) found that on Facebook, users' profiles, profile pictures of friends and even the number of friends one has, jointly influence the impressions that others have of them. Self-presentation thus relies on the approval of the presented self by those in the online social network, which in turn helps to manage impressions. One's social network is therefore no longer confined to personal relationships but also includes what Marwick and boyd (2011) call the "imagined audience". Although the authors discuss the imagined audience in the context of Twitter where one does not know much about the audience, boyd (2007) notes that participants take cues from the social media environment to imagine and construct the community in order to present themselves appropriately. Furthermore, online networked environments also complicate the process of segregating an individual's different audiences from one another (Strano & Wattai, 2010) due to the problem of context collapse (Wesch, 2009), where significant others from diverse spheres of your life (i.e., family, friends, co-workers etc.) converge in the online space. In such circumstances, discrepancies can emerge between the online and offline self-presentations of individuals due to varied expectations and preferences among different audiences, leading to self-presentations that may run counter to what is otherwise known of that person (DeAndrea & Walther, 2011). Furthermore, acts of self-presentation targeted at one audience "may be construed as embellishments, distortions, or dishonesties" by a different audience (DeAndrea & Walther, 2011, p.2). The latter audience may come to consider the individual as untrustworthy, unreliable, and dishonorable. Pertinently, Hall, Pennington, and Lueders (2013) note that friends with whom individuals are acquainted both offline and online may keep users' temptations to enhance self-presentations in check.

Impression Management

Over time, discrete and seemingly unrelated acts of self-presentation by an individual accrue towards a durable, overarching impression that people form of them. Impression management is the term Goffman (1959) used to refer to the process of individuals constantly tweaking their behaviors, and selectively sharing personal details. While Goffman made his observations with regard to face-to-face interaction, online social networks have since become spaces where individuals refine their behaviors virtually to provide selective details about themselves (Hogan, 2010). In this exercise of individual agency, impression management can thus be seen as "the process by which individuals attempt to control the impressions others form of them" (Leary & Kowalski, 1990, p. 34) via strategic tactics of self-presentation. Indeed, online impression management involves active engagement in creating, maintaining, and modifying an image that reflects one's ideal self

(Gonzales & Hancock, 2008). The public nature of social networks may further motivate individuals to manage their impressions more carefully because the formation of a favorable impression is considered to be the ultimate goal (Rosenberg & Egbert, 2011).

However, impression management is by no means a unilateral process. Goffman (1972) observed that people constantly take into consideration the impression that others have of them. Impression management of one's public image involves establishing a certain public social position in relation to group expectations. Knowledge of such expectations, as well as how to negotiate them, can only be achieved through sustained social interactions. These interactions then help to shape people's views of themselves, which are then reflected in the ways they present themselves during further interactions (Rosenberg & Egbert, 2011). "Impression management stems from a desire for approval, the self-presentation strategies we employ are dependent on our understanding of the social values of the group we hope to impress" (Strano & Wattai, 2010, p. 289). In other words, impression management should also be viewed as a social value that people strategize to achieve or maintain through self-presentation. Therefore, impression management is critical for fostering social relationships, and the two can be considered co-constitutive.

Whither Face?

As the preceding discussion shows, self-presentation and impression management are strategic acts of maintaining impressions of self and a certain public self-image and are highly congruent with the concept of face. If we superimpose the preceding discussion with the Asian conception of face that comprises self-face, concern for one's own image; other-face, concern for another individual's image; and mutual face, concern for the images of both parties and the image of their relationship, we can derive an appreciation for how face may add valuable nuance to our understanding of social interactions on online social networks. Research on self-presentation on SNS has largely ignored the notion of face. However, Lim, Vadrevu, Chan and Basnyat (2012) found that youths' online practices on Facebook were geared toward gaining face, giving face, and not losing face among their friends and were instrumental in sustaining peer dynamics and relationships. Remarkably, therefore, even though face is a centuries-old concept, it appears to be eminently suitable for analyzing social interactions in online social networking sites because it incorporates personal, social, and relational dimensions of self.

Self-presentation and impression management are ultimately motivated by a desire to influence one's reputation and regard among peers and as currently theorized resonate with the positive aspects of self-face, such as "gaining," "keeping," and "saving" face. Much research on online social networks focuses on gaining face through self-presentation (i.e., self-face) which then is presumed to create and maintain a certain image of the person. Studies have looked at different aspects of self-presentation such as narcissism (Carpenter, 2012; Davenport et al., 2014; Ong et al., 2011) and various ways of self-presentation online (Peluchette & Karl, 2009; Rosenberg & Egbert, 2011; Rui & Stefanone, 2013; Strano, 2008). Self-presentation is considered to be active self-promoting behavior, which leads to gaining, keeping, and saving face on online social networks by establishing certain self-images. Ultimately, what complicates and compounds online social interactions is the observability and transparency of communication on these online social networks. Friendship ties and whatever is (or is not) articulated in such networks are patently visible to the multiple, often overlapping, social networks to which individuals belong. Functions such as "liking," "sharing," "commenting," "favoriting," and "retweeting" posts enable the social network to demonstrate affiliation, affirmation, and even affection, thus giving face to the person in question in a very public manner. "Liking" or sharing someone's humorous post is often interpreted as a pat on someone's back or appreciation for witticisms; commenting in a sympathetic manner on a post of lamentation is likely to be viewed as a display of moral support and kinship; and responding to requests for information or assistance is read as a kind and magnanimous gesture that also signals regard for the individual in question. The person in question thus gains face from the public and observable social validation.

When we consider the dimension of losing face, however, this is where the analysis of self-presentation and impression management may assume a more complex tenor. The ramifications of losing face are just as important as those of saving, giving, and keeping face. While acts of self-presentation contribute to impression management through self-face, loss occurs when one fails to gain face from others in a social relationship. The Chinese notion of *lian* used in the context of loss of face can be understood online in the response from one's *guanxi* network. Behaving within the expected and accepted social norms of one's social network can prevent loss of face, thereby not being condemned within or by the social network. Similarly, the Vietnamese concept of face also revolves around loss of face. Loss is therefore dependent on how others respond to one's self-presentation. While self-presentation is aimed at image management, the successful conveyance of the desired image is dependent on whether others affirm it through their responses. Publicness is online social networks' critical affordance, displaying network members' responses to a person's efforts at self-presentation and impression management. While a great deal can indeed be expressed through the commission of communicative acts such as "liking," "sharing," "commenting," "favoriting," and "retweeting" posts, their very omission can also speak volumes. If an individual's efforts at self-presentation and impression management should fail to elicit positive responses from close friends and acquaintances, and this indifference from the social network is also publicly visible, the person in question thus loses face from the *absence* of public and observable social validation. Loss of face is therefore a potent indicator of one's social standing or more specifically, the lack thereof. Current research on online social networks has indeed captured the active response of the social network to individuals' self-presentation efforts by measuring how they are positively or negatively perceived by network members (see, for example, Hall, Pennington, & Lueders, 2013; Tong, Van Der Heide, Langwell, & Walther, 2008; Utz, 2010). However, situations of non-response by the social network have largely been overlooked. From the perspective of face, non-response on online social networks is tantamount to the lack of recognition of other-face. Online, this may be represented through comments that express affirmation and show concern for other-face by giving face within one's social network. The Korean notion of *Chemyon* is simultaneously self-face and other-face, where self-face can only be gained by respecting other-face. Similarly, the Thai concept of *Nâa* also relates to other-face in that one's face exists in relation to not making others lose face. Rather than the advancement of self-presentation alone, it encompasses the critical relational task of giving face to others. Therefore, it would be valuable to delve more deeply into how non-response and the possible loss of face that follows is perceived by both the individual in question and members of the social network.

Of course, another critical dimension of face is mutual face, where members of a social network seek to shore up the images of all parties and the image of their relationship. Mutual face is best advanced through an understanding and acknowledgment of the relationships of hierarchical interdependence undergirding social connections. For instance, the Japanese concept of *Mentsu* can only be derived through others' judgment and by maintaining relationships within one's social network. This mutual face online becomes a way to display harmony, respect, and affirmation of a relationship within one's online social network. Often positive acts that reinforce relationship status such as hierarchy and interdependence in the relationship are amplified through SNS when performing mutual face. For instance, Strano (2008) found that women tend to change profile pictures to emphasize the nature and status of friendships or family and romantic relationships. These images openly signal the status of the relationship, thereby giving face to these significant others. Similarly, *izzat* relates to mutual face where one avoids shame and loss of honor vis-à-vis others and emphasizes maintaining face in accordance to social norms. In the online realm, these iterations may take the form of maintaining hierarchy that remains visible to others, the choice of images presented, or the language used to refer to each other that shows respect and avoids dishonor. For instance, Strano and Wattai (2010) argue that the deletion and untagging of photos and explicit verbal communication on the user's page ensure managing the desired impression, while indicating to others the nature of the relationship. These visible acts avoid shame and dishonor and highlight the positive aspects of the relationship. This understanding is then put into practice by giving face to others through acts of affirmation, support, and even deference. Current research on self-presentation and impression management in online social networks do shed light on the relational dimension of network interactions but primarily from the perspective of external endorsement and sanction of projected self-images or lack thereof, as well as individual responses to the same (see, for example, DeAndrea & Walther, 2011; Hall, Pennington, and Lueders, 2013). While this approach has definite utility, if we accept that much social interaction is contingent upon mutual face, there is also a need to think about how reciprocal relationships in online social networks are sustained. With the perspective of mutual face, there is a greater illumination of both parties' efforts to preserve and give face in light of mutual interdependence. To best capture the dynamics of mutual face and their impact on online social network interactions, future research can comprise a greater effort to chart the pre-existing relationships undergirding people within a network, the length of their acquaintance, the nature of their interdependence, and their relative status. The feelings (both positive and negative) that are elicited by the enactment or omission of communicative acts necessarily vary according to the mutual relationships linking the parties involved, their shared expectations, and the social norms to which they subscribe. Given the relative novelty of online social networks, social norms influencing how they are to be used in social and professional interactions are already emerging, but these standards of social acceptability are constantly in flux as both technology and individual attitudes evolve.

Conclusion

A central trope across the different Asian conceptions of face is "social face," which reflects a stronger relational dimension of self than in the Western conception. This pronounced social dimension lends itself particularly well to online social networks that are designed to be deeply social, while allowing for individual introspection. Face management within online social networks requires active strategies that take on new forms in computer-mediated communication. For online face, all aspects—self, other, and mutual face—simultaneously come together as face management to create and maintain a desired public image. It also implies that deliberate acts of self-presentation must be reciprocated online for impression management. In online social networking sites, face management transpires in technologically facilitated ways where the structural design of these networks can amplify, constrain, and complicate facework. Individuals can take to online social networks to announce personal triumphs or milestones that invite salutations. Conversely, personal difficulties may also be publicly aired, eliciting gestures of support and proclamations of assistance. However, the absence of social affirmation is not without consequences for both the self and the peer group. The Asian concept of face thus sensitizes researchers to different dimensions of social, cultural, and possibly economic capital that individuals can derive when giving, saving, and gaining face via their online network interactions.

When we consider current research on online social networking, a great deal of emphasis is placed on the dimension of gaining face but insufficiently focused on losing face. Little or no research attention has been paid to situations where face is not given to someone, for example, where a post or tweet is not liked or shared, wherein the person who is actively self-presenting then loses face as a consequence of peer indifference. All of these online articulations, whether employing or subverting the technical tools the platforms afford, be they textual or visual, can be consciously or unwittingly made in the interest of face management. Ho (1976) noted that face has not gained extensive traction as a concept in the social sciences. We would add that extrapolation of the concepts of face and facework to online social networks is also limited. Yet the inherently ego-driven and community-oriented nature of face is highly congruent with the logics and characteristics of online social networks that impel people to interact while individually showcasing themselves. Hence, we posit that the dominant analytical frames for studying online social networking, while justifiably concerned with social capital, would be enriched if the principles of gaining, saving, giving, and losing face and the dimensions of self, other, and mutual face are incorporated. Furthermore, future research that incorporates the dimension of face in online social networking can also seek to integrate online and offline "face" and explore how and to what extent online practice and offline social relationship dynamics surrounding face complement and complicate each other.

References

Baig, N., Ting-Toomey, S., & Dorjee, T. (2014). Intergenerational narratives on face: A South Asian Indian American perspective. *Journal of International and Intercultural Communication*, 7: 127–147.

Bakhshi, S., Shamma, D. A., & Gilbert, E. (2014, April). Faces engage us: Photos with faces attract more likes and comments on instagram. In Proceedings of the SIGCHI Conference on Human Factors in Computing Systems (pp. 965–974). ACM.

Boiger, M., Güngör, D., Karasawa, M., & Mesquita, B. (2014). Defending honour, keeping face: Interpersonal affordances of anger and shame in Turkey and Japan, *Cognition and Emotion*, 28: 1255–1269.

boyd., d. (2007). Why youth (heart) social network sites: The role of networked publics in teenage social life. In D. Buckingham (Ed.) *Youth identity and digital media* (pp. 119–142). Cambridge, MA: MIT Press.

Brown, P. & Levinson, S. (1978). Universals in language usage: Politeness phenomena. In E. N. Goody (Ed.), *Questions and politeness* (pp. 57–324). Cambridge: Cambridge University Press.

Brown, P. & Levinson, S. (1987). *Politeness: Some universals in language usage*. Cambridge: Cambridge University Press.

Carpenter, C.J., (2012). Narcissism on Facebook: Self-promotional and anti-social behaviour. *Personality and Individual Differences, 52*: 482–486.

Davenport, S., Bergman, S.M., Bergman, J.Z., Fearrington, M.E. (2014). Twitter versus Facebook: Exploring the role of narcissism in the motives and usage of different social media platforms. *Computers in Human Behavior, 32*: 212–220.

DeAndrea, D.C., & Walther, J. (2011). Attributions for inconsistencies between online and offline self-presentations. *Communication Research, 38*(6): 805–825.

Gao, G., Ting-Toomey, S. & Gudykunst, W. B. (1996). Chinese communication processes. In M. H. Bond (Ed.), *The handbook of Chinese psychology* (pp. 49–54). Hong Kong; New York: Oxford University Press.

Gilbert, P., Gilbert, J., & Sanghera, J. (2004). A focus group exploration of the impact of izzat, shame, subordination and entrapment on mental health and service use in South Asian women living in Derby. *Mental Health, Religion & Culture, 7*(2): 109–130.

Goffman, E. (1959). *The presentation of self in everyday life*. New York, NY: Doubleday.

Goffman, E. (1972). On face-work: An analysis of ritual elements in social interaction. In E. Goffman (Ed.), *Interaction ritual: Essays on face-to-face behaviour* (pp. 5–46). London: Penguin.

Gonzales, A. L., & Hancock, J. T. (2008). Identity shift in computer-mediated environments. *Media Psychology, 11*(2): 167–185.

Hall, J., Pennington, N., & Lueders, A. (2013). Impression management and formation on Facebook: A lens model approach. *New Media & Society, 16*(6): 958–982.

Haugh, M., & Watanabe, Y. (2009). Analysing 'face-in-interaction' in Japanese: Insights from intercultural business meetings. In F. Bargiela-Chiappini & M. Haugh (Eds.), *Face, communication, and social interaction* (pp. 289–304). London, UK: Equinox Publishing.

Ho, D. Y.-F. (1976). On the concept of face. *American Journal of Sociology, 81*(4): 867–884.

Hogan, B. (2010). The presentation of self in the age of social media: Distinguishing performances and exhibitions Online. *Bulletin of Science Technology & Society, 30*: 377–386.

Hu, H. C. (2004). 中国人的面子观 [Face, from a Chinese perspective]. In H. C. Hu & G. G. Huang (Eds.), *Face: Chinese power games* (pp. 57–83). Beijing: China Renmin University Press.

Huang, K. P., & Wang, K. Y. (2011). How guanxi relates to social capital? A psychological perspective. *Journal of Social Sciences, 7*(2): 120.

Kim, Y., & Yang, J. (2010). The influence of *Chemyon* on facework and conflict styles: Searching for the Korean face and its impact. *Public Relations Review, 37*(1): 60–67.

Kim, Y-H., & Cohen, D. (2010). Information, perspective, and judgments about the self in face and dignity cultures. *Personality and Social Psychology Bulletin, 36*: 537–550.

Leary, M. R., & Kowalski, R. M. (1990). Impression management: A literature review and two-component model. *Psychological Bulletin, 107*(1): 34–47.

Liang, H., & Walker, G. (2011) Does "face" constrain Mainland Chinese people from starting new leisure activities? *Leisure/Loisir, 35*(2): 211–225.

Lim, S.S., Vadrevu, S., Chan, Y.K., & Basnyat, I. (2012) Facework on Facebook: The online publicness of juvenile delinquents and youths-at-risk. *Journal of Broadcasting & Electronic Media, 56*(3): 346–361.

Lin, L.-H. (2011). Cultural and organizational antecedents of *guanxi*: The Chinese Cases. *Journal of Business Ethics*, 99(3): 441–451.

Marwick, A. E., & boyd, d. (2011). I tweet honestly, I tweet passionately: Twitter users, context collapse, and the imagined audience. *New Media & Society*, 13(1): 114–133.

Matsumoto, Y. (1988). Reexamination of the universality of face: Politeness phenomena in Japanese. *Journal of Pragmatics*, 12(4): 403–426.

Ong, E. Y., Ang, R. P., Ho, J. C., Lim, J. C., Goh, D. H., Lee, C. S., & Chua, A. Y. (2011). Narcissism, extraversion and adolescents' self-presentation on Facebook. *Personality and Individual Differences*, 50(2), 180–185.

Pham T. H. N. (2014). How do the Vietnamese lose face? Understanding the concept of face through self-reported, face loss incidents. *International Journal of Language and Linguistics*, 2: 223–231.

Peluchette, J., & Karl, K. (2009). Examining students' intended image on Facebook: "What Were They Thinking?!" *Journal of Education for Business*, 85(1): 30–37.

Qi, X. (2011). Face: A Chinese concept in a global sociology. *Journal of Sociology*, 47(3): 279–295.

Rosenberg, J., & Egbert, N. (2011). Online impression management: Personality traits and concerns for secondary goals as predictors of self-presentation tactics on Facebook. *Journal of Computer-Mediated Communication*, 17: 1–18.

Rui, J., & Stefanone, M. (2013). Strategic self-presentation online: A cross-cultural study. *Computers in Human Behavior*, 29: 110–118.

Strano, M. M. (2008). User descriptions and interpretations of self-presentation through Facebook profile images. *Cyberpsychology: Journal of Psychosocial Research on Cyberspace*, 2(2), 5. Retrieved from http://www.cyberpsychology.eu/view.php?cisloclanku=2008110402&article=5.

Strano, M., & Wattai, J. (2010). Covering your face on Facebook: Managing identity through untagging and deletion. In F. Sudweeks, H. Hrachovec, and C. Ess (Eds.), Proceedings cultural attitudes towards communication and technology (pp. 288–299). Murdoch University, Australia.

Stritzke, W. G. K., Nguyen, A., & Durkin, K. (2004) Shyness and computer-mediated communication: A self-presentational theory perspective, *Media Psychology*, 6: 1–22.

Ting-Toomey, S. (1994). *The challenge of facework: Cross-cultural and interpersonal issues*. New York, NY: SUNY Press.

Ting-Toomey, S., Gao, G., Trubisky, P., Yang, Z., Kim, H. S., Lin, S. L., & Nishida, T. (1991). Culture, face maintenance, and styles of handling interpersonal conflict: A study in five cultures. *International Journal of Conflict Management*, 2(4): 275–296.

Ting-Toomey, S. & Oetzel, J. G. (2002). Cross-cultural face concerns and conflict styles. In W. B. Gudykunst & B. Mody (Eds.), *Handbook of international and intercultural communication* (pp. 143–163). Thousand Oaks, CA: Sage.

Tong, S., Van Der Heide, B., Langwell, L., & Walther, J. (2008). Too much of a good thing? The relationship between number of friends and interpersonal impressions on Facebook. *Journal of Computer-Mediated Communication*, 13: 531–549.

Ukosakul, M. (2003). Conceptual metaphors motivating the use of Thai 'face.' In E. Casad and G. Palmer (Eds.), *Cognitive linguistics and non-Indo-European Languages* (pp. 275–302). Berlin, New York, NY: Mouton de Gruyter.

Ukosakul, M. (2005). The significance of 'face' and politeness in social interaction as revealed through Thai 'face' idioms. In R. T. Lakoff and S. Ide (Eds.), *Broadening the horizon of linguistic politeness* (pp. 117–128). Amsterdam, Philadelphia, PA: John Benjamins Publishing.

Ukosakul, M. (2009). Significance of 'face' and politeness in social interaction as revealed through Thai 'face' idioms. In F. Bargiela-Chiappini & M. Haugh (Eds.), *Face, communication, and social interaction* (pp. 289–304). London, UK: Equinox Publishing.

Utz, S. (2010). Show me your friends and I will tell you what type of person you are: How one's profile, number of friends, and type of friends influence impression formation on social network sites. *Journal of Computer-Mediated Communication, 15*: 314–335.

Wesch (2009). YouTube and you: Experiences of self-awareness in the context collapse of the recording webcam. *Explorations in Media Ecology, 8*(2): 19–34.

Yang, J. (2015). The influence of culture on Koreans' risk perception, *Journal of Risk Research, 18*(1), 69–92.

3 My Letter to Heaven via E-mail

Translocal Piety and Mediated Selves in Urban Marian Piety in the Philippines

Manuel Victor J. Sapitula and Cheryll Ruth R. Soriano

Introduction: Popular Religion and the Internet

The continuing relevance and growth of religious practices in many parts of the world belie "predictions" regarding the decline of religion in modern society. This perspective, known as the "secularization thesis," presupposes that modern ethos is incompatible with religion, so that the advance of modernity *de facto* results in the decline of the religious in favor of secular values and ways of thinking. Studies have demonstrated that religion need not be adversely affected by modernizing conditions if it can utilize opportunities afforded by changing conditions in making religious practices more accessible (Fuller, 2004; Parker, 2002; P. Taylor, 2002). Studies in Christianity have particularly noted the means by which ecclesiastical structures respond to "the modernity question" (McAvoy, 1968; O'Dea, 1968), leading to notable changes in the social life of denominations, parish communities, and religious institutes, among others.

Premised on this adaptive capacity of religion, especially in the Asian context, this chapter looks into the salience of religion as "mediated piety" in the Philippines. In particular we explore the practice of importing offline religious practice of the devotion to Our Mother of Perpetual Help (henceforth *Popular Help Devotion)* to the online platform in order to craft its relevance to a broader range of devotees. We demonstrate how notions of interiority of the self (*loob* in Filipino) and shared identity (*kapwa* in Filipino) intersect with religious practices uploaded and practiced online. In this regard it is relevant to look into cultural notions informing the devotees' "religious imaginaries" and how these imaginaries are crafted by agents as reliance on communication technologies increases. *Religious imaginaries* refer to representations of identities that become the basis for determining authenticity and legitimate innovation in devotional practice. Its implications for devotional practices conceived as *online religion* (see Brasher, 2001) may be perceived on two dimensions: first, the formation and maintenance of relationships with the divine figure and other devotees and second, the ties that bind online devotional practice and individual identities. These two foci are in turn intimately linked to culturally sensitive notions of relationship (*kapwa*) and selfhood (*loob*). We then interrogate whether there is a significant difference between devotees availing themselves of actual novena sessions and those who, being unable to come to the shrine, utilize online devotional platforms.

The Perpetual Help Devotion in the Philippines

The Perpetual Help Devotion, considered one of the most popular Catholic devotions in the country, refers to a set of devotional practices surrounding a popular icon of the Virgin Mary that is venerated in a shrine in the Baclaran district in Paranaque in southern Metro Manila. Considering nearly five centuries of Catholic presence in the country, the Perpetual Help Devotion is relatively recent, as it started only during the American colonial period with the arrival of the Redemptorist Missionaries in 1906. The Redemptorists brought with them an icon of the Virgin Mary with the Child Jesus and displayed it at the chapel they built in Baclaran district in 1932. The Redemptorists also built mission churches outside Manila and often named them after Our Mother of Perpetual Help; these shrines in due course also became centers of devotional activity in Visayas and Mindanao. The Perpetual Help shrine in Baclaran district, however, assumed a significant role in spreading the devotion throughout the Philippines and has become a pilgrimage site for residents of Metro Manila and environing provinces. In recognition of its importance, the Perpetual Help shrine in Baclaran was declared a "national shrine" by the bishops of the Philippines in 1958 and was renamed henceforth as the "National Shrine of Our Mother of Perpetual Help."

What catapulted the shrine in Baclaran to popularity is the weekly communal recitation of the Novena to Our Mother of Perpetual Help (or the Perpetual Novena) in 1948, which has continued uninterrupted since (Figure 3.1). The one-hour novena consists of prayers, hymns, and the reading of a sample thanksgiving letter and homily and is integrated with the Mass or the Benediction of the Holy Sacrament. Priests in the Perpetual Help shrine relate how the novena became phenomenally successful in ways that their earlier confreres were not able to anticipate. A cursory review of the growth of the novena devotion suggests that it was rapidly well received by devotees: from the first novena session conducted in June 1948, the number of attendees grew by almost 300% one year later. This popularity is largely explained by the purported "effectiveness" of the novena prayers. Devotees writing thanksgiving letters since 1948 noted countless cases of "answered prayers" that they attribute to praying the novena.

A unique and central feature of the Perpetual Help Devotion is the offering of thanksgiving and petition letters to the Virgin Mary under the title of "Our Mother of Perpetual Help." Based on our interviews with priests, the letters are significant testaments of the devotees' everyday-life concerns in the context of faith and prayerful attention. This has inspired the practice of reading selected petition and thanksgiving letters during the novena itself. After the collection of the letters from boxes every Tuesday, priests and lay staff gather to read thanksgiving letters (petition letters are counted but not

Figure 3.1 Photo of Wednesday novena mass at the National Shrine of Our
Mother of Perpetual Help (Baclaran Shrine). Photo by Manuel V.
Sapitula (6 Jan 2010).

read individually). Thanksgiving letters are classified according to predetermined categories of blessings (e.g., spiritual favors, peace in the home,
financial help, seeking a partner in life, among others). Together with letters
collected from drop boxes, letters submitted online are pooled together and
printed; from this pile five to ten "thanksgiving letters of the week" are
selected. These letters then constitute a pool from which priests choose a
letter to be read in the Wednesday novena sessions. Priests have also occasionally used these letters to frame their homilies so as to better resonate
with the experiences of devotees who come to the shrine.

Online and Offline Religious Worship in the Philippines

Owing to the country's predominant number of Catholic adherents (which
is currently at 81 percent of the population), various devotions to Christ,
Mary, and patron saints have become salient features of religiosity in the
Philippines. Many of these devotions are traceable to the influence of
Iberian Catholicism, which significantly shaped the religious culture in predominantly Christian jurisdictions throughout the archipelago. These forms
of popular piety usually exist alongside official church rites like the Mass and
other sacraments. Most of them are also shrine-based and figure importantly
in the life of local communities. Although ways of venerating patron saints

vary significantly from place to place, they typically have an image or icon enthroned in a local shrine and a recitation of a set of prayers and performance of certain ritual acts. In some localities religious associations are also organized so that devotees may be enrolled as full-fledged members.

While most of these devotional practices remained community oriented and local, a few others (particularly those in urban areas) underwent significant changes due to increasing urbanization and mobility of devotees. There was, first, the challenge of remaining relevant in the midst of societal transformations. As people's expectations and lifestyles change due to novel urban arrangements, there is an increasing desire to adapt prayers, ritual acts, and practices to suit new realities. In some devotions, changes were made in prayer texts to make their language more accessible to modern temperaments and to reflect new conditions more efficiently. There were also changes in ritual acts, with some devotions streamlining certain practices to suit the fast-paced lifestyle of urban residents and the introduction of new expressions of religious piety.

Another change occurred with the dissemination of devotional practices—in this regard the internet became an important tool for reaching increasingly mobile devotees. Particularly with regard to this mode of innovation, the Perpetual Help Devotion proved to be an exemplary case in its increasing

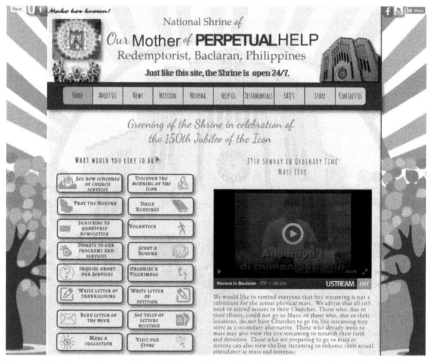

Figure 3.2 Screenshot of the official website of the National Shrine of Our Mother of Perpetual Help. (Source: www.baclaranchurch.org, screenshot taken on 22 October 2015.)

openness to virtual space. Similar to a few other devotions, the Perpetual Help Devotion is online: it has a dedicated website that includes live streams of novena prayers, online facilities for submitting petition and thanksgiving letters, and a virtual tour of the shrine (Figure 3.2). The recent use of internet platforms to engage with more devotees has further extended the reach of devotional practice beyond the geographical confines of the shrine compound.

This move of religious organizations to facilitate religious self-expression online has raised normative debates presenting either a utopian celebration of faith communities' use of the internet to strengthen or expand religious traditions (Zaleski, 1997; Goethals, 2003) or dystopic views that internet technologies will destroy established religion, casting questions on the authenticity of online religious practices (Dawson & Cowan, 2004). The concern with the authenticity of online religious practices centers on the issue of co-presence, which is altered when religious rituals are enacted in cyberspace and as virtual communities distance people from their physical religious institutions (Casey, 2006). Yet, studies also found that people join such online congregations primarily for their ability to harness relationships, to enact some sense of co-presence that enlivens their religious practice (H. Campbell, 2007; Cheong, Poon, Huang, & Casas, 2009). Recent research explored the dichotomy between *religion online* (or how the use of the internet to disseminate information allows religious institutions to maintain relevance by opening up multiple channels of communication), and *online religion* (where people are given the opportunity to participate in and practice religious activity such as masses, prayer, meditation, spiritual counseling, or devotion and enables new forms of traditional religious expression) (Dawson & Cowan, 2004).

Extending extant literature that examines practices of religion online or online religion as separate entities, we explore the use of the internet to understand how the nature and authenticity of religious meanings or imaginaries in relation to the Perpetual Help Devotion are influenced by the shrine's initiative of offering religious services online. By looking into the interconnected relationships of people's devotional practices online and offline, and through the lens of local concepts *loob* and *kapwa,* we explore the nature of mediated piety and how individual connection to the divine is affirmed or altered in online practices.

The Perpetual Help Devotion in particular is useful in assessing how the continuing relevance of religion in modern society is skillfully crafted by agents through the use of the internet. As a form of "modern popular religion," the Perpetual Help Devotion demonstrates a turn toward self-reliance and interiority by enabling meaning-making at the practical levels of life, while at the same time instituting enduring forms of community life (see Parker, 1998; C. Taylor, 1989). Internet communication technologies have generally facilitated the individualization process of religion as online resources make access to devotional resources more personalized (H. Campbell, 2007). It has, however, also led to new forms of connectivity among individuals (Brasher, 2001), insofar as online resources like Facebook pages, internet forums, live streams, and websites enable the "translocalization" of religious practices. As will be shown below, this co-occurrence of individualization and new social forms is premised not only on the use of internet communication technologies, but on culturally salient notions of selfhood, togetherness, and community.

Methodology

In view of this increasing turn to media technologies, the paper focuses on the interplay of material, spatial, and virtual modes of devotional practice. The material and spatial modes mostly refer to the actual conduct of devotional activities in the Perpetual Help shrine. Wednesday is the typical devotion day and the shrine's busiest time of the week because devotees coming for novena sessions reach 100,000 and as many as 120,000 during the first Wednesday of the month (Hechanova, 1998). In the course of the research we observed the shrine compound in order to assess how media technologies were utilized there. We also participated in some of the activities pertaining to the novena, particularly the weekly reading and tallying of petition and thanksgiving letters by the priests and staff.

The letters of thanksgiving cited in this paper were obtained from www. baclaranchurch.org, the official website of the Perpetual Help Devotion in the shrine in Baclaran. When comparisons between online and written letters were necessary, we obtained samples of written letters with the permission of the Rector of the shrine. While the general content of the letters is cited verbatim in this paper, we refrained from indicating personal details of devotees in order to protect their identities. In order to supplement data obtained online we also conducted interviews with members of the Media Team, as well as Redemptorist priests who are involved in media production, mostly in advisory and decision-making capacities. The Perpetual Help shrine shared with us the website analytics for April 2014, which provided us a glimpse of how the website is used, where the website visitors are located, and the nature of devotees' engagement with the website. We also monitored responses to the official website and the shrine's official Facebook page by looking at the number of hits and visits.

Innovation and Imagination in "Online Religion"

The Perpetual Help shrine has invested in a range of multimedia initiatives hosted on or linked to an interactive website. The first website, www. baclarannovena.org was set up in 2007 to allow devotees to observe weekly devotions through a live stream of its Wednesday novena sessions. Besides the novena prayers, the website also provides updates on shrine activities and links to religious-themed YouTube videos, most of which are produced by the shrine's Liturgy Ministry. The website facilitated a "simulation" of weekly novena experiences for devotees (J. Echano, Personal communication, May 12, 2014), thus allowing overseas Filipinos to feel that they are "participants" in the performance of devotional activities *in situ*.

The website also features a facility that allows devotees to send petition and thanksgiving letters online. Filipino Catholics are firm believers in writing and sending these letters because they believe that it is one of the most effective ways of communicating their struggles and concerns with the Virgin Mary. Devotees may write letters and mail them to the shrine or send letters to the shrine's official e-mail address. The 2007 website explains that the thanksgiving letters "are a testament to answered prayers which manifest the abundant graces that comes from God through perseverance in prayer." Thousands of these letters are received each week, and the online facility has further increased the number of received letters. When devotees send letters through the website facility they are directed to an e-mail address that can be accessed only by the Rector of the shrine or his secretary (V. Cueto, Personal communication, February 8, 2014).

Although discussions as to the proper content of multimedia initiatives have taken place among Redemptorists and lay collaborators, there is implicit consensus regarding the need to reach devotees who have migrated overseas. This complements the increasing involvement of the Perpetual Help shrine with the migrants and their left-behind families.[1] At present the Perpetual Help shrine refers mostly to website analytics, Facebook likes, network extensiveness, and Ustream views in assessing the reach of the new website facility. For the period April 1 to May 1, 2014, the website's homepage had 7,394 page views from visitors from various continents (Figure 3.3).

Figure 3.3 Geographic location of the website visitors of www.baclaranchurch.org. (Website analytics for 1 April 2014–1 May 2014, shared by Fr. Joey Echano of the National Shrine of Our Mother of Perpetual Help.)

The 2007 website continued to function until March 2014 when shrine authorities launched an updated website, this time with the domain address of www.baclaranchurch.org. The intent of the new website was to address the limitations of the older (2007) website; it is currently maintained by Fr. Joseph Echano, C.Ss.R., a member of the Redemptorist Baclaran community. The 2014 website adopted a more interactive design and included more options in terms of content and services. The updated website offers facilities for more active engagement, for instance tabs for "pray the novena," "volunteer," "start a novena," "donate to our programs and services," "start a pilgrimage," "make a suggestion," and "visit our store." Even the page on the "History of the Icon" has an interactive format: whenever the pointer is hovered over a replica of the icon, a corresponding explanation of theological significance and other highlights may be read. Fr. Echano explained that this wide range of services in the website's homepage draws devotees to the site, encouraging them to experiment with any of the available services. The facility for uploading letters of petition and thanksgiving is complemented in the new website by a tally of thanksgiving letters received (Figure 3.4), as well as an uploaded copy of the "Letter of the Week," which can be read by the website visitor (Figure 3.5). This feature is updated weekly to include the new letters; the old letters are not archived as they are replaced.

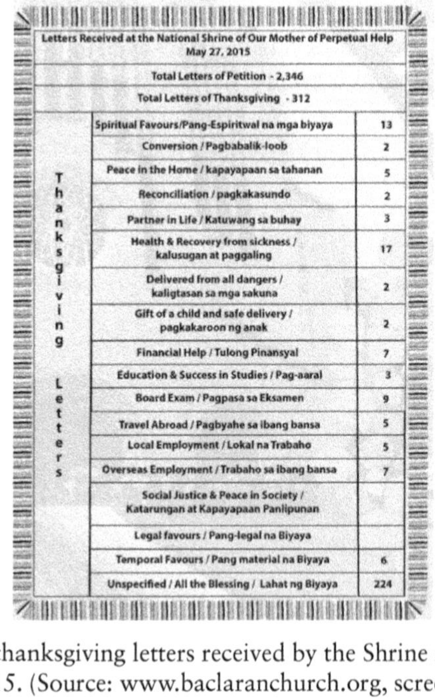
Letters Received at the National Shrine of Our Mother of Perpetual Help
May 27, 2015

Total Letters of Petition - 2,346

Total Letters of Thanksgiving - 312

Thanksgiving Letters		
	Spiritual Favours/Pang-Espiritwal na mga biyaya	13
	Conversion / Pagbabalik-loob	2
	Peace in the Home / kapayapaan sa tahanan	5
	Reconciliation / pagkakasundo	2
	Partner in Life / Katuwang sa buhay	3
	Health & Recovery from sickness / kalusugan at paggaling	17
	Delivered from all dangers / kaligtasan sa mga sakuna	2
	Gift of a child and safe delivery / pagkakaroon ng anak	2
	Financial Help / Tulong Pinansyal	7
	Education & Success in Studies / Pag-aaral	3
	Board Exam / Pagpasa sa Eksamen	9
	Travel Abroad / Pagbyahe sa ibang bansa	5
	Local Employment / Lokal na Trabaho	5
	Overseas Employment / Trabaho sa ibang bansa	7
	Social Justice & Peace in Society / Katarungan at Kapayapaan Panlipunan	
	Legal favours / Pang-legal na Biyaya	
	Temporal Favours / Pang material na Biyaya	6
	Unspecified / All the Blessing / Lahat ng Biyaya	224

Figure 3.4 Tally of thanksgiving letters received by the Shrine for the week of 27 May 2015. (Source: www.baclaranchurch.org, screenshot taken on 22 October 2015.)

Posting the tally of the letters online also signals the importance of the virtual community as an integral part of the shrine's community of devotees. In the same way the chosen "letter of the week" is read to devotees

> *September 21*
>
> *2014*
>
> *Thank you oh Lord, though Jesus Christ and with intercession of Mama Mary our Mother of Perpetual Help.*
>
> *Thank you for the freedom after being jailed for one year at UAE. It is only 5 days since I was freed and back here in the Philippines to live a normal life.*
>
> *Thank you for the great chance for me to lead another life. And hope that you will continue to grant me more blessings to continue to be a good son who have been found again by You and back to your sweet embrace Oh God.*
>
> *Thank you for this gift of life. Grant me the peace of mind so I can continue to live a good life and be a blessing for others. Thank you for the material and spiritual blessings that you have granted me all my life since I was born and thank you for giving me a good family whom I can turn to in all times I need them!*
>
> *Your son,*
> *(signed)*

Figure 3.5 Sample letter of the week posted at the website of the National Shrine of Our Mother of Perpetual Help, www.baclaranchurch.org (dated 21 September 2014, with permission from the National Shrine of Our Mother of Perpetual Help as custodian of the letter).

present in the novena devotions in the shrine, uploaded letters are made known to devotees who access the website. Members of the Media Team explained that the "tally" and the "letter of the week," which are important components of the Wednesday novena in the shrine and are posted with the live stream of the novena sessions, facilitate a fuller and "more accurate" experience of the novena devotion for those tapping the online services.

The agility that characterizes the Perpetual Help shrine's openness to modern communication technologies signals a change in the way religious devotion is deployed to meet certain needs. The use of online media has provided important support for the shrine's continuing orientation toward translocality. The intent behind the newly renovated website is not mere information dissemination but the "simulation" of the novena by utilizing technologies like live streaming, which transcends geographical distance through real-time broadcasting. As some members of the Media Team pointed out, the vision guiding recent innovations is "re-creating the experience of entering the shrine as one enters the website." All of these innovations aim at creating a more "holistic" online experience so that devotees accessing online interfaces of the novena are not deprived of the full experience of praying as if they were actually at the shrine (R. Pantua & B. Mayor, Personal communication, February 15, 2014). At the same time, however, Shrine administrators reflect that the online facilities resulted in a considerable change in the perception of the role of the church, both from the regulative and "consumption" dimensions of devotional practice. Online initiatives reconfigure hierarchical relationships such that ecclesiastical authorities are disposed to actively engage with devotees, respond to their requests, and catalyze community-building initiatives beyond the confines of the church's existing structures.

Portraying Devotional Authenticity Through the *Loob* (Inner Self)

The notion of "authenticity" is an important, sometimes even crucial, feature of devotional practice. It mainly refers to the expectation that devotion ought to be centered on human (not merely ritual) considerations and factors. In Hinduism it is widely regarded that *bhakti* (devotional practice) has a reciprocal and mutual character between devotee and god, and also among devotees themselves, which is a condition for its authenticity (O'Connell, 2014). In European Christianity the matter of "true devotion" hinged on the "religion of the heart" that stressed the affective dimension of experience as opposed to cerebral and mystical excesses that characterized seventeenth and eighteenth century spirituality (T. A. Campbell, 1991). That devotion ought to be "authentic" is already assumed in many devotional traditions; what matters, however, is the standard by which devotional practices are assessed as such.

In Filipino cultural repertoire, the notion of *loob* (innermost self) plays an important role in assessing the authenticity of the devotional relationship with the divine figure and is thus an important platform in assessing culturally sensitive notions of popular religion. The *loob* refers to a quality of one's personhood that stresses interiority and hence a certain freedom from external constraints and pressures. As the innermost self, *loob* is the seat of subjectivity and intentionality and the ground of relationships with one's *kapwa* (Alejo, 1990). In the context of popular religion the *loob* is crucial in establishing an enduring relationship with the divine figure, which begins with the opening up of oneself (*pagbubukas ng loob*) to the divine figure's influence and care (Sapitula, 2013a). This opening up is not ritualistic in character (despite the fact that rituals figure prominently in the devotion) but is based on the sincerity of one's purpose.

A close reading of letters at the Perpetual Help shrine from the 1940s to the present reveals that the authenticity of one's devotion strongly hinges on notions of interiority, sincerity, and truthfulness that is presupposed in one's *loob* (see Sapitula, 2013b). The writing of letters has thus facilitated a trend toward the individualization of religious practice. The virtual spaces of the internet have, however, fostered the creation of a new platform supporting the continuing personalization of religious practice, as internet platforms condition the flexibility of bringing everyday-life struggles into the context of devotional practice. By "authentic," devotional practices mediated online effect the same experience of closeness to the divine figure and feelings of assurance that petitions will be heard.

The devotional letters reveal it is the *loob* that establishes the authenticity of one's devotional practices. The task of the devotee is to open his/her *loob* to the patronage of the divine figure—this counts as "authentic" devotion, as opposed to "counterfeit" devotion that performs religious acts devoid of faith in the goodwill of the divine figure. This character of devotional practice at the shrine has remained fundamentally unchanged in the course of six decades (see Sapitula, 2013b). A migrant devotee, writing in 1959, perceived her successful trip to the United States as a debt of gratitude (*utang na loob*) to the Virgin Mary. She wrote:

> I left our native land on December 11, 1957. I am very happy and thankful, and I regard this as a significant debt of gratitude (*malaking utang na loob*) to you, our helpful Mother. While sailing I prayed the novena, imploring that we reach our destination safely and without encountering any accidents [at sea]. I reached America on January 2, 1958, a little anxious [of my life here] although my grandfather and my friends are also here with me … There are times when I am short of funds and encounter problems in my studies, prompting me to think of not finishing school. But after praying to you I feel strengthened (*lumalakas ang loob*) in finding solutions to my problems.
>
> (Letter dated July 20, 1959; translated from Tagalog original)

Another woman devotee, writing in 2005, emphasizes the importance of *loob* in her devotion with these words:

> Mama Mary, because of continuous trials that come our way, I just found myself attending Mass here in Baclaran every week. As I draw closer to you and have a change of heart (*pagbabalik-loob*), I found true peace inner peace and peace of mind (*kapayapaan ng loob at isipan*) that I have not experienced for a long time because I have forgotten you.
>
> (Letter undated [c. 2005]; translated from Tagalog original)

These brief testimonials allude to "authentic" devotion by highlighting intimate links in the performance of religious acts (attending Mass and praying the novena), debt of gratitude (*utang na loob*), change of heart (*pagbabalik-loob*) and inner peace (*kapayapaan ng loob*). This involvement of the *loob* is not incidental but central to the devotees' religious experience.

As the Perpetual Help shrine administration expands its web-based services, however, forms of devotional practice resulting from new technologies (including letter-writing through internet platforms) assert themselves as legitimate means of fostering authentic devotion. The issue here basically

concerns the role of *loob* in such internet platforms: is *loob* still the significant indicator of devotional authenticity in letters submitted online, assuming that such is the case for letters submitted in the conventional facility (i.e.,
drop box or postal mail)? A close reading of devotional letters submitted
online strongly suggests that there is no significant difference between conventional and online forms, as both rest on the perceived need for reciprocity with the divine figure. Thus, the religious imaginary of devotees engaged
in the virtual realm are pegged to the same notions of "authentic devotion"
despite the use of a different platform. Consider the letter submitted online
by a female devotee in 2013:

> I also claim,[2] Mother of Perpetual Help, that with your help the love
> and concern of my husband for me will return. You already know
> why … Mother of Perpetual Help I ask for your help, please watch
> over our relationship. Give me a lot of patience so that I can under-
> stand him, so that I can understand him completely, loving Mother.
> I claim, Mother of Perpetual Help, that with your help he will stop
> engaging with in his vices like smoking and gambling. Please help me.
> Thank you for all the blessings, Mother of Perpetual Help.
> (Letter undated [c. 2013]; translated from Tagalog original)

As can be seen, the devotee banks on the same notion of being honest and
truthful, qualities emerging from one's *loob*, when requesting something
from the Virgin Mary. She claims, quite candidly, that there are things that
the divine figure already knows, which suggests feelings of closeness with
the divine figure. Another devotee, conscious of using the internet facility for
submitting letters, remarks:

> I am very speechless. You never failed me. I don't know how to express
> how thankful I am right now. My visa has been approved. I hope it
> gets to me safely. But THANK YOU SOOOOO MUCH. Not even an
> all caps can fathom how thankful I am right now. I don't know how
> I can repay this, but I will try my hardest. Lord, You are amazing. After
> all the sins I have done, You still accepted me and blessed me. Lord,
> YOU ARE AMAZING!
> (Letter dated May 2, 2014;
> from verbatim English letter posted at
> http://www.baclaranchurch.org/letter-of-the-week.html)

The words "not even an all caps can fathom how thankful I am right now"
insinuates that while the devotee is using the internet as a platform to communicate with the divine figure, importance is accorded to the actual experience of joy welling up from one's *loob*. These and similar testimonies point
to the *loob* as the animating principle of devotional practice, whether it is
performed in the shrine, in the home, or on the internet.

Framing 'Translocal' *Pakikipagkapwa* in Devotional Practice

Previous studies have claimed that Filipino variants of popular religion are not merely transactional but are hinged on notions of authenticity and mutuality between the divine figure and devotees (e.g., Balajadia, 1991; Bautista, 2010; Cannell, 1999). It was particularly Cannell's (1999) anthropological research with devotees of an image of the Dead Christ (*Amang Hinulid*) in Bicol that alluded to an "exchange motif," noting that popular religion implies devotees' expectations of mutuality with divine figures. This resonates with Cerulo and Barra's (2008) assertion that divine figures assume the role of "legitimate co-interactants" in prayer, as well as Martin's (2009) observation that the saint's interventions in everyday affairs are assumed, if not openly expected, by devotees.

Such notions of intimacy with divine figures are highlighted in the notion of *kapwa*[3] (usually translated as *others*) in Filipino cultural psychology. In Maggay's (2002) analysis of Filipino interpersonal communication, *kapwa* encompasses the sphere of *ibang tao* (people who are "different from me/us," implying distance) and *hindi ibang tao* (people who are "not different from me/us," implying closeness). Many thanksgiving letters have implied that the divine figure is a person who is not far-off (*iba*) from the devotee, and that the devotional relationship is enacted with someone who is deemed to be close to oneself (*pakikipagkapwa sa hindi ibang tao*) (Sapitula, 2013a). Devotees display *pakikipagkapwa* (forming a relationship) by resorting to quite casual and straightforward language in addressing the divine figure, seemingly oblivious to its authority and power over them. Consider how one devotee casually addressed the Virgin Mary as "Ma" (mother) in one of the letters:

> Ma, I hope you'll help me to ask forgiveness from (sic) all my trespasses, from my words, deeds, thoughts and failed (sic) to do the things that should be done. I hope I receive forgiveness from other people whom I have wronged. Ma, help me to bring myself (*loob*) to Jesus. Please, Ma, I can't understand myself, if my faith in him is really strong.
>
> (Letter dated June 4, 1997; some parts translated from Tagalog original)

This sense of closeness is also extended to loved ones, especially members of one's family, significant others, close friends, or anyone who is deemed as special. The letters are replete with instances of devotees praying for people whom they hold dear, like a woman devotee who prayed for a good life (*magandang buhay*) for her former husband:

> Thank you, beloved Mother, that you have not abandoned him [N.B. the devotee's ex-husband]. I hope he continues with the good things

he has planned for his life even if we are already separated from each other. Loving Mother, I pray that you continue to guide him toward the good life (*mabuting buhay*), for I also desire his happiness. I wish the best of everything for him and for his future partner. I really hope he finds someone who will be his life-long companion.

(Undated letter [c. 1990s];
some parts translated from Tagalog original)

As devotees commenced using the shrine's website and official Facebook page in sending letters, a close reading of e-mailed letters demonstrates that notions of *pakikipagkapwa* have basically remained the same: there is reason to suppose that the modalities of engaging with the divine figure are premised on the formation of real, albeit invisible, bonds. Consider this letter (submitted online) by a female devotee in 2008:

> Mother of Perpetual Help, I know that you might be getting impatient with me already because I always pray that I and my friends may pass [the Board Exams], and also for those students who are in dire need. I know that you will give me what I ask for when the right time comes. Loving Mother, I pray that this time I can pass the Local Board [Exams]. Let that be your gift for me this Christmas. I promise that I will use it [my profession] in a good way and I will help everyone to the best of my abilities.
>
> (Undated letter; translated from Tagalog original)

This brief testimonial illustrates the same notions of closeness, with the devotee even alluding to the fact that the divine figure is "getting impatient" (*nakukulitan*) with her persistence. She also alludes to her *kapwa* (fellow exam takers) and prays that they pass the licensure exams.

Especially for migrant devotees, the utilization of online devotional platforms effects strong bonds that connect them to "the homeland," which is also an *imagined community* (see Anderson, 2006) of fellow devotees. This is the sense that can be obtained from a letter from a migrant devotee:

> I thank the Lord for giving me this chance in my life to pray with all the Filipinos in this website. Every minute in my life I wait and anticipate for (sic) every opportunity to speak to you, my Mother … Every time I turn on (sic) to this website, I feel I am home in the Philippines. I can feel the warmth of your love. The direction you have given our lives … You are our stairway to eternal life.
>
> (Letter dated April 27, 2014; verbatim English letter posted at http://
www.baclaranchurch.org/letter-of-the-week.html)

The position of the Virgin Mary as "mother" further reinforces this bond because the ties are perceived to be *familial* in nature: devotees regard themselves as "children" of the Virgin Mary because she has proved herself ready to assist devotees in their time of need. Thus, while the mode of engaging migrant devotees has expanded to include the "cybertemple" motif, expectations pertaining to the stability of the devotional relationship have not changed. This is significant because expectations and obligations flowing from the devotional relationship, insofar as they are guided by cultural notions of *pakikipagkapwa*, tend to remain the same regardless of the medium used by devotees.

Concluding Remarks

In the course of the discussion the paper explored how the Perpetual Help shrine was able to utilize the internet to extend devotional practice beyond geographical space and toward virtual space. The findings confirm Miller and Slater's (2000) assertion that the internet "can be exploited for the purposes of religious practice, which go well beyond the bland concept of 'communication' and enter into a dialogue about the nature of relationships both personal and theological" (pp. 186–187). We demonstrated the active role of communication technologies in crafting the continued relevance of popular religion and facilitating the emergence of translocal modes of producing religious meanings.

We noted in the course of the paper that religious piety mediated through the internet veers toward imaginaries that are premised on strong bonds with the divine figure through the enactment of one's *loob* (innermost self). In the course of the discussion we demonstrated how *loob* provides resources that maintain devotional practice, in that it is as disposed to sociality as it is to interiority. The social dimension of *loob* and *kapwa* conditions the interaction between religious piety and devotees' engagement with institutional agents. We demonstrated how mediation afforded by internet technologies enabled a two-way regulation of virtual space so that shrine authorities and devotees are able to mutually influence each other in the process of continued engagement.

In assessing how online mediation of novenas and letter writing change the nature of devotional practices, we note a parallel analysis suggested by Baudrillard's (1998) notion of the simulacra. He queries, "Does it [the icon] remain the supreme authority, simply incarnated in images as a visible theology?" (Baudrillard, 1998, p. 352). He alluded to the threat posed by the simulacra to the "real," which may be taken as the threat posed by online technologies on "true devotion." This issue is certainly relevant in the reproduction of iconic representations of the divine, especially because, in the case of the Perpetual Help Devotion, there is the notion of the "original icon" that is purported to be miraculous. What the Perpetual Help shrine in Baclaran (and other shrines) possesses is a replica of the original icon, which underwent a process of sacralization to acquire the same properties as the original icon (Garcia-Paz, n.d.). In this regard the explosion of replicas (both officially recognized and popular reproductions) may indeed cast a question on the necessity of the original icon.

The direction of our inquiry in this study, however, went beyond "the iconic" and emphasized practice. We thus differ from Baudrillard's estimation that mediation of devotional acts will tend to compromise its authenticity. Hjarvard (2006, p. 8) in fact claims that media "have become society's main purveyor of enchanting experiences." What we found is that the importation of devotional practices online has facilitated the continued relevance of popular religion itself. The continuing relevance is crafted through investment in technological updating and the production and diversification of religious imaginaries. These mutually reinforcing mechanisms transform online technologies so that they become vehicles for making the sacred accessible to more people. Thus, the live stream of novena prayers and online facilities for submitting letters documented here do not necessarily negate the general orientation toward authenticity and reciprocity; instead, they build on it to make "direct contact with the sacred" (Carroll, 1989, p. 38) possible for these devotees. Perceiving the internet as technology that can promote the interests of devotional practice allows religiously motivated users to cultivate religious practice online, while scholars look into mechanisms that underlie such cultivation and maintenance of such practices. This discourse frames the internet as "sacramental space" (see H. Campbell, 2010) where people can connect with their faith commitments as well as with like-minded believers. In the course of the inquiry we found that online initiatives resonate with the dynamics of "mediatization," wherein core elements of a social or cultural activity (for instance politics and religion, among others) assume media form (Hjarvard, 2006). This process of virtual importation of a social practice transforms the cultural field, as the symbolic content and the structure of the social and cultural activity are influenced by media environments upon which they gradually become more dependent. In the case of devotional practice, the turn to internet technologies has facilitated the "construction of collective emotions" (Hjarvard, 2006, p. 10) outside the confines of holy places and shrines. This need not be perceived as a threat to religious practice *per se*, as alternative forms of community have not posed a threat to the authenticity of devotional practice. We demonstrated that the standards of authenticity from the practitioners' perspective neither lie between the "real" and "simulacra" of iconic representation nor in mere performance of religious ritual. Devotees' accounts demonstrate that devotional authenticity is premised on the interplay of *loob* and *kapwa*, which makes devotional practice deeply personal yet overwhelmingly social in character. It is in this regard that we find Brasher's (2001) notion of *online religion* particularly salient: as virtual spaces online religion is also "inhabited" by people, albeit in different ways from geographical inhabiting.

In the course of this paper, we were able to demonstrate that an intimately personal activity such as devotional practices need not be dismissed as merely individualistic or eccentric and thus devoid of social relevance.

Rather than appealing to this usual notion of religious devotion, we located devotional acts in the broader cultural context of selfhood (*loob*) and shared identity (*kapwa*). By looking at devotional letters, both written and submitted online, we found that individual devotees are always located within webs of relationships; indeed, this web of encounters with one's *kapwa* is activated even in intimately personal activities like prayer and the performance of ritual acts. We are thus convinced that religious devotion, far from removing individuals from engagement with their social worlds, actually invite them to engage with them in creatively accessible and viable ways.

In the course of the research, we also came to the conclusion that the turn to notions of self (*loob*) and shared identity (*kapwa*) creates new trajectories of inquiry regarding the nature and role of religious practice in contemporary societies. The non-duality of *loob* and *kapwa* featured here shows that the devotees' perception of a divine *Other* need not imply distance and coercive power, but may also entail feelings of closeness and involvement with the banal affairs of everyday life. Such close resonance between devotee and divine patron is so deeply entrenched that it remains a vital force even when devotional practices are performed in virtual space. This finding spurs further inquiry regarding alternative modes of expressing individuality apart from oppositional- and other-oriented discourses that have characterized notions of selfhood in typical Western societies. The possibilities offered by the non-duality of self (*loob)* and shared identity (*kapwa*) allow a more nuanced inquiry into the modes of togetherness that coexist with aspirations for personal well-being in the context of modern life and aspirations.

Notes

1. There is currently a weekly Mass for migrants, where left-behind families as well as returnees are invited to participate. After the Mass, volunteers conduct support sessions and group sharing activities with willing participants.
2. "Claiming" something in prayer is a manifestation of faith that the request will be granted. This form of prayer is frequently used in charismatic circles. Based on the other contents of the letter, the devotee is a member of *El Shaddai*, a local Catholic charismatic group founded by Mike Velarde (or Brother Mike to his followers).
3. *Kapwa*, on closer inspection, is different from the English word "other" because the notion of *kapwa* regards other people as closely connected to oneself or even extensions of oneself, while "other" implies difference and separation from oneself.

References

Alejo, A. (1990). *Tao po! Tuloy!: Isang landas ng pag-unawa sa loob ng tao.* Quezon City: Ateneo de Manila University Press.

Anderson, B. (2006). *Imagined communities: Reflections on the origin and spread of nationalism.* London/New York: Verso.

Balajadia, B. (1991). Mass mediums: An initial study of spirit possession groups as popular church in the making. In Belita, J. (Ed.), *And God said: Hala!* Manila: De La Salle University Press.

Baudrillard, J. (1998). The precession of the simulacra. In J. Storey (Ed.), *Cultural theory and popular culture: A Reader.* Athens, GA: University of Georgia Press.

Bautista, J.J. (2010). *Figuring Catholicism: An ethnohistory of the Santo Niño de Cebu.* Quezon City: Ateneo de Manila University Press.

Brasher, B.E. (2001). *Give me that online religion.* San Francisco, CA: Jossey-Bass.

Campbell, H. (2007). Who's got the power? Religious authority and the internet. *Journal of Computer-Mediated Communication, 12*: 1043–1062.

Campbell, H. (2010). *When religion meets new media.* London and New York, NY: Routledge.

Campbell, T.A. (1991). The *religion of the heart: A study of European religious life in the seventeenth and eighteenth centuries,* Columbia, SC: University of South Carolina Press.

Cannell, F. (1999). *Power and intimacy in the Christian Philippines.* Cambridge: Cambridge University Press.

Carroll, M.P. (1989). Italian Catholicism: Making direct contact with the sacred. In R. O'Toole (Ed.), *Sociological studies in Roman Catholicism: Historical and contemporary perspectives.* Studies in Religion and Society Vol. 24. Lewinston, NY: The Edwin Mellen Press.

Casey, C. (2006). Virtual ritual, real faith, the revirtualization of religious ritual in cyberspace, *Online Journal of Religions on the Internet, 2*(1): 73–90.

Cerulo, K.A., and Barra, A. (2008). In the name of …: Legitimate interactants in the dialogue of prayer. *Poetics 36*: 374–388.

Cheong, P.H., Poon, J.P.H., Huang, S.H., Casas, I. (2009). The internet highway and religious communities: Mapping and contesting spaces in religion-online. *The Information Society, 25*(5): 291–302.

Dawson, L. & Cowan, D. (2004). *Religion online. Finding faith on the internet.* London & New York, NY: Routledge.

Fuller, C.J. (2004). *The camphor flame: Popular Hinduism and society in India.* Revised and expanded edition. Princeton, NJ: Princeton University Press.

Garcia-Paz, A.M. (n.d.). *Holy Mary of Perpetual Help: History and interpretation of the icon.* 3 volumes. Translated by J. Campos. No publication details.

Goethals, G. (2003). "Myth and ritual in cyberspace." In Jolyon Mitchell & Sophia Marriage (Eds.), *Mediating religion: Conversations in media, religion and culture.* (pp. 257–269). New York, NY: T&T Clark.

Hechanova, L.G. (1998). *The Baclaran story.* Photos by J. de Guzman, C.Ss.R. Quezon City, Philippines: Claretian Publications.

Hjarvard, S. (2006). *The mediatization of religion. A theory of media as an agent of religious change.* Paper presented to the 5th International Conference on Media, Religion and Culture: Mediating Religion in the Context of Multicultural Tension The Sigtuna Foundation, Stockholm/Sigtuna/Uppsala, Sweden, 6–9 July.

Maggay, M.P. (2002). *Pahiwatig: Kagawiang pangkomunikasyon ng Filipino.* Quezon City: Ateneo de Manila University Press.

Martin, E. (2009). From popular religion to practices of Sacralization: Approaches for a conceptual discussion. *Social Compass, 56*(2): 273–285.

McAvoy, T.T. (1968). American Catholicism and the Aggiornamento. *The Review of Politics, 30*(3), July: 275–291.

Miller, D. and Slater, D. (2000). *The Internet: An ethnographic approach*. Oxford and New York, NY: Berg.

O'Connell, J.T. (2014). Caitanya Vaiṣṇava ethics in relation to devotional community. In R.M. Gupta (Ed.). *Caitanya Vaiṣṇava philosophy: Tradition, reason and devotion* (pp. 135–162). Surrey: Ashgate Publishing.

O'Dea, T. (1968). *The Catholic crisis*. Boston, MA: Beacon Press.

Parker, C.G. (1998). Modern popular religion: A complex object of study for sociology. *International Sociology, 13*(2): 195–212.

Parker, C.G. (2002). Religion and the reawakening of indigenous peoples in Latin America. *Social Compass, 49*(1): 67–81.

Sapitula, M.V.J. (2013a). Ang pagiging deboto bilang pakikipagkapwa: Isang panimulang pagsusuri sa mga liham pasasalamat ng mga deboto ng Ina ng Laging Saklolo sa Baclaran. *Daluyan: Journal ng Wikang Filipino, 19*(2), August: 111–132.

Sapitula, M.V.J. (2013b). *Marian piety and modernity: A Sociological assessment of popular religion in the Philippines*. Unpublished Ph.D. dissertation. Singapore: Faculty of Arts and Social Sciences, National University of Singapore.

Taylor, C. (1989). *Sources of the self: The Making of the modern identity*. Cambridge, MA: Harvard University Press.

Taylor, P. (2002). *Modernity and re-enchantment: Religion in post-revolutionary Vietnam*. Vietnam Update Series. Singapore: Institute of Southeast Asian Studies (ISEAS).

Zaleski, J. (1997): *The Soul of Cyberspace*. San Francisco, CA: Harper Press.

4 Exploring Confucianism in Understanding Face-ism in Online Dating Sites of Eastern and Western Cultures

Michael Prieler

Introduction

Face-ism is the phenomenon in which media visually depict men with more facial prominence than women. Experiments have shown that greater facial prominence is associated with intelligence, attractiveness, and dominance (Archer, Iritani, Kimes, & Barrios, 1983; Zuckerman, 1986). Considering that women are generally shown with less facial prominence than men, such depictions might have real-life consequences for the perceptions of men and women, because people learn from the media and other visual depictions (Bandura, 2009). In this regard, we conducted a content analysis that sought to shed more light on the phenomenon of face-ism from an international perspective. This content analysis is one of the first to employ cross-cultural data (from four cultures) and to study gender representations on the internet (Collins, 2011). It is also the first to employ self-representations from online dating sites for studying face-ism.

Online dating sites are websites where individuals can search for contacts with the aim of fostering a romantic and/or sexual relationship. These websites can be accessed over the internet through mobile devices or computers, and users can search for relationships based on criteria such as age, gender, location, education, and height. Online dating sites have become increasingly popular over the last few years. The Pew Research Center reported that 38% of those who are single in the United States used online dating sites (A. Smith & Duggan, 2013). Research in the Netherlands found that people between 30 and 40 years of age and people low in dating anxiety were the most active online daters, and that online dating was unrelated to income and educational level (Valkenburg & Peter, 2007). Research has also indicated that men and women have a strong preference for similarity when seeking an online partner, as is the case offline (Fiore & Donath, 2005; Hitsch, Hortaçsu, & Arieli, 2010).

In contrast to traditional media (such as magazines or TV) where a photo is chosen by professional photographers and journalists, online dating sites use self-presentations. In other words, the user posts his or her own photographs. Prior research has found that users create their "ideal

self" in such an environment and are strategic in their online presentations (Ellison, Heino, & Gibbs, 2006; Whitty, 2008). This attempt to create
an ideal self has been manifested in men misrepresenting their personal
assets, relationship goals, personal attributes, and heights and women
misrepresenting their weights through online dating sites (J. A. Hall, Park,
Song, & Cody, 2010; Toma, Hancock, & Ellison, 2008). These misrepre-
sentations of height and weight indicate the perceived importance of physical attributes for online daters. Physical attributes are especially visible in
the profile photographs that are posted by users. Attractiveness and other
qualities shown in photographs have been found to be strong predictors
of overall profile attractiveness (Fiore, Taylor, Mendelsohn, & Hearst,
2008), although this was found to be more true for male observers than
for female ones (Hitsch et al., 2010). Online daters have been found to be
the least accurate with their photographs (in comparison to other online
self-presentations, such as height, age, and relationship information), and
this was especially true for less attractive online daters (Toma & Hancock,
2010; Toma et al., 2008). A study by Hancock and Toma (2009) found
that around 1/3 of photographs are inaccurate, occurring more frequently
among women than men. Inaccurate profile photographs included those
that were outdated, retouched, or taken by a professional photographer
to create a more attractive impression overall (Hancock & Toma, 2009).
In short, online daters face a tension between the pressure of appearing
attractive and the need to use a photo that is not judged as deceptive when
meeting face-to-face.

   This study will compare face-ism in online dating sites in Japan, South
Korea, Sweden, and the United States to broaden our understanding of this
under-researched area of media representation. We also seek to investigate
whether there is a relationship between our face-ism results and an inter-
nationally recognized gender index (Hofstede's masculinity index) or indigenous philosophical traditions (Confucianism).

Literature Review and Research Questions

Research on Face-ism

While much research has been done on gender representations in the media
(Collins, 2011), face-ism is one area that has received little attention (Sparks,
2006). The term *face-ism* (or relative facial prominence) was introduced by
Archer et al. (1983), who first measured facial prominence with an index.
The face-ism index measures the distance (in millimeters or any other unit)
of a facial depiction from the top of the head to the lowest point of the chin
divided by the distance from the top of the head to the lowest visible part of
the subject's body. This index can range from 0 (i.e., the face is not shown
at all) to 1 (i.e., the picture shows only the face). In other words, the face-ism
index indicates the height of the head compared to the height of the body
in a photo.

Most prior research finds that men are represented with greater facial prominence/face-ism scores than women (and thus women with greater prominence of their bodies). Such findings certainly coincide with the sexualization of women and show that face-ism is a form of gender stereotyping. According to Archer et al. (1983), this difference reflects gender stereotypes that highlight personality and intellect in men but physical attractiveness in women. Regardless of the reasons for the differences in facial prominence, they have real consequences. As pointed out by Archer et al. (1983), intelligence, ambition, and physical appearance are associated with greater facial prominence. Zuckerman (1986) found a significant relationship between high facial prominence and dominance but not intelligence. Schwarz and Kurz (1989) found that more facial prominence is associated with more competence, while Costa and Bitti (2000) found that more facial prominence is preferred when evaluating photographs of other people (but not of oneself) and that it is associated with attractiveness. While previous studies found differing results for the effects of face-ism, all came to the conclusion that a higher face-ism score/facial prominence generally led to more positive associations. Thus, face-ism has real social consequences.

Several studies have applied content analysis and concluded that men are depicted with more facial prominence than women. The first study was by Archer et al. (1983), who found that, compared to the visual depictions of women, those of men show more of the face and less of the body. This was true for U.S. and international magazines featuring artwork produced across six centuries depicting men and women. Other studies have confirmed these findings in magazines (Nigro, Hill, Gelbein, & Clark, 1988; Zuckerman, 1986) and television (Copeland, 1989; C. C. I. Hall & Crum, 1994). However, some recent studies have shown that face-ism is not equally pervasive across all cultures (Konrath, Au, & Ramsey, 2012). In light of such mixed findings, we formulate the following research question:

RQ1: *Will the face-ism score of men be significantly higher than that of women in the profile photographs of online dating sites?*

Some studies have found moderating factors of face-ism. Zuckerman (1986) found smaller differences in facial prominence between men and women in magazines featuring women's issues, and Sparks and Fehlner (1986) found occupation to be related to facial prominence: both men and women in higher-level occupations were portrayed with greater facial prominence. Similarly, Matthews (2007) found no gender differences but an overall higher facial prominence among people engaging in intellectually focused occupations. However, Konrath and Schwarz (2007) found gender differences in facial prominence among politicians in the United States, Canada, Australia, and Norway, observing an inverse correlation between level of political office and facial prominence, which led to parity among genders for face-ism at the gubernatorial level. A follow-up study conducted across 25 cultures yielded similar results (Konrath et al., 2012). Szillis and Stahlberg (2007) found gender differences in facial promi-nence among German university professors and members of parliament. Specifically, they found that higher face-ism scores among younger female politicians might indicate a generational change in terms of gendered self-representations, assuming that politicians had some influence on the choice of their photographs on the homepage of the parliament. Last but not least, some studies found education to play a role in face-ism. Konrath and Schwarz (2007) found that face-ism among politicians in the United States did not differ based on their levels of academic achievement. However, men with three university degrees exhibited smaller faces than men with one degree, and women with three degrees had larger faces than those with one degree. Men and women with 3 degrees were represented simi-larly. However, education was found to play no role in Canada, Australia, or Norway. Because information about occupation was not consistently provided by the online dating sites we used, we focused our next research questions on age and education:

RQ2: *What role does age play for gender differences in face-ism scores?*
RQ3: *What role does education play for gender differences in face-ism scores?*

Confucianism and Hofstede's Masculinity Index: The Role of Culture in Face-ism

There have been several cross-cultural studies on face-ism. Archer et al. (1983) found face-ism to be present in publications from 11 countries. Very few studies have focused on online representations of men and women and analyzed whether gender differences persist (Konrath et al., 2012; Konrath & Schwarz, 2007; L. R. Smith & Cooley, 2012). Konrath and associates (2012; 2007) evaluated photographs of politicians shown on government websites, but L. R. Smith and Cooley (2012) used photographs posted on Facebook. Although both studies claimed to analyze face-ism of self-representations, we argue that this is the case only in the latter, because government websites have their own rules and tend toward standardized portrait photographs.

Self-perception theory (Bem, 1967) states that self-perception is influ-enced by the cultural influences on the individual, and thus individuals will try to self-present in a way that is considered most desirable within a cul-ture. For example, women are expected to show more parts of their bodies than men. People might have internalized these gender stereotypes of their respective cultures and unwittingly expressed them through online venues. Thus, it is only natural to investigate whether culture has an influence on gender differences in face-ism scores. L. R. Smith and Cooley (2012) found significantly more facial prominence in photographs of men than women in Facebook profiles posted from seven nations. In addition, they found an association between face-ism and Hofstede's cultural dimensions. Konrath and Schwarz (2007) found that the number of women in parliament was not associated with gender bias (e.g., a more similar face-ism score between genders). Konrath et al. (2012) analyzed the representations of politicians and came to the surprising result that face-ism was higher in cultures with less gender inequality, especially those with more educated and professional women; they expected to find lower face-ism in more gender egalitarian societies. They interpreted the findings to suggest that macro-level structural sexism is not the same as individual and micro-level sexism.

In this study, we also relate our results to the masculinity dimension from Hofstede's cultural dimensions (Hofstede, 2001) and to Confucianism. Hofstede's cultural dimensions (including power distance, individualism, uncertainty avoidance, masculinity, and long-term orientation) have received much attention, and they have been used in various research areas. For this study, Hofstede's masculinity dimension is of special interest. Cultures that score higher on this dimension are said to have more gender differentiation compared to cultures that score lower on this index (Hofstede, 2001). Thus, we have selected some of the highest- and lowest-scoring cultures on this index. It should be noted that Japan's culture scores high in the masculinity index (MAS = 95), and South Korea's scores in the middle (MAS = 39), seemingly at odds with their shared Confucian heritage, which should imply that gender differences should be rather similar.

Confucianism is a philosophy (some consider it a branch of ethics or a form of religion) based on the teachings of the Chinese philosopher, Confucius (551–479 B.C.). Confucianism was established in China around 200 B.C. when it became the official state ideology. Confucian teachings were also influencing other parts of Asia, such as Taiwan, Hong Kong, Macau, Singapore, Vietnam, Korea, and Japan, where it continues to be a strong influence in many aspects of life (Park & Chesla, 2007). Although Confucianism was well known in Korea around 400, it was only from the Chosun dynasty (around 1400) when it became orthodox teaching and started to play a more important role in society (Berthrong & Berthrong, 2000). When the Ming dynasty in China fell to the Manchus in 1644, the Koreans proclaimed themselves to be the only state in East Asia that followed orthodox Confucianism, and they sought to create an ideal Confucian state (Berthrong & Berthrong, 2000; Rainey, 2010). Today, Confucian influence is very much alive in Korean attitudes toward their families, teachers, and even in international affairs (Rainey, 2010). In Japan, Confucianism was known and studied from around 600, but it was only around 1600 that it became an important part of society and was incorporated into the Tokugawa shogunate's ruling ideology. Confucianism was more adapted to the environment in Japan than in Korea, but it was not as dominant there. Nevertheless, it continues to play a role in Japan for teaching moral virtues such as loyalty and filial piety (Rainey, 2010).

Confucius taught that social and political order would prevail if every individual knew his role in society and fulfilled his responsibilities (Park & Chesla, 2007). Confucianism's five principal relationships are central to social life and must be maintained to keep a healthy society. Through these five relationships, each person defines a sense of identity, duty, and responsibility. These relationships are husband and wife, parent and child (father and son), older sibling and younger sibling, older friend and younger friend, and ruler and subject. These relationships are regarded as reciprocal, where the former should show benevolence and the latter should show respect; each side has responsibilities, and one learns to put others' interests before one's own (Rainey, 2010). That three of these relationships are connected with the family shows the important role of the family in Confucianism, which is still seen in Confucian societies. In short, Confucianism posits the family as the fundamental unit of society, and the state is modeled on the family (Park & Chesla, 2007; Rainey, 2010).

Nonetheless, the Confucianism legacy is often blamed for the continuing low status of women, rigid gender role divisions, and male dominance in these cultures. In Confucianism, a clear division between husband and wife exists (and, more generally, between male and female members of society). The husband is the dominant partner and is expected to show responsibility and benevolence to the latter, who is subordinate in the relationship and is expected to show obedience, loyalty, and respect (Hyun, 2001). However, the underlying idea of the relationship is not dominance but a separation of sexes and a division of labor and responsibilities (Park & Chesla, 2007; Rainey, 2010). Confucian societies seem to be particularly interesting venues for gender research because scholars claim that the patriarchal Confucian philosophy has exerted a negative impact on women, and it has been blamed for both historical and contemporary gender discrimination. While economic development is challenging these traditional values, and the status of women has improved (Kendall, 2002; Liddle & Nakajima, 2000), women in Confucian societies continue to face significant cultural disadvantages. This can be seen, for example, in the Global Gender Gap Report of 2014 (Hausmann, Tyson, Bekhouche, & Zahidi, 2014), which ranked Japan number 104 and South Korea number 117 out of 142 investigated countries (as compared to Sweden, 4, and the United States, 20).

In summary, while Japan and South Korea rank rather differently in Hofstede's masculinity index, both cultures are often regarded as gender unequal, which might be connected with their Confucian heritage. Based on these contradictory facts, we formulate our final research question:

RQ4: *Are the differences of the mean face-ism scores between men and women within each culture better reflected by Hofstede's masculinity index or by Confucianism?*

Research Method

As in previous research (Konrath et al., 2012; L. R. Smith & Cooley, 2012), we applied content analysis to determine face-ism. The content analysis was conducted using one online dating site from each of the four chosen cultures. The selection of cultures is consistent with Hofstede's masculinity index (2001) because they span the spectrum of the index, including the highest-scoring culture, Japan (MAS = 95), and the lowest-scoring culture, Sweden (MAS = 5). In addition, we chose South Korea, which scored relatively low compared to other East Asian cultures (MAS = 39). Finally yet importantly, we also included the United States as a country of reference, because most previous studies were conducted in the United States; it scored between South Korea and Japan (MAS = 62). For each of the four cultures, we selected one representative online dating site: www.sweden-dating.com from Sweden, www.yyc.co.jp from Japan, http://cinemating.com from South Korea, and www.match.com from the United States.

From each dating site, we randomly selected and downloaded the profiles of 450 men and 450 women. We also extracted their profile photographs. From each of these profiles, we noted demographic information such as gender, age, and educational background (university vs. no university), if available. After providing training in coding, two students independently coded all variables and measured the profile photographs using the software KLONK Image Measurement Professional to create a face-ism score. The coding rules for the photographs were adapted from previously published methods (Archer et al., 1983) and excluded photographs showing more than one human being, those emphasizing some particular body region, those with co-subjects (e.g., a person next to a car), repeating photographs, and those with disembodied heads. Intercoder reliabilities were measured on 30% of the overall sample using Krippendorff's Alpha, and reliabilities were above .98 for all variables (gender, age, culture, education, face-ism score).

Results

Research question 1 (RQ1) asked if the face-ism score of men would be significantly higher than that of women in the profile photographs. Our results showed that men had a higher face-ism score ($M = .621$; $SD = 0.211$) than women ($M = 0.593$; $SD = 0.191$; $t = 4.194$; $p < .001$). By culture, only Japan (men: .724; women: .686; $t = 2.997$; $p = .003$) and South Korea (men: .629; women: .530; $t = 8.344$; $p < .001$) showed significant gender differences between face-ism scores. This was not the case for Sweden (men: .617; women: .636; $t = -1.538$; $p = .124$) and the United States (men: .514; women: .519; $t = -0.400$; $p = .689$).

Research question 2 (RQ2) asked whether the age of the person in the photo had an influence on gender differences in face-ism scores. For this analysis, we split the sample at the median age (32 years) into two sub-samples (Iacobucci, Posavac, Kardes, Schneider, & Popovich, 2015). An analysis of the face-ism scores of the two age groups showed that in the younger age group, no significant gender differences were found (men: .623; women: .608; $t = 1.626$; $p = .104$), while significant differences were found in the older age group (men: .620, women: .575; $t = 4.643$; $p < .001$). After further splitting the groups by culture, we found that in South Korea, gender differences for face-ism scores emerged in both age groups. Among the younger, the scores were .651 and .548 for men and women, respectively ($t = 7.165$; $p < .001$), while among the older, they were .599 and .503, respectively ($t = 4.904$, $p < .001$). In the United States, gender differences for face-ism scores were found in neither age group. Among the younger, the scores were .490 and .520, respectively ($t = -1.391$; $p = .165$), while among the older, they were .529 and .519, respectively ($t = -0.555$; $p = .579$). The same was found for Sweden, where the scores among the younger were .607 and .642, respectively ($t = -1.891$; $p = .059$), and among the older, they were .626 and .629, respectively ($t = -0.179$; $p = .858$). These results reflect the overall results from RQ1 and show that age had little influence on face-ism. In contrast, however, we found face-ism in Japan was based on age, where only the older age group showed significant gender differences for face-ism scores. They scored .737 among men and .679 among women ($t = 2.967$; $p = .003$), while the younger age group scored .712 among men and .690 among women ($t = 1.279$; $p = .201$).

Research question 3 (RQ3) asked what role education (university versus no university qualifications) played for gender differences in the face-ism score. We found gender differences in both groups. Among those who had not attended university, men and women had face-ism scores of .658 and .625, respectively ($t = 2.159$; $p = .031$) while among those who attended university, they were .605 and .554, respectively ($t = 5.412$; $p < .001$). By culture, the results did not change significantly. In South Korea, gender differences for face-ism scores were found in both groups. Men and women who attended university scored .632 and .530, respectively ($t = 6.691$; $p < .001$), similar to those who did not attend university (men: .615; women: .545; $t = 3.082$; $p = .002$). In Sweden, men and women who attended university scored .636 and .592, respectively ($t = 1.490$; $p = .138$) while those who did not scored .654 and .661, respectively ($t = -0.273$; $p = .781$). Similarly, in the United States, the scores were .513 and .519, respectively ($t = -0.469$, $p = .639$) for those who attended university and .551 and .483, respectively ($t = 0.962$; $p = .342$) for those who did not. All these findings indicate that education had little influence on face-ism. In contrast, Japanese photographs showed significant gender differences among those who attended university (men: .710; women: .664; $t = 2.338$; $p = .020$) but none among those who did not (men: .728; women: .694; $t = 1.240$; $p = .216$).

Research question 4 (RQ4) asked whether differences in the mean face-ism scores for men and women within each culture were better represented by Hofstede's masculinity index or Confucianism. While this research question cannot be answered *per se* because the sample of four cultures is rather small, and Confucianism provides information about only South Korea and Japan, we can nevertheless draw some tentative conclusions based on our results. Gender differences in the mean face-ism score (male mean minus female mean) were .099 for South Korea, .038 for Japan, –.0.005 for the United States, and –0.019 for Sweden. The largest gender gap was for South Korea followed by Japan. No significant differences were seen for the United States and Sweden (and in fact, they had higher mean face-ism scores for women). Comparing these results with each country's ranking in Hofstede's masculinity index, where the order was Japan (95), the United States (62), South Korea (39), and Sweden (5), there seems to be little relationship between gender differences in face-ism scores and Hofstede's masculinity index. We note that in both rankings, Sweden was the lowest and Japan was relatively high. Thus, Hofstede's masculinity index provides little explanation for the results we found.

Discussion and Conclusion

When considering the entire sample of dating site photographs, our findings resonate with those of extant research: men are shown with more facial prominence than women. However, when analyzing the data by culture, more facial prominence among men was found only in Japan and South Korea. Such a finding raises questions regarding the overall validity of face-ism theory, because within our four investigated cultures, face-ism theory was valid only for the two East Asian cultures of Japan and South Korea, not for Sweden or the United States. It might be that facial prominence has become more similar between men and women in the United States and Sweden over the years, while face-ism remains very much alive in East Asia. The similar results between men and women in the United States and Sweden do, however, coincide with two recent studies. L. R. Smith and Cooley (2012) also found few significant gender differences in face-ism scores, which they interpreted as a possible shift in gender presentation in the digital world. Konrath and associates (2012) found that within 25 cultures investigated, only 15 showed a higher face-ism score for men, and three (Zimbabwe, Rwanda, and South Korea) showed a higher face-ism score for women. However, caution must be taken when comparing our results with these examples of previous results because the latter featured photographs of politicians taken from official government websites. Although there might be some influence of the politician in choosing the photographs, such websites generally have fixed standards and use portrait photographs; they may not be comparable to websites where people can truly self-represent, such as Facebook or online dating sites.

When investigating whether there is a relationship between Hofstede's masculinity index and differences in the face-ism scores of the two genders, none was found. There was clearly a different rank using the two methods. While in Hofstede's masculinity index, Japan was ranked highest, followed by the United States, South Korea, and Sweden, gender differences among face-ism scores were greatest for South Korea, followed by Japan, the United States, and Sweden. This lack of relationship agrees with previous research (L. R. Smith & Cooley, 2012). One reason for this result might be that macro-level sexisim (e.g., Hofstede's masculinity index) and micro-level sexism (e.g., photographs of individuals online) are not the same (Konrath et al., 2012).

On the other hand, that Japan and South Korea had rather similar results and were the only cultures that showed significant gender differences in face-ism scores, indicates that Confucianism might be a better way to explain our results. Confucianism is naturally unable to tell us anything about the United States and Sweden. Confucianism's strong emphasis on gender role divisions (Park & Chesla, 2007; Rainey, 2010) is reflected in the gender differences seen in the face-ism scores. In addition, as with the findings of previous research associating higher face-ism scores with better evaluations, women showing lower face-ism scores than men underlines Confucianism's perspective that women are subordinate to men in patriarchal Confucian societies (Hyun, 2001). One could hypothesize that in Western cultures, such as the United States and Sweden, face-ism scores between men and women are increasingly similar because of increasing gender equality and growing sensitivity and awareness of face-ism in these cultures. These results contradict previous and rather surprising findings (Konrath et al., 2012) that face-ism was greater in cultures with higher levels of gender equality. Both Japan and South Korea are generally regarded as less gender equal than Sweden and the United States (Hausmann et al., 2014), and thus our results are more in line with expectations.

We found that face-ism was not largely influenced by the age of the person in the photo when viewing results by culture. Only in Japan was there an influence; gender differences in face-ism scores appeared in the older age group but not in the younger one. This result might indicate that in Japan, gender differences in face-ism scores are disappearing with time, possibly because of a general decrease in the influence of Confucian values in Japanese society, thus the older generation holds Confucian values in greater regard than the younger. The older users of Japanese online dating sites may follow the more traditional gender depictions, thereby confirming face-ism theory. The only culture where gender differences in face-ism scores was prominent among both age groups was in South Korea. Thus, South Korea displayed the strongest gender differences in this respect. Considering that South Korea is generally regarded as the country with the strongest form of Confucianism (Berthrong & Berthrong, 2000; Rainey, 2010), our findings appear to be in accordance with Korea's Confucian heritage. The strong role that Confucianism continues to still play in South Korea can be seen in many parts of life, such as the importance of seniority and age, as well as in areas of gender inequality. South Korea is seen as gender unequal in many dimensions. For example, the Global Gender Gap Report by the World Economic Forum ranks South Korea 117 out of 142 countries. Notably, women in South Korea only receive 51% of men's salaries for similar work, and women constitute only 19% of parliament (Hausmann et al., 2014).

Similarly, we found little influence of education on gender differences in face-ism scores when viewing the results by culture, confirming previous research (Konrath & Schwarz, 2007). However, differences again could be noted for Japan, where those with university qualifications showed significant gender differences, while those without manifested no gender differences. This finding runs counter to previous research, which found that education played no role. It also runs in contrast to the finding in the United States that politicians with higher degrees showed no gender differences in face-ism scores (Konrath & Schwarz, 2007). One could speculate that those who were more educated in a Confucian society might have more actively imbibed the ideology of Confucianism, and thus more of them behaved in accordance with Confucian gender role divisions, including for self-presentation through online dating sites. Nevertheless, the unexpected finding that the highly educated people with profiles on Japan's dating site displayed more gender differences (compared to less educated ones) definitely requires further research.

In conclusion, even though we found some support for previous results that men had higher face-ism scores/facial prominence than women, we also found contradictions to previous research in multiple ways. For example, gender differences in face-ism scores were found only among the Japanese and South Koreans, which might indicate that Confucianism is a better way to understand the use of face-ism in East Asia than is Hofstede's masculinity index. While Hofstede's masculinity index (Hofstede, 2001) showed large differences between Japan and South Korea, the common heritage of Confucianism points toward a strong gender division (Park & Chesla, 2007; Rainey, 2010), which was reflected in the gender differences we found. We also found that the age of the person in the photo played a role in gender differences in face-ism scores only in Japan. The differences were found only for the older age group, which might indicate shifts in Confucian-based values over time. Finally, education was found to be relatively unimportant for gender differences in face-ism scores, except in Japan, where those with a university education clearly ran against expectations. This could also be interpreted as an influence by the length of education in Confucian ideology; the longer people follow this ideology, the more they are committed to gender roles. Nevertheless, it is difficult to draw any final conclusion except that face-ism seems to be very much alive in more traditional societies with a Confucian heritage, such as Japan and South Korea, and might have become less so in other places, coinciding with a general shift toward more gender equality.

As previous research has indicated, a higher face-ism score might lead to more positive associations such as intelligence, ambition, dominance, and competence (Archer et al., 1983; Schwarz & Kurz, 1989; Zuckerman, 1986). Thus, women might be evaluated less favorably than men when generally depicted with a lower face-ism score. Such depictions might have social consequences and subsequently lead to perceptions that women are less intelligent, ambitious, or competent than men. Hence, it is of importance that future research and educators focus on the concept of face-ism.

In addition, showing women with lower face-ism scores/facial prominence than men coincides with the criticism that women are more sexually objectified. South Korea and Japan were found to be highly stereotypical for gender representations in general and for sexual objectification of women in particular (Prieler, 2012; Prieler, Ivanov, & Hagiwara, 2015). Our findings support the gender differences. Previous research has indicated that sexual objectification of women could lead to anxiety, shame, depression, and eating disorders, among other problems (Fredrickson & Roberts, 1997). As a result, face-ism should be taken seriously.

As with every research project, this project has limitations. First, the results are representative only of the cultures we studied, at the time when the samples were taken, and for the specific online dating sites chosen. Second, other online dating sites might represent photographs in a different way, and we could imagine that online self-representations are different from representations by traditional media, such as newspapers or magazines, which were the objects of study for most research to date. Future research conducting content analysis of photographs to measure face-ism should use a transmedia approach that includes diverse media and not only self-representations through online dating sites. This could lead to a finding that traditional media represent gender quite differently than do self-representations. Future research should also further analyze possible relationships between face-ism and gender indices in addition to Hofstede's masculinity index. Suggestions are the gender egalitarianism index by the Project GLOBE (Emrich, Denmark, & Den Hartog, 2004; House, Hanges, Javidan, Dorfman, & Gupta, 2004) and the Global Gender Gap Index (Hausmann et al., 2014), which seems to agree more with our findings. For doing so, we also recommend extending the number of cultures studied so that a wider range of statistical analyses can be performed. In this context, we would like to mention that we have decided to use t-tests for this chapter as we are interested mainly in comparing the means of two groups (mean face-ism scores of men and women) and in order to make the results as understandable as possible to a wide audience (not necessarily that familiar with advanced statistical methods). However, we acknowledge that such an approach involves potential limitations and problems. As a result, we suggest using more advanced statistical methods (such as regression) in future research. Finally, one should keep in mind that the few existing studies (Archer et al., 1983; Costa & Bitti, 2000; Schwarz & Kurz, 1989; Zuckerman, 1986; Zuckerman & Kieffer, 1994) on the face-ism effect all were conducted in the United States or in Europe; studies have yet to be conducted in other geographical areas. Therefore, it is questionable whether face-ism has the same effect in, for example, East Asia as it has in Western cultures. For example, previous research has revealed that different cultures perceive visual depictions in different ways (Nisbett, 2003), which might be also true for face-ism. It is therefore of major importance to study face-ism effects in a non-Western context and understand whether face-ism has the same effect in South Korea or Japan, where this study found significant gender differences.

Acknowledgment

This work was supported by the National Research Foundation of Korea Grant funded by the Korean Government (NRF-2013S1A5A8020741).

References

Archer, D., Iritani, B., Kimes, D. D., & Barrios, M. (1983). Face-ism: Five studies of sex differences in facial prominence. *Journal of Personality and Social Psychology, 45*(4): 725–735. doi: 10.1037/0022-3514.45.4.725.

Bandura, A. (2009). Social cognitive theory of mass communication. In J. Bryant & M. B. Oliver (Eds.), *Media effects: Advances in theory and research* (3rd ed., pp. 94–124). New York, NY: Routledge.

Bem, D. J. (1967). Self-perception: An alternative interpretation of cognitive dissonance phenomena. *Psychological Review, 74*(3): 183–200. doi: 10.1037/h0024835.

Berthrong, J. H., & Berthrong, E. N. (2000). *Confucianism: A short introduction.* Oxford, UK: Oneworld.

Collins, R. L. (2011). Content analysis of gender roles in media: Where are we now and where should we go? *Sex Roles, 64*(3/4): 290–298. doi: 10.1007/s11199-010-9929-5.

Copeland, G. A. (1989). Face-ism and primetime television. *Journal of Broadcasting & Electronic Media, 33*(2): 209–214. doi: 10.1080/08838158909364075.

Costa, M., & Bitti, P. E. R. (2000). Face-ism effect and head canting in one's own and others' photographs. *European Psychologist, 5*(4): 293–301. doi: 10.1027//1016-9040.5.4.293.

Ellison, N., Heino, R., & Gibbs, J. (2006). Managing impressions online: Self-presentation processes in the online dating environment. *Journal of Computer-Mediated Communication, 11* (2): 415–441. doi: 10.1111/j.1083-6101.2006.00020.x.

Emrich, C. G., Denmark, F. L., & Den Hartog, D. N. (2004). Cross-cultural differences in gender egalitarianism: Implications for societies, organizations, and leaders. In R. J. House, M. Javidan, V. Gupta, P. Dorfman & P. J. Hanges (Eds.), *Culture, leadership, and organizations: The GLOBE study of 62 societies* (pp. 343–394). Thousand Oaks, CA: Sage.

Fiore, A. T., & Donath, J. S. (2005). Homophily in online dating: When do you like someone like yourself? *CHI EA '05 CHI '05 Extended abstracts on human factors in computing systems* (pp. 1371–1374). New York, NY: Association for Computing Machinery.

Fiore, A. T., Taylor, L. S., Mendelsohn, G. A., & Hearst, M. (2008). Assessing attractiveness in online dating profiles. *Proceeding of the twenty-sixth annual SIGCHI* conference on *Human factors in computing systems* (pp. 797–806). New York, NY: Association for Computing Machinery.

Fredrickson, B. L., & Roberts, T.-A. (1997). Objectification theory: Toward understanding women's lived experiences and mental health risks. *Psychology of Women Quarterly, 21*(2): 173–206. doi: 10.1111/j.1471-6402.1997.tb00108.x.

Hall, C. C. I., & Crum, M. J. (1994). Women and "body-ism" in television beer commercials. *Sex Roles, 31*(5/6): 329–337. doi: 10.1007/BF01544592.

Hall, J. A., Park, N., Song, H., & Cody, M. J. (2010). Strategic misrepresentation in online dating: The effects of gender, self-monitoring, and personality traits. *Journal of Social and Personal Relationships, 27*(1): 117–135. doi: 10.1177/0265407509349633.

Hancock, J. T., & Toma, C. L. (2009). Putting your best face forward: The accuracy of online dating photographs. *Journal of Communication, 59*(2): 367–386. doi: 10.1111/j.1460-2466.2009.01420.x.

Hausmann, R., Tyson, L. D., Bekhouche, Y., & Zahidi, S. (2014). Global gender gap report. Retrieved from http://www3.weforum.org/docs/GGGR14/GGGR_CompleteReport_2014.pdf.

Hitsch, G. J., Hortaçsu, A., & Arieli, D. (2010). What makes you click? Mate preferences in online dating. *Quantitative Marketing and Economics, 8*(4): 393–427. doi: 10.1007/s11129-010-9088-6.

Hofstede, G. (2001). *Culture's consequences: Comparing values, behaviors, institutions, and organizations across nations* (2nd ed.). London, UK: Sage.

House, R. J., Hanges, P. J., Javidan, M., Dorfman, P. W., & Gupta, V. (Eds.) (2004). *Culture, leadership, and organizations: The GLOBE study of 62 societies.* Thousand Oaks, CA: Sage.

Hyun, K. J. (2001). Sociocultural change and traditional values: Confucian values among Koreans and Korean Americans. *International Journal of Intercultural Relations, 25*(2): 203–229. doi: 10.1016/S0147-1767(01)00009-8.

Iacobucci, D., Posavac, S. S., Kardes, F. R., Schneider, M. J., & Popovich, D. L. (2015). Toward a more nuanced understanding of the statistical properties of a median split. *Journal of Consumer Psychology, 25*(4): 652–665. doi: 10.1016/j.jcps.2014.12.002.

Kendall, L. (Ed.) (2002). *Under construction: The gendering of modernity, class, and consumption in the Republic of Korea.* Honolulu, HI: University of Hawai'i Press.

Konrath, S., Au, J., & Ramsey, L. R. (2012). Cultural differences in face-ism: Male politicians have bigger heads in more gender-equal cultures. *Psychology of Women Quarterly, 36*(4): 476–487. doi: 10.1177/0361684312455317.

Konrath, S., & Schwarz, N. (2007). Do male politicians have big heads? Face-ism in online self-representations of politicians. *Media Psychology, 10*(3): 436–448. doi: 10.1080/15213260701533219.

Liddle, J., & Nakajima, S. (2000). *Rising suns, rising daughters: Gender, class and power in Japan.* London, UK: ZED Books.

Matthews, J. L. (2007). Hidden sexism: Facial prominence and its connections to gender and occupational status in popular print media. *Sex Roles, 57*(7/8): 515–525. doi: 10.1007/s11199-007-9276-3.

Nigro, G. N., Hill, D. E., Gelbein, M. E., & Clark, C. L. (1988). Changes in the facial prominence of women and men over the last decade. *Psychology of Women Quarterly, 12*(2): 225–235. doi: 10.1111/j.1471-6402.1988.tb00938.x.

Nisbett, R. E. (2003). *The geography of thought: How Asians and Westerners think differently … and why*. New York, NY: Free Press.

Park, M., & Chesla, C. (2007). Revisiting Confucianism as a conceptual framework for Asian family study. *Journal of Family Nursing, 13*(3): 293–311. doi: 10.1177/1074840707304400.

Prieler, M. (2012). Gender representation in a Confucian society: South Korean television advertisements. *Asian Women, 28*(2): 1–26.

Prieler, M., Ivanov, A., & Hagiwara, S. (2015). Gender representations in East Asian advertising: Hong Kong, Japan, and South Korea. *Communication & Society, 28*(1): 27–41.

Rainey, L. D. (2010). *Confucius & Confucianism: The essentials*. Malden, MA: Wiley.

Schwarz, N., & Kurz, E. (1989). What's in a picture? The impact of face-ism on trait attribution. *European Journal of Social Psychology, 19*(4): 311–316. doi: 10.1002/ejsp.2420190405.

Smith, A., & Duggan, M. (2013). Online dating & relationships. Retrieved from http://www.pewinternet.org/2013/10/21/online-dating-relationships/.

Smith, L. R., & Cooley, S. C. (2012). International faces: An analysis of self-inflicted face-ism in online profile pictures. *Journal of Intercultural Communication Research, 41*(3): 279–296. doi: 10.1080/17475759.2012.728771.

Sparks, G. G. (2006). *Media effects research: A basic overview* (2nd ed.). Belmont, CA: Wadsworth.

Sparks, G. G., & Fehlner, C. L. (1986). Faces in the news: Gender comparisons of magazine photographs. *Journal of Communication, 36*(4): 70–79. doi: 10.1111/j.1460-2466.1986.tb01451.x.

Szillis, U., & Stahlberg, D. (2007). The face-ism effect in the internet: Differences in facial prominence of women and men. *International Journal of Internet Science, 2*(1): 3–11.

Toma, C. L., & Hancock, J. T. (2010). Looks and lies: The role of physical attractiveness in online dating self-presentation and deception. *Communication Research, 37*(3): 335–351. doi: 10.1177/0093650209356437.

Toma, C. L., Hancock, J. T., & Ellison, N. B. (2008). Separating fact from fiction: An examination of deceptive self-presentation in online dating profiles. *Personality and Social Psychology Bulletin, 34*(8): 1023–1036. doi: 10.1177/0146167208318067.

Valkenburg, P. M., & Peter, J. (2007). Who visits online dating sites? Exploring some characteristics of online daters. *CyberPsychology & Behavior, 10*(6): 849–852. doi: 10.1089/cpb.2007.9941.

Whitty, M. T. (2008). Revealing the "real" me, searching for the "actual" you: Presentations of self on an internet dating site. *Computers in Human Behavior, 24*(4): 1707–1723. doi: 10.1016/j.chb.2007.07.002.

Zuckerman, M. (1986). On the meaning and implications of facial prominence. *Journal of Nonverbal Behavior, 10*(4): 215–229. doi: 10.1007/BF00987481.

Zuckerman, M., & Kieffer, S. C. (1994). Race differences in face-ism: Does facial prominence imply dominance? *Journal of Personality and Social Psychology, 66*(1): 86–92. doi: 10.1037/0022–3514.66.1.86.

Part III

Group Processes and Collective Imaginaries

5 Credibility, Reliability, and Reciprocity

Mobile Communication, *Guanxi*, and Protest Mobilization in Contemporary China

Jun Liu

Introduction

The past decade has seen an increasing use of the mobile phone as a facilitator for contentious politics around the world (e.g., Castells, Fernandez-Ardevol, Qiu, & Sey, 2007, pp. 185–214; Howard & Hussain, 2011; Liu, 2013a, in print; Rafael, 2003; Suárez, 2006). Yet, the role of the mobile phone as a means for mobilizing protests remains largely unclear. In particular, current scholarship mainly focuses on the analysis of discrete contentious events, failing to establish a conceptual framework to scrutinize possible similarities between these contentions. To fill this gap, this study examines the role that mobile phones play in protest mobilization by investigating mobile-phone-facilitated political protests in China. It analyzes the influence of "*guanxi*," understood as "interpersonal relationship" or "personal connections" in Chinese and embodied in mobile communication, on protest mobilization and recruitment. Drawing on evidence from four protest cases in rural and urban China with more than 40 in-depth interviews conducted between 2007 and 2011, this study demonstrates the relevance and effectiveness of mobile communication in mobilizing participants' *guanxi,* as it relates to issues of credibility, reliability, and reciprocity for protest mobilization. The embedding and relevance of *guanxi* via mobile communication for protest mobilization call for a nuanced understanding of the dynamics of mobile communication in contentious politics by incorporating the concepts of trust, social capital, and reciprocity.

I first provide a critical review of current studies of mobile communication and protest mobilization, addressing the relevance of approaching such a topic from the perspective of social ties—*guanxi* in this case—that underline the influence of interpersonal relationships for mobilization. I then elaborate on case selection, data collection, and analysis methods, followed by a brief overview of four protests in rural and urban China that exemplify how the Chinese people have taken advantage of the mobile phone in initiating and mobilizing protests against the authorities. I further explore how mobile communication facilitates protest participation and recruitment by exploiting the dynamics of *guanxi* and discuss the political implications of *"guanxi*-embedded mobile communication" (Liu, 2010) in China before suggesting avenues for further research.

Mobile Phones and Protest Mobilization: A Critical Review

There has been considerable academic interest in the use of mobile phones as a means of recruitment and mobilization in sociopolitical movements (e.g., Ibahrine, 2008; Rafael, 2003; Rheingold, 2008; Suárez, 2006). Studies on the most recent wave of protests in Arab countries have credited new communication technologies in general, and mobile phones in particular, as playing an essential role in articulating and mobilizing activists for protests and demonstrations (e.g., Allagui & Kuebler, 2011; Howard & Hussain, 2011, p. 39). Although scholars have recognized the relevance of the mobile phone for mobilization in political contentions, the exact contribution of mobile phone use in protest mobilization remains less understood. To be clear, most studies have addressed the technological affordances of mobile phones—such as availability (i.e., the ubiquity of wireless devices), affordability (low-cost terminals and telecommunication fees), efficiency (rapid diffusion of information), and autonomous communication networks—for mobilization (Castells et al., 2007, p. 188; Hermanns, 2008; Rafael, 2003; Rheingold, 2008; Suárez, 2006). Nevertheless, no causal relationship has been established between these affordances and the mechanisms of protest mobilization. A few studies identify the relevance of context and inter-media dynamics (Qiu, 2008; Rafael, 2003, p. 415) beyond mobile communication for protest mobilization. Here, the mobile phone has been regarded as a tool (e.g., Qiu, 2008, p. 49) that largely relies on *external* forces for legitimating mobilization appeal.

However, as mobile communication studies persuasively argue, apart from instrumental functions, mobile communication engenders mediated social ties that strengthen social cohesion on the basis of mutual engagement and rituals of interaction (e.g., Ling & Yttri, 2002; Ling, 2004, 2008). Thus, beyond its instrumental functions, what is the contribution of mobile communication to mechanisms of protest? Specifically, which dimension of mobile communication contributes to recruitment and participation in protest mobilization?

Social Ties and Protest Mobilization: From Face-to-Face to Mediated Relationships

To understand the mechanism of protest mobilization in the age of new media, it is crucial to assess the influence of social ties. They were seen as a basic but relevant recruitment and mobilization agent before new communication technologies such as mobile phones became affordable and accessible (e.g., Diani & McAdam, 2003). Such ties integrate "networks of trust" (Tilly, 2005), identify shared individual preferences and perceptions (Passy, 2003), engender movement identity (Friedman & McAdam, 1992), and exercise social control during movement actions (Snow, Zurcher, & Ekland-Olson, 1980).

Previous studies have recognized the importance of the embedding of social ties and interpersonal relationships via the mobile phone in protest mobilization (Castells et al., 2007; Suárez, 2006). Nevertheless, these studies rarely probe the questions of *how* mobile-phone-mediated social ties affect protest mobilization and participation, leaving them as a taken-for-granted consequence of mobile communication. As Gould states in his critical viewpoint of social ties as a basis for social movements, "simply observing that social ties affect mobilization is not much of a contribution. It is a bit like noticing that people who are stricken with plague have had contact with other plague victims" (2003, p. 237). Similarly, McAdam offers the critique that "showing that these activists were linked to the movement by some prior social tie does not prove the causal potency of that tie" (2003, p. 287). The question of how an existing social tie and interpersonal relationship matter in protest mobilization, whether or not it is mediated by mobile communication technology, still needs to be clarified and theorized. As Bennett, Breunig, and Givens (2008) suggest, more refined questions are needed to understand, at an in-depth level, "the kinds of communication that individuals use to activate personal networks" (p. 286) during protests. By examining the influence of mobile-phone-mediated social ties and interpersonal interactions on protest mobilization in detail, this study provides a nuanced portrait and expounds on the role of mobile phones in protest mobilizations.

Mobile Phones, *Guanxi*, and Protest Mobilization in China

In 2014, China had the world's largest population of mobile phone users, surpassing 1.2 billion, or 90 percent of its total population (Shen, 2014). As in other parts of the world, the ubiquity of mobile phones in China enables the growth of mobile-phone-mediated contentious activities, with the increasing use of mobile phones as a major tool for mobilizing mass protests (e.g. Liu, 2013a, 2013b, 2015; Weber, 2011). As an emerging yet rarely touched upon topic in both communication studies and China studies, mobile-phone-mediated contentious activities in China offer cases worthy of closer examination for understanding the role of mobile phones in protest mobilization.

To understand interpersonal interactions in China, however, it is imperative to consider *guanxi*, the fundamental basis of the intricate social ties that constitute Chinese culture. In Mandarin Chinese, the word *guan* signifies "to connect" or "to close up," while *xi* denotes chain, "to tie up," or "to link." In combination, *guanxi* connotes pervasive social ties among parties that make up social networks in Chinese society (Gold, Guthrie, & Wank, 2002b; Yan, 1996b; Yang, 1994).

Similar to the "old boy network" in the West, *guanxi* involves more complex, unwritten, and implicit rules than most relationship systems (Gold et al., 2002a; Kipnis, 1997; Yan, 1996b). Beyond literal translations such as "relation" or "personal connections," *guanxi* implies intangible emotional bonds and ethical obligations between two or more individuals (Christensen & Levinson, 2003, p. 573; Gold et al., 2002a, p. 4). More specifically, *guanxi* has three key characteristics.

First, *guanxi* takes root in familiarity or intimacy, which means the totality of personal connections rather than those that are based only on money. When two people share a bond, their *guanxi* implies that both sides must "know a great deal about each other and share with each other frequently" (Bian, 1997, p. 369). In other words, *guanxi* includes not only a utilitarian view of relationship but also *ganqing* (affection, attachment), the rapport of an emotional interpersonal relationship. In this way, *guanxi* accounts for the trustworthiness and *credibility* of information exchange and thus effectively inhibits the occurrence of opportunistic or dishonest acts, for example, furnishing false diplomas or certifications for education, training, and work experiences (e.g., Bian, 2002, p. 131). The significance of credibility arising from *guanxi* has been reinforced in a Chinese environment characterized by inadequate social infrastructure, and weak legal institutions that have failed to provide "a trusted third party adjudication and enforcement of private agreements" (So & Walker, 2006, p. 114) with concomitant "unpredictable risks of arbitrary bureaucratic intervention" (Smart, 1993, p. 404).

Second, *guanxi* involves varying degrees of *reliability* of personal relations and social support, including friendship, loyalty, and solidarity, according to the extent of *guanxi* between people. Individuals thus appeal to and draw strength from each other within their *guanxi* network, and given this ethos of reliability, the individual in Chinese society is always considered part of a social ecology of relational interdependence. As Tong and Yong observe, "[t]he closer the *guanxi*, the higher the expectation of its reliability by both parties, and vice versa" (2014, p. 47). Moreover, when rules are still not as important as personal relations in China always focus on the exceptionality of present circumstances and make their decisions and judgments "based on acquaintance or lack of acquaintance with others" (Michailova & Hutchings, 2006, p. 394) instead of resorting to law or other formal rules.

Third, *guanxi* carries a norm of *reciprocity*. *Guanxi* usually develops between persons who are strongly tied to each other, thereby imposing a mutual obligation on both sides to respond to requests for assistance. As a reciprocal process, *guanxi* not only stimulates endless circulations of favors and gifts (Yan, 1996a, 1996b; Yang, 1994), but also embeds itself within Chinese society to a far greater extent as "a dynamic process embedded in social interactions in everyday life" (Yan, 1996a, p. 4; Yang, 1994, p. 6). Those who fail to fulfill their obligations will be isolated in society and suffer from losing face (*mianzi*) and may even risk the ultimate price of losing their *guanxi* networks and the social resources embedded within (Cheng & Rosett, 1992; Hwang, 1987; Smart, 1993). Therefore, Chinese people not only rely heavily on *guanxi* to obtain social resources to meet their needs and adapt to changing environments, but also actively engage in *guanxi* to perform reciprocity, fulfill obligations, maintain solidarity, and anchor their roles in social networks.

Reciprocity also implies that both sides will share each other's social circles after they set up *guanxi*. Therefore, *guanxi* acts as an intermediary to tap into others' social connections and resources. Consequently, *guanxi* extends to *guanxi* networks that permeate Chinese society and are sustained by intricate, hidden rules of social interactions and network structures (Walder, 1986: Chapter Three and Five).

To sum up, *guanxi* entails credibility, reliability, and reciprocity among actors in China. Credibility introduces reliability to personal networks and social support, while reliability strengthens the trustworthiness of information and renders reciprocity important for solidarity. Reciprocity, in turn, reinforces the sense of reliability and credibility among social actors. These three characteristics are intertwined with each other and shape the process of interpersonal interactions in China.

While the widespread proliferation of new communication technologies shapes the individual as the focus and conduit for numerous networks to which he/she is attached, in China, the dynamics of *guanxi* as social ties still largely dominates contemporary social life. As a potent asset for interaction and survival in Chinese society, *guanxi* is naturally imbricated in mobile interactions (Chu, Fortunati, Law, & Yang, 2012; Chu & Yang, 2006). Liu (2010) proposes the concept of a "*guanxi*-embedded mobile social network," in which *guanxi* dynamics have been incorporated into both mobile communication and interpersonal networks in the wake of the increasing popularity of mobile devices and the sharp rise in phone use in maintaining social relations in Chinese society. In her ethnographic studies of mobile phone use among female migrant workers in Beijing, Wallis (2013) reveals the women's heavy reliance on existing *guanxi* and, particularly, the participants' norms of reciprocity during mobile communication practice to build network capital. How does mobile communication, infused with the dynamics of *guanxi* and its characteristics of credibility, reliability, and reciprocity, influence protest mobilization?

Methods

To present a nuanced picture of the use of mobile phones in protest mobilization, this study employs a multiple case-study design (Yin, 2009, p. 18). The main criterion for case selection was the use of mobile phones as a key means of mobilization (in contrast to the internet, for example). Four cases were therefore identified as follows: the anti-Para-Xylene ("anti-PX" for short) protests in Xiamen in 2007, the Weng'an mass incident in 2008, and the taxi driver strikes in Fuzhou and Shenzhen in 2010. The case descriptions will be provided in the next section.

Subsequent to the case selection, this study adopted snowball sampling and in-depth interviews. Snowball sampling allowed researchers to recruit "hidden populations" or individuals and groups that are not easily accessible through other sampling strategies (Salganik & Heckathorn, 2004). As an increasingly relevant interpersonal communication channel for social connections, mobile phones facilitate access to the individuals within one's network (Katz & Aakhus, 2002; Ling, 2008). The mobile network accordingly provides snowball sampling with a similar network based on personal contacts and structured around interaction. To recruit protest participants for my interviews, I tracked the flow of mobilizing messages within the mobile network. More specifically, I asked a few people in four cities, as "the seeds," to provide details about whom they received mobilizing messages from, and to whom they distributed these messages via their mobile phones. Then I replicated this process to identify and recruit more participants in the protests. Given that the mobile phone is both a private tool and the crucial conduit in sample protests, the mobile network-based sampling procedure guaranteed the interviewees' privacy and safety and ensured their participation in protests. Meanwhile, approaching participants through their mobile connections not only kept issues (i.e., protest participation) low profile, but also easily created a rapport and gained the trust of interviewees, as the researcher, an "outsider," had been introduced to them by people they already knew. Such rapport and trust thus assured the validity of research by entailing both a degree of honest dialogue and accurate information from participants and smooth compliance with sampling procedures. 65 participants were initially recruited.

Next, to foreground ethical practices, this study operated with permission from interviewees in all cases. Due to the politically sensitive nature of protest participation in China, the researcher wanted interviewees to be not only voluntary but also safe after joining this research. The sample was subsequently reduced to 43 after some withdrew from the research due to the sensitive subject matter.[1]

All interviews were conducted in Chinese in person by the researcher in friendly environments or in spaces that the interviewees would often inhabit or visit. Each interview lasted for around one and a half hours. A semi-structured interview guide was designed to explore how interviewees employed their mobile phones and perceived mobile communication in protests through a focused, conversational procedure (for more details about the interview guide, see Liu, in press). The researcher felt that most interviewees did their best to recall and elaborate on their practices, interpretations, and perceptions regarding the use of mobile phones in protests.

After data collection, an explanation-building approach and cross-case synthesis (Yin, 2009, p. 18) were employed to figure out questions of how participants adopted their mobile phones as a facilitator for protest mobilization, what kinds of mobile interaction was generated, and how mobile interaction affects protest participation and recruitment.

Mobile Communication and Protest Mobilization in China: Cases

I now provide an overview of the four cases: the anti-PX protest in Xiamen, the Weng'an mass incident, and the taxi driver strikes in Fuzhou and Shenzhen. The anti-PX protest in Xiamen is one of the largest middle-class protests in recent years (*The Economist*, 2007). Residents challenged the local government's decision on a chemical factory they perceived to be a health threat by distributing text messages[2] and calls and by urging people to join a street protest to demonstrate their concern over the environmental issue and to voice their dissatisfaction with the government's decisions. This incident is thought to be the first time a protest was primarily organized by mobile phones in China. Social commentators lauded "the power of text messaging" (Xie & Zhao, 2007). Similarly, on June 28, 2008, thousands of mobile-phone-mobilized residents assaulted and torched a police station and smashed county government office buildings in southwest China's Guizhou Province. The unrest was triggered by allegations of a cover-up of a 16-year-old girl's "unusual death" and the injustice her relatives suffered at the hands of the government and policemen (Yu, 2008).[3]

The taxi drivers' strikes in Fuzhou and Shenzhen further exemplified mobile-phone-mediated mobilization (for detailed information about mobile communication in both strikes, see Liu, 2014). Discontent with the controversially rigid manner of enforcing traffic regulations by local police and long-standing concerns including unlicensed competition, high fuel prices, and rising rental fees due to the inaction of local government prompted taxi drivers in several cities to stage strikes, one after another, between 2008 and 2013, by primarily using calls and texts via their mobile phones. On April 23, 2010, in response to an unbearable surge in penalties handed out by the police, taxi drivers in Fuzhou went on strike (*"Taxi drivers go on strike,"* 2010). In addition to face-to-face interactions, mobile calls became the major conduit for the strikes (taxi drivers in Fuzhou, personal communication, December 2010). Similarly, over 3,000 taxi drivers took part in a three-day strike that was organized largely through mobile communication in Shenzhen at the end of October 2010 to protest at the failure of the government to address the problems of suburban drivers and the city's inequitable cab fare structure. As strikes by taxi drivers have become more frequent due to soaring costs that squeeze profits for drivers, the mobile phone has emerged as a key channel for distributing strike calls and organizing protests.

In short, although these four cases took place in different sets of circumstances (urban and rural areas), they include different groups (the middle class, the rural population, and the working class), with varying causes (environmental concerns, justice-seeking, and complaints against the government), all of them embraced the mobile phone as a key means of organizing and facilitating protests.

Findings and Discussions: Mobilizing *Guanxi* for Protest Mobilization

The multiple-case-study analysis shows that the mobile phone allows participants to communicate and distribute mobilizing messages in an inexpensive, immediate, and independent way. Inexpensiveness, first, pertains to the low-cost, easy-to-use mobile device as the key mobilizing platform and affordable telecommunication prices for information dissemination, be it through voice calls or text messaging. The capability for lowering the threshold for organizing and coordinating protests is thus immense, as mobile phones—cheaper to own and easier to run than computers—gain ground as a *mundane* tool for facilitating political protests. Second, immediacy refers to the instantaneous information transfer via mobile phones, in particular the synchronous voice call, which enables rapid mobilization for protests. In other words, the immediate communication via mobile phones allows the proliferation of mobilizing messages within a short period, making it difficult for the authorities to predict when and where mobilization will ensue, thus undermining their ability to intervene in any protest outbreaks. Relying largely on voice calls, the taxi drivers in the Fuzhou case initiated and organized strikes *overnight* (Liu, 2014). Immediacy thus raises the *potential* for rapid mobilization, which may leave the authorities unprepared for protests. Third, independence refers to the fact that mobile communication is an autonomous process. A protester can decide on the kind and amount of information he or she wishes to share, with whom, and at what time. In the case of protests, the communicator is able to independently decide on the *specific* recipients with whom s/he would like to share mobilizing messages and, more importantly, which individuals are most likely to be recruited into protests, or even to mobilize more people for protests. This process provides participants with the autonomy to maximize their control over the procedure of mobilization, which then activates and incorporates *guanxi* into mobilization and greatly increases the possibility of protest participation and recruitment.

Guanxi-Mediated Mobile Communication and Protest Mobilization

The interviews revealed that in the process of mobile interactions, participants have the autonomy to activate and mobilize their *guanxi* for protest mobilization. The activation and involvement of *guanxi* and the associated credibility, reliability, and reciprocity thus served as the driving force for both recruitment and participation in protests.

First, with trustworthiness strengthened through *guanxi* networks, information via mobile communication enjoys high credibility, which makes people more likely to trust and disseminate these messages further. For instance, in the Weng'an case, people kept disseminating messages regarding the controversial death of the female student as these messages were coming from "[their] reliable sources from *guanxi* networks," (a merchant, personal communication, October 2010)[4], even after local government had labeled such messages "rumors" (Lai, 2011). As one interviewee explained, "it is a matter of mutual trust [toward people from your *guanxi* networks], not verification [of facts]" (a primary school teacher, personal communication, October 2010). The statement demonstrates that the mutual trust in the bilateral relations within the *guanxi* tie imbues mobile messages with high credibility. Similarly, in the Xiamen case the interviewees noted that they would trust messages directed against the PX project they received via their mobile interactions, even if "the senders do not have enough knowledge about the topic (i.e., the impact of PX plants on the local environment)" (a white-collar, personal interview, September 2010). Importantly, the high credibility of mobile messages obtained through *guanxi*-mediated mobile communication does not mean that people take for granted that the information is factually accurate. As in the Xiamen case, it is impossible for people with little background in chemical knowledge to make a judgment about the potential impact of the petrochemical PX plants on the local environment. Nevertheless, with the trustworthiness and perceived credibility vested by *guanxi* ties, the interviewees were willing to give senders and their messages the benefit of the doubt. As one respondent argued, "it's better to believe it than not, especially when messages are coming from the people you trust" (an editor, personal communication, September 2010). In this way, given established *guanxi* relationships and the perceived high credibility, people were encouraged to trust such messages from their *guanxi* networks and distribute them further via mobile communication.

Second, the reliability stemming from *guanxi* ties contributes to both the proliferation of mobilizing messages and the recruitment and mobilization process. As one interviewee noted when she received the mobile text from her friends,

> the [mobilizing] texts show care and kindness from my friends' network, as they wanted to inform me of the potential pollution from the [PX] project. It also shows that they are asking me to increase [the text's] dissemination. Likewise, it is my *duty* to forward this information to my friends, as I also care about them and hope they are aware of this issue and spread it within their [mobile] social network to get more support.
>
> (emphasis mine, a university student, personal communication, December 2010)

The above statement suggests that when people received messages via their mobile devices, they not only received factual information, they were also reminded of the *guanxi* between senders and themselves and their own duties in their *guanxi* network regarding such relevant information. Such sentiments, largely self-perceived, encourage people to diffuse mobilizing messages throughout their *guanxi* network as both a form of social support and a fulfillment of their duties in maintaining *guanxi*. As one interviewee explained, mobilizing your network resources by disseminating messages via a mobile device "is a crucial way to demonstrate that you are a reliable friend, even if it concerns joining a protest [about a political sensitive issue]" (a taxi driver, personal communication, October 2011). Similarly, a large majority of the interviewees noted that they had immediately passed the message on, via their mobile phones, to people in their *guanxi* networks. As several interviewees mentioned, "if the message is important to me, it becomes important to my friends" (a resident in Xiamen, personal communication, September 2010). It is clear here that, through mobile communication, a stable, relational reliability among people emerges readily by disseminating messages that they perceive as relevant to those within their *guanxi* network. Meanwhile, the above statement shows that the proliferation of mobilizing messages expands the collective action's influence not only by informing more people, but also by recruiting more *guanxi* network resources into the distribution practice. In short, circulating messages through one's mobile phone has become a crucial way to activate one's *guanxi* network resources or social capital (Gold et al., 2002a, p. 7; Putnam, 2000) as social support, which consequently becomes a crucial force for promoting the proliferation of mobilizing calls through a mobile network.

Third, the reciprocity from *guanxi* greatly shapes the response to mobilizing messages, driving people to engage in protest participation and recruitment as a fulfillment of their obligations on the basis of *guanxi*. In practice, when people received mobilizing messages via mobile communication, they viewed such a message as an appeal from their *guanxi* networks and as more than a mere piece of (mobilization) information. As one interviewee explained, "[the message] is a piece of information from *a specific sender*, who could be your friend, colleague, relative, and so on from your *guanxi* networks" (emphasis mine, a university lecturer, personal communication, September 2010). For receivers, whether and how to respond to the [mobilizing] request in this message from *a specific sender* (Ling, 2004, p. 151) depends not just on the information itself, but more importantly on *guanxi*, specifically the reciprocal obligation in *guanxi* between the communicators. Another interviewee said, "beyond informing you about protest issues, the message actually seeks your participation as a kind of reciprocal help relating to your *guanxi*" (a taxi driver, personal communication, October 2010). In this situation, responding positively to the request enabled the recipient to demonstrate reciprocity, thereby strengthening the mutual relationship.

In this way, reciprocity from *guanxi* legitimizes mobilization appeals by underlining the norm of responding to requests for support from one's social networks, thus *shifting* the attention from "should I respond to and participate in the call for collective action?" to "should I respond to the request for help/support from my social network?" As such, the reciprocity inherited from *guanxi* imposes pressure to respond to the request to participate in protest. Given the duty and obligation to reciprocate, in particular the fear of losing social support in the long run, there is a greater inclination to agree. As such, the norm of reciprocity decisively exerts influence over people's decisions concerning recruitment and participation in protests. On the contrary, if people refuse to respond to the appeal from *guanxi* networks, as one said, "you will probably lose your *guanxi* resource, and people will in turn not respond to your request in future, as you have failed to fulfill your role and duty in *guanxi* practice" (a taxi driver, personal communication, October 2010).

Furthermore, the more often people receive mobilizing messages from their *guanxi* networks, the more willing they are to distribute these messages and join the protest mobilization. One interviewee elaborated, "The multiple [mobilizing] messages illustrate that the people you know all agree with this issue [of whether to participate in strikes or demonstrations]. And they are urging you to be one of them. You would not want to be isolated" (a taxi driver, personal communication, October 2011). Through involving themselves in the participation and recruitment via mobile communication, people are also demonstrating their attitudes toward mobilization, while sharing their feelings about mobilization: The implicit meta-message is "I agree with and support this action." Mobilization through mobile phones thus articulates a sense of solidarity. In the cases discussed, when people received mobilizing messages, they realized that the people in their social network were "not only sharing information, but also their attitudes towards this event and their engagements in it. In other words, you are not alone!" (a taxi driver, personal communication, October 2011). Consequently, mobile phone users realize that others in their social network have a common understanding of certain situations that every individual in the same social network may have to face. In other words, individuals in the same [mobile] network realized that they were not alone when disseminating mobilizing messages; instead, they were networked individuals who enjoyed support from one other due to their shared awareness. The perception thus engenders a sense of cohesion and solidarity within participants during mobilization, as they know that those in their personal networks are "in the same camp" (a taxi driver, personal communication, October 2011). As more people distribute and receive the messages via mobile communication, their sense of solidarity grows stronger.

In short, circulating messages through one's mobile phone has become a crucial way to activate one's *guanxi* resources as social support, which consequently becomes a crucial force not only to proliferate mobilizing calls through a mobile network, but also to facilitate recruitment and participation in protests. More specifically, in the process of mobilization, mobile communication distributes messages with high credibility from established social ties, encouraging people to trust such messages and disseminate them further to a larger audience. The reciprocal nature of social ties engenders mutual reliability and reinforces obligation for both sides. To positively respond to messages and circulate them through one's mobile phone has become a crucial way to fulfill one's duty and obligation as social support in *guanxi* practice. Reliability also strengthens the feeling of reciprocity in protests, while reciprocity in turn secures and intensifies mutual reliability and enhances feelings of solidarity.

Conclusion: Embedding Social Ties for Protest Mobilization

This study has shown that mobile interaction embeds and incorporates social ties and interpersonal networks, or *guanxi*, as the key mobilization agent for protests. More specifically, *guanxi* ensures credibility, engenders reciprocity, and reinforces reliability, which consolidates solidarity for protest mobilization. In this way, the mobile phone establishes itself as a relevant means of protest mobilization in China.

Nevertheless, the emphasis on *guanxi* may limit the long-term impact of mobile-phone-facilitated protests on China's contentious politics. For participants, a key motivation to protest against the authorities may have more to do with one's social ties than the politics at hand. The interviews confirmed that participants normally did not consider how they would achieve the aim of the protest (e.g., request that the government amend the management regulation for the benefit of taxi drivers) or what kind of strategies they would adopt to expand the influence of their protests (for a detailed discussion, see Liu, in print). Against this backdrop, the use of mobile phones appears to be more of a tactic for articulating social ties for collective action than a strategic way of acting against the authorities so that substantial change can be wrought.

By addressing the embedding and relevance of *guanxi* as social ties in protest mobilization, this study also offers implications for future research regarding mobile phone use and protest mobilization in a broader context. For instance, similar to the situation in China, Gouldner emphasizes "a generalized moral norm of reciprocity which defines certain actions and *obligations* as repayments for benefits received" (emphasis in original, 1960, p. 170) in the Western context. As a self-perpetuating phenomenon with regard to social support, reciprocity here carries the connotation that "each party has rights *and* duties" to support others with whom they share social ties (emphasis in original, Gouldner, 1960, p. 169). As the dynamics of social support binding social ties, reciprocity has the potential to act as a reservoir or resource for recruitment and mobilization. For Tilly (1978), reciprocity from "netness," or relational connectedness, is crucial in engendering mutual obligations and encouraging collective action mobilization. Given norms of reciprocity, Putnam (2000, p. 21) also believes that such networks facilitate coordination and communication for political contention. A promising question that scholars should explore as they further theorize the role of mobile phones in protest mobilization would be the extent to which our current understanding of *guanxi*-embedded mobile communication can serve as a facilitator of protest mobilization in other contexts beyond China by integrating concepts such as trust, social capital, and reciprocity.

Notes

1. Among them, 18 from the Xiamen case (11 male, seven female); eight from the Weng'an case (seven male, one female); six from the Shenzhen case (all male); and 11 from the Fuzhou case (all male).
2. One of the most renowned texts read: "For the sake of our future generations, take action! Participate among 10,000 people, June 1st at 8 a.m., opposite the municipal government building! Hands tied with yellow ribbons [as a symbol associated with environmental protection]! Pass this message on to all your Xiamen friends!"
3. Some mobile messages read: "Without conducting a full autopsy, the police believed the girl committed suicide by jumping in a river, and they did not take mandatory measures against the suspect and ignored the family's call for a full autopsy" (Buckley, 2008).
4. All translations are mine unless otherwise noted.

References

Allagui, I., & Kuebler, J. (2011). The Arab Spring and the role of ICTs. *International Journal of Communication,* (5): 1435–1442.

Bennett, W. L., Breunig, C., & Givens, T. (2008). Communication and political mobilization. *Political Communication,* 25(3): 269–289. doi:10.1080/10584600802197434.

Bian, Y. (1997). Bringing strong ties back in: Indirect ties, network bridges, and job searches in China. *American Sociological Review,* 62(3): 366–385.

Bian, Y. (2002). Institutional holes and job mobility process. In T. Gold, D. Guthrie & D. Wank (Eds.), *Social connections in China* (pp. 117–136). New York, NY: Cambridge University Press.

Buckley, C. (2008). Girl's death sparks rioting in China. Accessed November 2, 2008, from http://uk.reuters.com/article/latestCrisis/idUKPEK27256220080628?sp=true.

Castells, M., Fernandez-Ardevol, M., Qiu, J. L., & Sey, A. (2007). *Mobile communication and society: A global perspective.* Cambridge, MA: The MIT Press.

Cheng, L., & Rosett, A. (1992). Contract with a Chinese face. *Journal of Chinese Law,* 5(2): 143–244.

Christensen, K., & Levinson, D. (2003). *Guanxi.* In K. Christensen & D. Levinson (Eds.), *Encyclopedia of community* (pp. 572–574). London: Sage.

Chu, R. W.-c., Fortunati, L., Law, P.-l., & Yang, S. (2012). *Mobile communication and greater China.* London: Routledge.

Chu, W.-c., & Yang, S. (2006). Mobile phones and new migrant workers in a south China village. In P. Luo, L. Fortunati, & S. Yang (Eds.), *New technologies in global societies* (pp. 221–244). Singapore: World Scientific Publishing.

Diani, M., & McAdam, D. (Eds.). (2003). *Social movements and networks.* New York, NY: Oxford University Press.

Friedman, D., & McAdam, D. (1992). Collective identity and activism. In A. D. Morris & C. M. Mueller (Eds.), *Frontiers in social movement theory* (pp. 156–173). New Haven, CT: Yale University Press.

Gold, T., Guthrie, D., & Wank, D. (2002a). An introduction to the study of *guanxi*. In T. Gold, D. Guthrie, & D. Wank (Eds.), *Social connections in China* (pp. 3–20). Cambridge: Cambridge University Press.

Gold, T., Guthrie, D., & Wank, D. (2002b). *Social connections in China*. Cambridge: Cambridge University Press.

Gould, R. V. (2003). Why do networks matter? Rationalist and structuralist interpretations. In Mario Diani & Doug McAdam (Eds.), *Social movements and networks* (pp. 234–257). New York, NY: Oxford University Press.

Gouldner, A. W. (1960). The norm of reciprocity: A preliminary statement. *American Sociological Review, 25*(2), 161–178.

Hermanns, H. (2008). Mobile democracy: Mobile phones as democratic tools. *Politics, 28*(2): 74–82. doi: 10.1111/j.1467–9256.2008.00314.x.

Howard, P. N., & Hussain, M. M. (2011). The role of digital media. *Journal of Democracy, 22*(3): 35–48. doi: 10.1353/jod.2011.0041.

Hwang, K.-k. (1987). Face and favor: The Chinese power game. *American Journal of Sociology, 92*(4): 945–947.

Ibahrine, M. (2008). Mobile communication and sociopolitical change in the Arab world. In J. E. Katz (Ed.), *Handbook of mobile communication studies* (pp. 257–272). Cambridge, MA: The MIT Press.

Katz, J. E., & Aakhus, M. (2002). *Perpetual contact: Mobile communication, private talk, public performance*. Cambridge: Cambridge University Press.

Kipnis, A. B. (1997). *Producing guanxi: Sentiment, self, and subculture in a North China village*. Durham, NC: Duke University Press.

Lai, H. (August 19, 2011). High growth can't hide problems. *China Daily*. Accessed from http://www.china.org.cn/opinion/2011-08/19/content_23246056.htm.

Ling, R. (2004). The mobile connection: The cell phone's impact on society. San Francisco, CA: Morgan Kaufmann.

Ling, R. (2008). *New tech, new ties: How mobile communication is reshaping social cohesion*. Cambridge, MA: The MIT Press.

Ling, R., & Yttri, B. (2002). Hyper-coordination via mobile phones in Norway. In J. Katz & M. Aakhus (Eds.), *Perpetual contact: Mobile communication, private talk, public performance* (pp. 139–169). Cambridge: Cambridge University Press.

Liu, J. (2010). Mobile social network in a cultural context. In E. Canessa & M. Zennaro (Eds.), *M-SCIENCE: Sensing, computing and dissemination* (pp. 211–240). Trieste: ICTP.

Liu, J. (2013a). Mobile communication, popular protests and citizenship in China. *Modern Asian Studies, 47*(3): 995–1018. doi: http://dx.doi.org/10.1017/S0026749X12000340.

Liu, J. (2013b). *Mobilized by mobile media — How Chinese people use mobile phones to change politics and democracy* (Unpublished doctoral dissertation), University of Copenhagen, Copenhagen.

Liu, J. (2014). Calling for strikes: Mundane mobile calls, mobilizing practices, and collective action in China. *Georgetown Journal of International Affairs, XV*(1): 15–24.

Liu, J. (2015). The dynamics of real-time contentious politics. In Anja Bechmann & Stine Lomborg (Eds.), *The Ubiquitous Internet* (pp. 74–92). London: Routledge.

Liu, J. (in print). Communicating beyond information: Mobile phones and mobilization to offline protests in China. *Television & New Media*. http://tvn.sagepub.com/content/early/2014/08/20/1527476414544972.refs, doi: 10.1177/1527476414544972.

McAdam, D. (2003). Beyond structural analysis: Toward a more dynamic understanding of social movements. In Mario Diani & Doug McAdam (Eds.), *Social movements and networks* (pp. 281–298). New York, NY: Oxford University Press.

Michailova, S., & Hutchings, K. (2006). National cultural influences on knowledge sharing. *Journal of Management Studies, 43*(3): 383–405. doi: http://dx.doi.org/10.1108/13673270910942691.

Passy, F. (2003). Social networks matter. But how? In M. Diani & D. McAdam (Eds.), *Social movements and networks* (pp. 21–48). New York, NY: Oxford University Press.

Putnam, R. D. (2000). *Bowling alone: The collapse and revival of American community*. London: Simon & Schuster.

Qiu, J. L. (2008). Mobile civil society in Asia. *Javnost — The Public, 15*(3): 39–58.

Rafael, V. L. (2003). The cell phone and the crowd. *Popular Culture, 15*(3): 399–425.

Rheingold, H. (2008). Mobile media and political collective action. In J. E. Katz (Ed.), *Handbook of mobile communication studies* (pp. 225–240). Cambridge, MA: The MIT Press.

Salganik, M. J., & Heckathorn, D. D. (2004). Sampling and estimation in hidden populations using respondent-driven sampling. *Sociological Methodology, 34*(1): 193–239. doi: 10.1111/j.0081-1750.2004.00152.x.

Shen, C. (2014). *Ministry of Industry and Information Technology of the People's Republic China: The number of mobile phone users is close to 1.3 million in China*. Retrieved from: http://tc.people.com.cn/n/2014/0625/c183175-25195976.html.

Smart, A. (1993). Gifts, bribes, and *guanxi*: A reconsideration of Bourdieu's social capital. *Cultural Anthropology, 8*(3): 388–408.

Snow, D. A., Zurcher, L. A. J., & Ekland-Olson, S. (1980). Social networks and social movements. *American Sociological Review, 45*(5): 787–801.

So, Y. L., & Walker, A. (2006). *Explaining guanxi: The Chinese business network*. New York, NY: Routledge.

Suárez, S. L. (2006). Mobile democracy: Text messages, voter turnout, and the 2004 Spanish general election. *Representation, 42*(2): 117–128. doi: 10.1080/00344890600736358.

Taxi drivers go on strike (2010, April 23). *China* Daily, p. 7.

The Economist (2007). China: Mobilised by mobile; Protest in China. *The Economist, 383*(8534): 68.

Tilly, C. (1978). *From mobilization to revolution*. Reading, PA: Addison-Wesley.

Tilly, C. (2005). *Trust and rule*. Cambridge: Cambridge University Press.

Tong, C. K., & Yong, P. K. (2014). *Guanxi* bases, *xinyong* and Chinese business networks. In Chee-Kiong Tong (Ed.) *Chinese business: Rethinking guanxi and trust in Chinese business networks* (pp. 41–61). New York, NY: Springer.

Walder, A. G. (1986). *Communist neo-traditionalism: Work and authority in Chinese industry*. Berkeley, CA: University of California Press.

Wallis, C. (2013). *Technomobility in China: Young migrant women and mobile phones*. New York, NY: The NYU Press.

Weber, I. (2011). Mobile, online and angry: The rise of China's middle-class civil society? *Critical Arts: South-north cultural and media studies, 25*(1): 25–45. doi: 10.1080/02560046.2011.552204.

Xie, L., & Zhao, L. (2007). The power of mobile messaging. *China Newsweek,* *326*(20): 16–17.

Yan, Y. (1996a). The culture of guanxi in a North China village. *The China Journal,* *35*(1): 1–25.

Yan, Y. (1996b). *The flow of gifts: Reciprocity and social networks in a Chinese village,* Stanford, CA: Stanford University Press.

Yang, M. M.-h. (1994). *Gifts, favors, and banquets.* Ithaca, NY: Cornell University Press.

Yin, R. K. (2009). *Case study research: Design and methods* (4th ed.). London: Sage.

Yu, J. (2008). A review of anger-venting mass incident. *South Wind View,* (15): 20–22.

6 The Local Sociality and Emotion of *Jeong* in Koreans' Media Practices

Kyong Yoon

Introduction

The rapid innovation and diffusion of information and communication technologies (ICTs) in South Korea (hereafter, Korea) since the late 1990s has been remarkable and has attracted global attention. To recover from the country's financial crisis in the late 1990s, the government proactively invested in ICT industries (Kang, 2014). As a result, the ICT industry's contribution to Gross Domestic Product (GDP) growth, which was just 4.5% in 1990, increased to 50.5% in 2000 (Hanna, 2010). Thus, Korea, which used to be known as "the land of morning calm," has recently been represented as a global ICT powerhouse (Jin, 2010).

With the extensive adoption of ICTs throughout the country, the increasing presence of technologically mediated communication in Koreans' lives over the past two decades raises questions of how local cultural norms are negotiated and redefined in emerging media environments. The conjunction of local culture with new media in the Korean context may be particularly intriguing because the country is known for the lingering influence of traditional cultural norms despite the extreme rate of modernization and urbanization (Alford, 1999; Yoon, 2003, 2006). In particular, Koreans' cultural characteristic of *jeong* (정),[1] which draws on face-to-face and family-like bonding as the prototype of human relationships (S-W. Lee, 1994), does not seem at first glance to be compatible with virtual communications enabled by new mobile personal technologies.

The emergence of web 2.0 and social media provokes contemplation about how mediation is locally negotiated in Koreans' media practices, especially in relation to the local cultural code of *jeong*. In the midst of the flourishing discourse of globalization and increasing media technologies, *jeong*-based relationships appear to remain a badge of collective identity amongst Koreans (Alford, 1999; S-W. Lee, 1994; Tudor, 2012). Thus, *jeong* is an important indigenous concept to be examined in the studies of emerging media technologies in the Korean context. However, media studies research, by both Korean and international scholars, has paid little attention to *jeong* and other related local cultural codes.

In this respect, this chapter explores how the locally specific cultural norm of *jeong* is articulated within emerging media environments and how the concept can help to illuminate Asians' media practices. The scholarly investigation of *jeong* in the realm of media studies can show how the Korean notion can be compared to other Asian concepts relevant to understanding mediated communication, on the one hand, and with those favored in Western media theories, on the other. This chapter suggests that *jeong* may not necessarily fade away with the emergence of mediated communication; thus it is important to address how this local norm is imbricated with the evolution of communication technologies. In so doing, while suggesting an alternative, non-Western understanding of selfhood in media environments, this chapter also critiques and cautions against essentializing the practice of *jeong*. In addition, by applying an insider perspective on Koreans' media practices, we can avoid the decontextualized formulation of media analysis and thus re-imagine emerging communication technologies and human communication (Dissanayake, 2009, p. 458).

Defining *Jeong* in the Era of Globalization

Jeong has been considered one of the key characteristics that govern Koreans' human relations (S-W. Lee, 1994). However, despite its frequent use in Koreans' everyday life and in the journalistic discourse on 'Koreanness' (*hanguginnon:* 한국인론), the concept has rarely been defined in academic terms (S. C. Choi & Choi, 2001). Although several attempts to define and analyze *jeong* have been made mostly by Korea-based scholars since the 1990s (e.g., Baek, 2002; S. C. Choi & Choi, 2001; S. C. Choi, Kim, & Kim, 2000; Ko, 2014; S-W. Lee, 1994; Yoon, 2003), the concept still lacks theoretical and empirical investigation. This paucity of research may be due to the intangible and subjective nature of the concept, which does not allow for an unequivocal analysis and comparison with any social scientific concepts developed in the West (H. Yang & Yu, 2012).

The Korean concept of *jeong* draws on the Chinese character 情 *(qing)*, which originally refers to emotion or feeling. However, the Korean notion of *jeong* has been so uniquely localized that its meaning is more complex than the original Chinese meaning (Chung & Cho, 1997). An authoritative Korean language institution defines *jeong* as "the mind arising from a feeling" or "the mind of feeling love or affection" (National Institute of the Korean Language, 2015). This definition captures an aspect of *jeong* in its ordinary use, where *jeong* is elucidated as a particular state of mind (*maeum*) and/or feeling (*neukkim*). However, the definition remains too ambiguous to be used for cultural analysis. In this respect, S-W. Lee's (1994) attempt to see *jeong* as a perspective or framework that defines Koreans' human relations and social lives offers leverage whereby we can analyze the process of *jeong* and compare it with its Western, or Asian, analogues. In particular, S-W. Lee (1994) analogizes *jeong* as a symbolic space that represents Koreans' human relations, drawing on family-like bonding. From this perspective, Koreans' sociality in the *jeong* space can be contrasted with Western societies' human relations predicated on social exchange between individuals who seek to advance their own self-interests. The *jeong* space comprises *uri* (우리: we), in which "I" and "You" exist as an inseparable unit (S-W. Lee, 1994). In a similar vein, S.C. Choi and Choi (2001, p. 80) state that "*jeong* embodies the emotional links among individuals that are bonded both socially and relationally." In this perspective, *jeong* refers to a mechanism of Koreans' social and interpersonal relationships between in-group members (Baek, 2002; S. C. Choi & Choi, 2001; S. C. Choi & Kim, 2006).

Given the aforementioned literature, *jeong* can be analyzed as a communication process that involves two dimensions—emotion and sociality, which are deeply intertwined. That is, *jeong* refers to locally bound affection or a particular state of emotion (Shim, Kim, & Martin, 2008), which is maintained within the family or family-like, small groups. Thus, it is necessary to consider *jeong* in relation to Koreans' mentality of *uriseong* (우리성: we-ness). As S.C. Choi, Kim, & Kim (2000) effectively analogized, *uriseong* is to *jeong* as structure is to substance. We-ness and *jeong* are deeply interwoven and interdependent (S. C. Choi et al., 2000). In the sociable and emotional space of *jeong* (S-W. Lee, 1994), which originally draws on face-to-face based, small circles of people (Alford, 1999), in-group members share a strong sense of togetherness and attachment to each other (S. C. Choi & Choi, 2001). The *jeong*-based relationship is also likely to emerge throughout a long period of time (S. C. Choi & Choi, 2001). Regardless of one's individual interests therefore, he or she cannot be easily exempt from the space of *jeong* and cannot do so volitionally.

In response to the rapid modernization of Korea, literature on the discourse of Koreanness (*hanguginnon*) tends to lament the decline of *jeong*, which is often discussed in parallel with increased individualism and Westernization (e.g., Tudor, 2012). In particular, the growing discourse of globalization since the mid-1990s has aroused in Koreans a mixture of concerns, fears, and hopes (Alford, 1999). In particular, the explosive diffusion of personal mobile technologies has ignited debates about their impact on traditional and local cultural norms. On the one hand, as shown in serial governmental policies such as Cyber Korea 21 (1999) and Korea Vision 2006 (2002), ICTs have been considered in the dominant discourse to be a key to Korea's transition to a globalized society, thus strengthening the we-ness of Koreans. At the same time, however, public discourse about ICTs has also involved concerns about the decrease of *jeong* due to the extensive use of communication technologies (Yoon, 2010). Particularly in the Korea of the late 1990s and the early 2000s, young people were represented in popular discourse as a group that was particularly exposed and vulnerable to excessive media use (Yoon, 2006). Regardless of their different evaluations of the role of emerging technologies, the two aforementioned dominant discourses seem to share an essentialized notion of Korean we-ness. That is, emerging media technologies were signified as contributing to or detrimental to the imagined essence of we-ness.

While Koreans have long acknowledged *jeong* as a foundational norm of sociality and emotion, it has been criticized for its restrictive roles in personal and public sectors (Alford, 1999; S. C. Choi et al., 2000; Ko, 2014; S-W. Lee, 1994). In particular, it is argued that family-like attachment of *jeong* among in-group members may intervene in private life. As *jeong* is created via a form of long-term, close attachment, it can be considered an inescapable relationship. It can be expressed as not only as "sweet" (*goun*) but also as "bitter" (*miun*) *jeong* (S. C. Choi et al., 2000). For example, Yoon's (2003) studies of young mobile phone users in Seoul showed how family attachment drawing on *jeong* could sometimes be perceived as "a nuisance" for individual members of the family. Furthermore, the blurred boundary between the private and the public in the *jeong* space may entail the management of public affairs through private connections, as shown in the management style of *jaebeol* conglomerates (Alford, 1999).[2] Such side effects of local sociality have been similarly observed in other East Asian countries, where affective and personal connections often command significant power in the public sector (Chang & Chu, 2006). As *jeong* tends to increase within certain temporal and spatial boundaries and to rely on cultural proximity, its formation and maintenance may inevitably exclude individuals who are not considered culturally proximate. Hence, the *jeong* space may not necessarily be an egalitarian and/or hospitable arena, since it clearly demarcates insiders from outsiders, even discriminating against the latter (Han & Choi, 2011; H. Yang & Yu, 2012). Overall, it appears that among Koreans, while *jeong* is an emotional resource to maintain and protect in response to globalizing forces on the one hand, it is also considered an outdated cultural code that may adversely affect modern ways of life.

Jeong in the Cross-Cultural Context

The concept of *jeong* seems to share a common ground with other East Asian based cultural norms such as *amae* in Japan and *guanxi* in China (M. H. Kim, 2012; Mao, Peng, & Wong, 2012; I. Yang, 2006). It has been argued that East Asians share "relationship cultures" or "collectivistic cultures," which are distinguished from cultures that draw on the individualistic conception of human beings and relations that are primarily prevalent in the West (Han & Choi, 2011; Sasaki & Marsh, 2011). In relationship cultures that "share a common emphasis on relational concerns across all domains from the dinner table to the office" (Sanchez-Burks et al., 2003, p. 364), *jeong*, *amae*, and *guanxi* tend to be identified as comparable concepts (Han & Choi, 2011). These concepts are often referenced in light of the individualism-collectivism comparison, or the cross-cultural examination of social trust (Han & Choi, 2011; Sanchez-Burks et al., 2003).

Amae, which can be translated as "permissive love" or "dependence" in English, has been compared to the notion of *jeong*, as both emphasize attached and obligatory relationships (M. H. Kim, 2012). *Amae* involves a feeling of dependency between children and parents and thus allows one to act "childish and dependent with a lover and feel comforted, forgiven and taken care of, or even be spoiled" (Han & Choi, 2011, p. 399). *Amae's* collectivist dependency is very similar to the emphasis on interdependency between members of an *uri* (we) in the *jeong* space. However, *amae* allows for a participant's privilege over other(s), which seems different from the way *jeong* functions, as the latter tends to be based more on reciprocal relationships between *uri* members (I. Yang, 2006, p. 291).

Jeong is also comparable to the Chinese concept of *guanxi*, which refers to "relationships of close ties" and now more widely refers to "connections" or "social ties" (M. M. Yang, 1994). "Practicing *guanxi* means engaging in a trust relationship through reciprocal interactions and seeking *guanxi* is to establish a trust relationship by searching familial ties" (Han & Choi, 2011, p. 397). The emphasis on familial ties in *guanxi* largely overlaps with the close bonding in the *jeong* space. While *guanxi* emphasizes "personal benefits rather than benefits to the collective," *jeong* relationships emerge from individuals' commitment to the collective of *uri* (I. Yang, 2006, p. 291).

Jeong, amae, and *guanxi* are "all intricately related to human connectedness and interpersonal relationships" (S. S. Kim, 2007, p. 727). Given its similarity with *guanxi* and *amae, jeong* can be situated in the East Asian tradition of human relations and communications, which tends to emphasize collective harmony, a highly context-oriented communication style, and clear in-group/out-group divisions (de Mooij, 2014). In this regard, East Asians' shared legacy of Confucianism and its particular role in Koreans' communication is noteworthy. Confucianism, based upon the lessons and canons of Confucius (551–479 B.C.), has significantly influenced Korea and other East Asian countries. Confucianism is a "value system that seeks to bring harmony to the lives of people in communities—the family, the village, and the state" (Shim et al., 2008, p. 27). Confucianism, introduced to and developed in Korea since the fifteenth century, defines the family relationship as the "prototype of all human relations" (S-W. Lee, 1994, p. 86), and thus social relations or public lives are considered an extension of family relationships (S-W. Lee, 1994). The imagination of the family as the origin (or inseparable part) of the self in the *jeong* space appears to reflect Confucian norms, and *jeong's* collectivism and emphasis on in-group harmony are also regarded as Confucian influences. It is often agreed that "Confucian codes of conduct" operate extensively in Koreans' everyday life (Shim et al., 2008, p. 46; See also Alford, 1999; Janelli, 1993).

Jeong can also be compared to a few Western concepts addressing networks and/or affective ties. The affective sociality of *jeong* seems to have particular significance in the era of social media, as the concept may offer an important reference point for the Western concept of "social network." The notion of social networks, which emerged as "a middle ground between individuals and communities" in sociology (Baym, 2011, p. 385), is defined as "structures of relationships linking social actors" (Marsden, 2001, p. 2727).

The Western concept of social networks can be compared to *yeonjul* in Korea, which is an actualized form of *jeong*-based close social ties. *Yeonjul* may be a good example of how the indigenous concept of *jeong* can be reified as a relatively concrete and tangible form of sociality. *Yeonjul*, which can be translated as "affective linkage," is a Korean mode of strong social ties that largely rely on the members' birthplace (blood and regional ties) or educational background (alumni status) (Lew & Chang, 1998). Whereas the Western concept of networks draws on rational individuals' pursuit of interest and/or collaboration, *jeong* and *yeonjul* are not necessarily grounded in a concept of solid selfhood but bear a more pronounced social stance. Notably, recent empirical studies show how *jeong* and *yeonjul* are enabled via emerging communication technologies and how young Koreans execute these different modes of sociality to negotiate the networked individualism of (Western-developed) social media and the collectivist space of *jeong*.

Jeong's affective dimension of social relations can also be compared to Western concepts of "caring" or "gift-giving." *Jeong* focuses on unconditional, unintentional, and ceaseless attachment and is thus differentiated from the Western concept of caring that tends to take into account the carer's intention (Ko, 2014). Gift-giving practices examined in Western-based studies address the "exchange of the tangible between both physically distributed and co-proximate groups" and imply strategic engagement with social exchange for enhancing intimacy (Taylor & Harper, 2002, p. 440). Such gift-giving appears to be significantly different from the way *jeong* operates; "simple exchanges of gifts or performing rituals are not enough for brewing *jeong* sentiment" (Han & Choi, 2011, p. 401) because *jeong* practices are more than intended social exchanges between individuals and need to develop over a long period of time, emphasising unintended, selfless commitment to the group.

Jeong 2.0 in the Era of Social Media

The integration of emerging media technologies with existing cultural norms has been actively examined throughout the development of media studies (e.g., Horst & Miller, 2006; Miller & Slater, 2000; Williams, 1974). In this regard, the ongoing cultural negotiation of new technologies is not entirely unique to the Korean context. However, the role of *jeong* in the web 2.0 era offers a particularly intriguing case for media studies as it reveals how social interactions in two apparently different spaces—*jeong*-based space and technologically mediated space—are articulated with each other.

To explore how *jeong* operates, or is redefined in response to new ICT environments, two major perspectives on technologically mediated communication are significant (Tomlinson, 1999): first, as a *facilitating* process of already existing cultural norms and second, as an *intervening* process that causes qualitative changes in the cultural norms. This framework identifying two aspects of mediation, albeit simplistic, may effectively address how the role of ICTs in society has been theorized. It also seems to resonate with the ongoing technological and cultural determinism debates (Lister, Dovey, Giddings, Grant, & Kelly, 2009). In this respect, while a new communication technology can be viewed as a means to efficiently maintain or intensify existing cultural norms, it can also be claimed that the introduction and diffusion of a new technology may entail new cultural norms that are qualitatively different from existing ones.

With regard to the sociality of *jeong*, it is important to explore how the *jeong* space as a small group-oriented, collectivist cultural norm interacts with the technologically mediated virtual space. Internet-mediated communication has been considered to decrease, transform, and/or supplement the traditional mode of community (Wellman et al., 2003). It is argued that the virtual space of the internet, and more recently online social networking sites (SNSs), involve particular affordances that incline users toward particular forms of media usage. In particular, Wellman et al. (2003) identified constant global connectivity, wireless portability, and individualization as critical technological affordances of the early internet. boyd's (2014, p. 11) study of the more recent trends in online social networking has illustrated four major features of social media design: 1) the durability of online content; 2) the existence of the potential audience; 3) the spreadability of content; and 4) searchability.

Western-based scholars have argued that the affordances of web 2.0 facilitate the emergence of "networked publics" (boyd, 2014) or "networked individuals" (Wellman et al., 2003). This view appears to draw on a Western perspective of the "the individual as the source of rational thought" (Bowers et al., 2000, p. 190). However, the internet itself has evolved differently depending on the user's cultural context. For example, the Cyworld phenomenon in Korea illustrates how the internet is localized, mediated, and signified among Korean users. Korea-developed Cyworld, an early form of social media (1999~), reflects local cultural norms that valorize the family as a foundational unit for communication. In particular, users on Cyworld create their own homes, and their friends are interpellated into family members (J. H. J. Choi, 2006; Shim et al., 2008). For example, the classification levels for Cyworld friends are referred to as *chon*, which means the unit of kinship; close contacts are called *ilchon,* which originally referred to parent-children relationships, and second level contacts are named *"ichon,"* which originally meant grandparent-children relationships. Jin (2012, p. 5) claims that the kinship metaphor "plays a significant role in promoting online social networking in Korea mainly because users' relationships are stronger than those seen in other SNSs due to the metaphor of family relationship, which cannot be easily broken."

This familial imagination among Korean internet users appears to be distinctively different from the networked individualism that seems to be reified in interfaces of Western-designed SNSs such as Facebook (Rainie & Wellman, 2012). In addition, Cyworld's indirect representations of user identity, often via avatars rather than photographs of oneself, can be contrasted with the public display of self that is observed on Facebook (boyd, 2014) or Instagram. Shim et al. (2008, p. 130) suggest that the avatar-mediated self-representation on Cyworld is a way to "express 'self' or to create an image of 'self' indirectly." Even so, the self exists in the *jeong* space, remaining largely inseparable from its family or familial communities. In this respect, Yoon (2015) has found that recent Korean Facebook users are not necessarily satisfied with the ways in which Facebook displays the self and facilitates networks. In the study, some Korean users tried not to directly present themselves on Facebook profile and timelines. For them, updating about their individual lifestyles and interests was not necessarily a cool thing to do, as they regarded Facebook as a virtual space for "showing off," something they were averse to doing. Conversely, they saw Cyworld as a more intimate virtual space where they were prepared to post personal stories and share feelings with their significant others.

In addition to its sociality dimension, *jeong* involves an emotion dimension in the context of web 2.0. The affective space of *jeong*, which originally draws on face-to-face intimacy, may be more complicated with highly mediated communication enabled by personal ICTs. In particular, Koreans still find it important to maintain such face-to-face intimacy even with the intensifying use of technologically mediated communication. For example, young Koreans, who are often depicted as a techno-savvy demographic, do not necessarily prefer technologically mediated communication. As explored in a case study (Yoon, 2003, p. 332), although young Koreans appropriated the mobile phone "as useful technology when it is based on a face-to-face relationship," they described it as "restrictive or boring when it is dissociated from such direct interaction." Similarly, in a recent study of smartphone use by transnational Korean families (Yoon, 2016), some young people questioned the value of mediated, virtual togetherness in favor of face-to-face communication.

The enduring importance of *jeong* as a form of close and intimate emotion implies that in the Korean context, communication technologies are not necessarily perceived as communicative, but are signified as technological and perhaps even incompatible with the humanizing space of *jeong*. In this respect, the practice of "cute customization" among young Koreans (Hjorth, 2009a, 2009b) shows how new technology is appropriated in a way that can be better integrated with the local emotion of *jeong*. According to Hjorth (2009a and 2009b), young Korean media users appropriated cute stickers, accessories, and avatars in an intimate way, so that affective sociality is enhanced and new technology is re-signified as having humanity and feelings. Koreans' preference for intimate interface design, stickers, and avatars has also been observed in the recent phenomenon of the Korean-developed messenger application (app) KakaoTalk (2010~), which has been nicknamed a "national messenger" due to its extensive popularity. Yoon's (2015) study of Korean KakaoTalk users suggests that the app's focus on inter-personal and small group talk on a smartphone and its affinity with voice calls have been identified as the key appeals to Korean users (see also Jin & Yoon, 2014). In the study, "doing KaTalk" (acronym for KakaoTalk) implied intimate feelings between participants who greatly value the close-ness and closed-ness of communication. Their intimate feelings are not only verbally shared, but often rely on non-verbal cues. Certain user inter-faces in cyberspace, such as avatars and gifts (on Cyworld), and stickers (on KakaoTalk), can contribute to non-verbal, indirect, and high context-oriented sharing of *jeong* (D. H. Lee, 2013b). In particular, the extensive use of stickers in mediated communication is considered a characteristic of mobile media cultures in Korea and other East Asian countries (Hjorth, 2009a; Lim, 2015; Russell, 2013). Lim (2015) attributes the popularity of stickers in the Asian context to the ability to explicitly visualize feelings, whereby the ambiguity that often occurs in Asians' high-context communication can be avoided; however, she also suggests that emotive stickers may paradoxi-cally help to facilitate emotional social bonding that relies on high context communication.

As was earlier discussed, the affective space of *jeong* draws on collectivist sociality predicated on the collective of *uri* (we) rather than the individual self. This affective and collective norm may be in conflict with the default settings of emerging communication technology, such as SNSs, which pri-marily draw on an individualist perspective and encourage individuals to showcase themselves to their networked publics (boyd, 2014). In Korea, however, technology is appropriated through the local sociality and emotion of *jeong* and has thus engaged with a local mediascape, in which techno-logical mediation is redefined by designers and users as a more affective, collective, and humanized process. It should also be noted that the *jeong* space of affection involves a strong sense of attachment, imbuing individual participants with a sense of obligation to respond all the time. Indeed, Kore-ans have difficulty turning down others' requests to meet or communicate online or offline. In Haddon and Kim's (2007, p. 11) study, an interviewee commented on how she would respond to such requests: "I can't say 'no'. It's so hard to say no. It's part of the culture in Korea. To say 'no' is not good." In this regard, *jeong* relationships can substantially limit one's free-dom, compelling users to respond and pay attention to others' requests for communication online. A recent study has also reported that young Koreans struggle with un-friending on social media and increasingly experience dig-ital fatigue caused by dealing with the extensive range of Facebook friends (Yoon, 2015).

In contrast to the aforementioned observations on the lingering influence of *jeong* in social media use, D.H. Lee's (2013a) study of young Koreans' use of Twitter explored how *jeong*-based *yeonjul* sociality can actually be modified by social media. The study found that Twitter's affordances, which allow for relatively egalitarian or open communication beyond the hierarchies involved within strong local ties, interplay with and transform the traditional norms of sociality. Notably, strong ties and instrumentally organized weak ties are blurred in Koreans' use of Twitter. Thus, D.H. Lee (2013a) claims that young Koreans seek ontological security not only through local norms of sociality, but also through a mixture of affective ties and technologically mediated virtual ties.

The observed transformation of *jeong* relationships may also be considered in light of the recent notion of "reflexive intimacy." In his study of Australia-based Facebook users, Lamberts (2013, p. 177) finds that social media users' emotional engagement with technology and other users are not simply dictated by social media's affordances. Rather, he argues, users may increasingly appropriate social networking media as a tool to enhance emotional competency or what he calls "reflexive intimacy." Reflexive intimacy, which seems to be inspired by the individualization thesis, focuses on the agentic force of individuals in negotiating relationships with an explosive range of others via technological mediation, such as via social media in particular. However, this concept does not accommodate the affective ties and ambiguous boundary of selfhood in the *jeong* space, which do not necessarily derive from agentic force but more from relational bonds. In the *jeong* space, we-ness constitutes a central unit of intimacy and indeed tends to be accompanied by the suppression of the self to some extent (Shim et al., 2008).

Conclusion

This chapter has addressed the unique cultural characteristic of *jeong* to develop an understanding of Koreans' media practices. Korea's rapid modernization over the past few decades, which has been accompanied by the phenomenal increase of ICT production and consumption, has seemed to be in conflict with indigenous ways of life to some extent. The remaining value of *jeong* in Koreans' sociality and emotion can be seen as a local response to globalization (Yoon, 2003). While some critics consider *jeong* to be no more than a myth that may not have any substance (e.g., Alford, 1999), this chapter has argued that the notion of *jeong* can illuminate how the local mediascape is constructed, signified, and maintained in the Korean context. Thus, the dimensions of local sociality and emotion that are salient in *jeong* can be further elaborated upon and utilized for internationalizing media studies.

The notion of *jeong* may offer an alternative framework for understanding selfhood in the social media era. Despite the increasing use of personal communication technologies, feelings of the collective of *uri* (we) are so fundamental in the affective and attached space of *jeong* that an "I--centered" perspective seems absent and silenced (S. C. Choi & Choi, 1990). The Western-dominated discourse of emerging communication technologies and internet-mediated communication tends to be predicated on a particular understanding of selfhood. That is, whether from a technologically or culturally deterministic perspective, the user is defined as a (be it active or passive) rational subject in emerging digital environments who can decide whether or not to be involved in diverse social networks. However, a conceptualization of selfhood that focuses on relations between rational individuals does not fully explain the inter-dependence of I, you, and we in the *jeong* space or the seamlessness of such relationships. This implies that a particular Western model of the "ideal" ICT user and its subject position may not be easily applicable to other contexts such as Asia-based users (Goggin & McLelland, 2009). Thus, for a better understanding of Koreans' media practices, it may be necessary to explore the ongoing role and meaning of local cultural norms.

With the explosive diffusion of social media and their associated apps, dominant social media's technological affordances have been considered to have significant influence on our daily communications and media use. For example, Facebook's interface, originally built upon the concept of "public-by-default and private-by-effort" (boyd, 2014, p. 12), may contribute to easily expanding the user's human networks, thus constructing a virtual public sphere that has been referred to as the arena of "networked publics" (boyd, 2014) or "networked individuals" (Rainie & Wellman, 2012). However, this conceptualization of networks may not fully explain how local affective ties, which are based upon local norms of sociality, such as *jeong* and *yeonjul*, engage with virtual, mediated communications.

The prevailing model of networked individuals also appears to adopt a technologically deterministic perspective, as it suggests that social media enhances a particular form of individualism. However, as evidenced in the significant Facebook fatigue amongst Korean users (Yoon, 2015), social media can be appropriated and signified as even an "unsociable" media form in the *jeong* space. The "sociability" of social media is based upon a specific form of individual and society and does not universally lead to intensifying and expanding social ties. Of course, individualist online user behaviors, or a mixture of individualist and collectivist orientations, have increasingly been observed in Korea-based cyberspace (D. H. Lee, 2013a; Shim et al., 2008). However, some Korean online forums that have encouraged overtly individualist user behaviors and discouraging *jeong*-based affective ties have ended up as extremist trolling sites. In this regard, K.H. Lee (2014) argues that the recent Korean trolling site *ilbe* and its hate speech phenomenon are partly due to its attempt to circumvent any possible *yeonjul*. Hence, Koreans' close and closed communication style, based on the norm of *jeong*, may not easily co-exist with the networked individualism afforded by the dominant forms of social media and the internet. We therefore need to engage in further discussion about how *jeong* space can evolve in the era of social media. Mediated space, which may often lack such characteristics as familial connections, embodied intimacy, a clear sense of local belonging, and/or the context and cue of communication, may be in conflict with the *jeong* space and thus remain uncomfortable for those who are more familiar with *jeong* relationships.

The incompatibility of social media-driven communication with the *jeong* space may be part of a bigger question about the cultural bias of the internet and social media. There have been discussions and suggestions about alternative online cultures in recent media studies (e.g., Fuchs, 2014). However, while most of the discussions seem to address aspects such as gender, race, and social class, they remain largely Western-centric perspectives. With few exceptions (e.g., Wong, 2013), there has been little discussion of how Asian cultural frameworks can be appropriated to challenge the Western-dominant design of communication technologies and their virtual spaces. In this respect, the concept of *jeong* can be a significant reference point for theorization about new media in Asia. In particular, an emic perspective from inside can contribute to exploring how Koreans carry, use, and negotiate *jeong* in their media practices. However, the emic perspective does not necessarily imply a celebratory introduction and revival of local norms in media studies. As has been addressed earlier in this chapter, *jeong* may (adversely) involve the voluntary suppression of the self and the exclusion of others (Ko, 2014; Yee, 2000). In this process, various subject positions—marginalized groups in particular—can be interpellated into the homogeneous national subject (Cho Han, 2000).

Thus, the use of *jeong* and other related concepts discussed in this chapter suggests that the theorization of *jeong* for internationalizing media studies may require bilateral efforts—exploring and re-signifying the indigenous concept in the language of media discourse, on the one hand, and critiquing the essentialized use of the local concept, on the other.

Notes

1. *Jeong* can also be romanized as *cheog, chŏng*, or *jung*. The romanization of Korean terms in this chapter follows the Revised Romanization of Korean system.
2. *Jaebeol*, also written as *chaebŏl*, refers to family-owned, Korean corporations. The term *jaebeol* literally means a wealth ("jae")-clan ("beol"). *Jaebeols* own dozens of affiliated companies across various industrial sectors. Samsung, Hyundai, SK, LG, and Hanhwa are the biggest five *jaebeol* in Korea as of 2015 (Marlow, 2015).

References

Alford, C. F. (1999). *Think no evil: Korean values in the age of globalization*. Ithaca, NY: Cornell University Press.
Baek, H. J. (2002). A comparative study of moral development of Korean and British children. *Journal of moral education*, 31(4): 373–391.
Baym, N. K. (2011). Social networks 2.0. In M. Consalvo and C. Ess (Eds.), *The handbook of Internet Studies* (pp. 384–405). Oxford: Wiley-Blackwell.
Bowers, C. A. et al. (2000). Native people and the challenge of computers: Reservation schools, individualism, and consumerism, *American Indian*, 24(2): 182–199.

boyd, d. (2014). *It's complicated: The social lives of networked teens*. New Haven, CT: Yale University Press.

Chang, E. C., & Chu, Y. H. (2006). Corruption and trust: Exceptionalism in Asian democracies? *Journal of Politics*, 68(2): 259–271.

Cho Han, H. (2000). "You are entrapped in an imaginary well": A feminist critique of modernity and Korean culture. *Inter-Asia Cultural Studies*, 1(1): 46–69.

Choi, J. H. J. (2006). Living in Cyworld: Contextualising cy-ties in South Korea. In A. Bruns & J. Jacobs (Eds.), *Uses of blogs* (pp. 173–186). New York, NY: Peter Lang.

Choi, S. C., & Choi, S. H. (2001). *Cheong*: The socioemotional grammar of Koreans. *International Journal of Group Tensions*, 30(1): 69–80.

Choi, S. C., & Kim, K. (2006). Naïve psychology of Koreans' interpersonal mind and behavior in close relationships. In U. Kim, K-S. Yang, & K-K. Hwang (Eds.), *Indigenous and cultural psychology: Understanding people in context* (pp. 357–369). New York, NY: Springer.

Choi, S. C., Kim, J. Y., & Kim, K. (2000). The structural relationship analysis among the psychological structure of *jung* (sweet *jeong*, hateful *jeong*), its behaviors, and functions. *The Korean Journal of Social and Personality Psychology (Hanguk-simnihakoeji: Sahoe mit seonggyeok)*, 14(1): 203–222.

Chung, C. K. & Cho, S. (1997). Significance of "jeong" in Korean culture and psychotherapy. HarborUCLA Medical Center. http://www.prcp.org/publications/sig.pdf.

de Mooij, M. (2014). *Human and mediated communication around the world: A comprehensive review and analysis*. New York, NY: Springer.

Dissanayake, W. (2009). The production of Asian theories of communication: Contexts and challenges. *Asian Journal of Communication*, 19(4): 453–468.

Fuchs, C. (2014). *Social media: A critical introduction*. New York, NY: Sage.

Goggin, G., & McLelland, M. (Eds.) (2009). *Internationalizing internet studies: Beyond Anglophone paradigms*. New York, NY: Routledge.

Haddon, L., & Kim, S. D. (2007). Mobile phones and web-based social networking: Emerging practices in Korea with Cyworld. *The Journal of the Communications Network*, 6(1): 5–12.

Han, G., & Choi, S. C. (2011). Trust working in interpersonal relationships: A comparative cultural perspective with a focus on East Asian culture. *Comparative Sociology*, 10(3): 380–412.

Hanna, N. K. (2010). *Transforming government and building the information society: Challenges and opportunities for the developing world*. New York, NY: Springer.

Hjorth, L. (2009a). *Mobile media in the Asia-Pacific: Gender and the art of being mobile*. New York, NY: Routledge.

Hjorth, L. (2009b). 'Gifts of presence: A case study of a South Korean virtual community, Cyworld's mini-hompy'. In G. Goggin & M. McLelland (Eds.), *Internationalizing internet studies: Beyond Anglophone Paradigms* (pp. 237–251). New York, NY: Routledge.

Horst, H., & Miller, D. (2006) *The cell phone: An anthropology of communication*, Oxford: Berg.

Janelli, R. L. (1993). *Making capitalism: The social and cultural construction of a South Korean conglomerate*. Stanford, CA: Stanford University Press.

Jin, D. Y. (2010). *Korea's online gaming empire*. Boston, MA: MIT Press.

Jin, D. Y. (2012). Critical analysis of user commodities as free labor in social networking sites: A case study of Cyworld. *Continuum: Journal of Media and Cultural Studies*. Ahead-of-print, 10.1080/10304312.2012.664115.

Jin, D. Y., & Yoon, K. (2014). Reimagining smartphones in a local mediascape: A cultural analysis of young KakaoTalk users in Korea. *Convergence: The International Journal of Research into New Media Technologies*. Ahead-of-print, doi:10.1177/1354856514560316.

Kang, I. (2014). It all started with a bang: The role of PC bangs in South Korea's cybercultures, In K. H. Kim and Cho. Y. (Eds.), *The Korean popular culture reader* (pp. 55–75). Durham, NC: Duke University Press.

Kim, M. H. (2012). A cognitive study on *jeong* in Korean and *amae* in Japanese, *Comparative Cultural Studies (Bigyomunhwayeongu)*, 27: 471–496.

Kim, S. S. (2007). Psychological contours of multicultural feminist hermeneutics: Han and relationality, *Pastoral Psychology*, 55(6): 723–730.

Ko, M-S. (2014). The establishment of ethic of *jeong*: Focused on the relation with ethic of caring, *The Korean Journal of Philosophy of Education (Gyoyukcheolhangnyeongu)*, 36(2): 1–29.

Lamberts, A. (2013). *Intimacy and friendship on Facebook*. New York, NY: Palgrave Macmillan.

Lee, C. (2014). Korea struggles to enact hate speech laws. http://www.koreaherald.com/view.php?ud=20141228000346.

Lee, D. H. (2013a). Smartphones, mobile social space, and new sociality in Korea. *Mobile Media & Communication*, 1(3): 269–284.

Lee, D. H. (2013b). Mobile snapshots: Pictorial communication in the age of tertiary orality. In M. Wise & H. Koskela (Eds.), *New visualities, new technologies: The new ecstasy of communication* (pp. 186–204). Farnham, Surrey: Ashgate.

Lee, K. H. (2014). How do we recognize "*ilbe*"? *Citizens and the World (Simingwa Segye)*, 25: 244–256.

Lee, S-W. (1994). The *cheong* space: A zone of non-exchange in Korean human relationships, In G. Yoon and S-C. Choi. *Psychology of the Korean people: Collectivism and individualism*, Seoul: the Korean Psychological Association.

Lew, S-C. & Chang, M-H. (1998). Functions and roles of the non-profit/nongovernmental sector for Korean social development: The affective linkage-group, *Korea Journal*, 38(4): 277–299.

Lim, S. S. (2015). On stickers and communicative fluidity in social media. *Social Media+ Society*, 1(1): 1–3.

Lister, M., Dovey, K., Giddings, S., Grant, I., & Kelly, K. (2009). *New media: A critical introduction (2nd Ed.)*. New York, NY: Routledge.

Mao, Y., Peng, K. Z., & Wong, C. (2012). Indigenous research on Asia: In search of emic components of guanxi. *Asia Pacific Journal of Management*, 29(4): 1143–1168.

Marlow, (2015). South Korea's *chaebol* problem. *The Globe and Mail*. April 24. http://www.theglobeandmail.com/report-on-business/international-business/asian-pacific-business/south-koreas-chaebol-problem/article24116084/.

Marsden, P. V. (2001). *Encyclopedia of Sociology: Vol. 4* (2nd Ed.). New York, NY: Macmillan.

Miller, D., & Slater, D. (2000). *The internet: An ethnographic approach*. Oxford: Berg.

National Institute of the Korean Language, 2015. http://krdic.korean.go.kr/.

Rainie, L., & Wellman, B. (2012). *Networked: The new social operating system.* Cambridge, MA: MIT Press.

Russell, J. (2013). Stickers: From Japanese craze to global mobile messaging phenomenon. http://thenextweb.com/asia/2013/07/12/stickers/.

Sanchez-Burks, J., Lee, F., Choi, I., Nisbett, R., Zhao, S., & Koo, J. (2003). Conversing across cultures: East-West communication styles in work and nonwork contexts. *Journal of personality and social psychology*, 85(2): 363–372.

Sasaki, M., & Marsh, R. M. (2011). Social trust: part two. *Comparative Sociology*, 10(3): 317–320.

Shim, T. Y. J., Kim, M. S., & Martin, J. N. (2008). *Changing Korea: Understanding culture and communication.* New York, NY: Peter Lang.

Taylor, A. S., & Harper, R. (2002). Age-old practices in the 'new world': A study of gift-giving between teenage mobile phone users. *Proceedings of the SIGCHI conference on Human factors in computing systems* (pp. 439–446). New York, NY: The Association for Computing Machinery (ACM).

Tomlinson, J. (1999). *Globalization and culture.* Chicago, IL: University of Chicago Press.

Tudor, D. (2012). *Korea: The impossible country.* North Clarendon, VT: Tuttle Publishing.

Wellman, B., Quan-Haase, A., Boase, J., Chen, W., Hampton, K., Díaz, I., & Miyata, K. (2003). The social affordances of the Internet for networked individualism. *Journal of Computer-Mediated Communication*, 8(3). http://onlinelibrary.wiley.com/doi/10.1111/j.1083-6101.2003.tb00216.x/full.

Williams, R. (1974). *Television: Technology and cultural form.* London: Fontana.

Wong, P. H. (2013). Confucian social media: An oxymoron?. *Dao*, 12(3): 283–296.

Yang, I. (2006). *Jeong* exchange and collective leadership in Korean organizations. *Asia Pacific Journal of Management*, 23(3): 283–298.

Yang, M. M. (1994). *Gifts, favors, and banquets: The art of social relations in Chinese society.* Ithaca, NY: Cornell University.

Yang, H., and Yu, M. B. (2012). A qualitative study of organization members' experiences of 'we-ness.' *Korean Journal of Administration Studies (Hangukaeng-jeonghakbo)*, 46(4): 325–355.

Yee, J. (2000). The social networks of Koreans. *Korea Journal*, 40(1): 325–352.

Yoon, K. (2003). Retraditionalizing the mobile: Young people's sociality and mobile phone use in Seoul, South Korea. *European Journal of Cultural Studies*, 6(3): 327–343.

Yoon, K. (2006). The making of neo-Confucian cyberkids: Representations of young users of mobile phones in South Korea. *New Media and Society*, 8(5): 753–771.

Yoon, K. (2010). The representation of mobile youth in the post-colonial techno-nation of Korea. In S. Hemelryk Donald, T. Anderson, & D. Spry (Eds.), *Youth, Society and Mobile Media in Asia* (pp. 108–119). London & New York, NY: Routledge.

Yoon, K. (2015). *Diasporic apps? An ethnography of young South Korean migrants' use of communication apps.* Paper presented at the Annual Conference of the International Association for Media and Communication Research, Montreal, Canada, July 14.

Yoon, K. (2016). The cultural appropriation of smartphones in transnational Korean families. In S.S. Lim (Ed.), *Mobile communication and the family: Asian experiences in technology domestication.* New York, NY, and Dordrecht, Springer. In press.

7 Ritual and Communal Connection in Mobile Phone Communication

Representations of *Kapwa, Bayanihan* and 'People Power' in the Philippines

Cheryll Ruth R. Soriano and Sun Sun Lim

Studies analyzing the theoretical relationship between culture and advertising (Lury, 2011; McCracken, 1988; Otnes & Scott, 1996; Williamson, 1978) argue that advertising brings consumer goods and representations of the culturally constituted world together within the frame of an advertisement. Advertising of goods necessarily requires a reflection of human culture and, consequently, advertisements need to be mediated by a culturally symbolic field in order to gain relevance in society (Appadurai, 1986; Ju, 2009; Meijer, 1998, p. 238). The present study builds on this line of inquiry by considering how Philippine television advertisements for mobile technology products and services use the frame of ritual and mobilize the various dimensions of *kapwa* (connecting to significant others) to appeal to consumers. We question how advertisements reify the importance of culturally embedded rituals and relationships that are underscored by shared values to shape the mobile phone's place in society. At the same time, we explore how advertising promotes the ritual of mobile communication and consumption through aspirational marketing campaigns that frame social reality through a ritualized system of symbolic production. The paper will argue that aside from engaging cultural rituals in mobile advertising, the advertising of mobile services can be considered a "media ritual" (Couldry, 2003) as it entrenches forms of social organization within a locale and the centrality of mobile communication in that social organization.

We focus on advertisements' representation and promotion of mobile adoption in society because advertisements are considered one of the most visible products of culture industries. Advertising and technology share the characteristic of double-edgedness. On the one hand, advertising and technology are seen as tools of the capitalist market for driving the consumer society (Sassatelli, 2007; Williams, 1980). On the other hand, both advertising and technology represent societal dynamics and shape culture. We focus specifically on mobile technology because of its explosive growth in the Global South, illustrated by its emergence as a primary form of telecommunication. In the Philippines, the local adoption of mobile technology has been profound and has evolved to have vital social, developmental, political, and spiritual roles woven into the daily lives of the masses (Goggin, 2006). In 2009, the average Filipino mobile phone user sent a monthly average of 600 texts, 43 percent more than their U.S. counterparts (Dimacali, 2010), earning it the moniker of "texting capital of the world" (Mendes, Alampay, Soriano, Soriano, 2007; Pertierra, 2005, p. 27). This prominence of the mobile phone in the Philippines amidst a state of relative poverty and economic development makes it a compelling case for analyzing technology and societal interactions.

Rituals in Advertising

The cultural approach to consumer culture and advertising presents a paradigm shift from the logic of seeing consumption as a purely individualistic activity. The cultural industries do not merely manipulate, but accommodate the view of consumers as they are involved in a continuous process of interaction or the "cultural circuit" (Johnson, 1986; Lury, 2011). In addition, advertising reflects a society's values, and effective advertising and marketing are indelibly linked to the underlying culture of the target group (Chang, Jisu, McKinney, Sar, Wei, & Schneeweis, 2009, p. 672). Advertisements are seen to convey the advertisers' collective knowledge and/or assumptions about what is appealing to a particular society. Advertising in turn transmits cultural values through associating material goods with qualities or values exalted by a particular culture.

Connected to this cultural approach to advertising is a body of literature on the relationship between advertising and ritual (McCracken, 1988; O'Reilly, 2005; Rook, 1985; Otnes & Scott, 1996). Otnes and Scott (1996) developed this association by describing a two-way relationship between advertising and ritual, in which advertising can influence existing rituals, while those same rituals can also be incorporated into advertisements in order to convey meaning. Rook (1985) applied grooming rituals to modern consumer behavior, where he defines ritual as incorporating both religious and non-religious behaviors: "a type of expressive, symbolic activity constructed of multiple behaviors that occur in a fixed, episodic sequence, and that tend to be repeated over time" (p. 252). Rituals are laced with emotion, symbolism, and even cognition and are performed either individually or in a group (Otnes & Scott, 1996). Rituals define the 'right way of doing things' and make symbolic statements about social order (Rook, 1985). Some public rituals are viewed as contributing to social cohesion (Ling, 2008) that bind a nation through symbolic nationalistic practices that work to prevent social conflict and promote social order (Levy & Zaltman, 1975). While ritual has long been recognized as a method for deriving meaning from consumer goods (Rook, 1985), ritual can also be used to derive meaning from a particular advertising text (Ritson & Elliott, 1999, p. 271).

But what is the relationship between media and rituals? Couldry (2003) developed the term 'media ritual' to refer "to the whole range of situations where media themselves 'stand in', or appear to 'stand in', for something wider, something linked to the fundamental organizational level on which we are, or imagine ourselves to be, connected as members of a society" (p. 4). He analyzed the 'media rituals' that characterize everyday talk about celebrities or the legitimation of 'surveillance' in reality TV through 'Big Brother' shows (Couldry, 2003), arguing that "certain practices around media ... have the transformative force of ritual in their own right ... as they 'construct themselves as socially central' or 'as a central access point to a wider centre'" (Couldry, 2012, p. 70). Advancing a critical position, he argued that while ritual can be seen as affirming social order and community via the expression of certain transcendent values, rituals are also seen to institute "natural and legitimate certain key category differences," ideologies (of the ruling class), and inequalities (Couldry, 2003, p. 28). This essentially shifts the emphasis of ritual analysis from mere questions of meaning, toward questions of power that are embedded, maintained, or communicated in rituals (Couldry, 2003). The repetitive form of rituals works because it reproduces categories and patterns of thought that bypass explicit belief. It is also in this ritualized form that advertisements can successfully reproduce cultural practices without questions being raised about their content (Couldry, 2003, 2012). Using this framework of 'media rituals' to analyze advertisements of mobile technology products and services, we ask:

> RQ1: How are traditional Philippine rituals appropriated as referential tools to promote consumer adoption of mobile communications and technology in the Philippines?
>
> RQ2: How do advertisements for mobile products and services depict the relationship between mobile technology and Philippine society? How do these advertisements showcase communication rituals that are enabled by these devices?

Mobile Communication, Culture and Ritual in the Philippines

Previous sociological works identified instances wherein mobile devices mediate ritual interactions that dictate a sense of social order and solidarity within a locale. First, the mobile phone's ritualized role is manifested by its salience for the maintenance of social relationships (Ling, 2008; Pertierra, 2005; Wajcman, Bittman, & Brown, 2009). For example, Ling (2008) has investigated the relationship between mobile phones and rituals in the European context and found that through the use of various social rituals the mobile phone strengthens social ties within the circle of friends and family—sometimes at the expense of interaction with those who are physically present—and creates what he calls 'bounded solidarity.' The ritualized function of the mobile phone was also explored in the amplification of collectivist cultures and facilitating new modes of cooperation and social cohesion (Burrell, 2010; Campbell & Kwak, 2010; Sreekumar, 2011).

Second, the mobile phone enacts ritualized roles. For example, studies have found that women's uses of the mobile phone fit the spheres of activity and interests traditionally designated to them, such as taking responsibility for the emotional and material needs of husbands and children, the elderly, the handicapped, or the sick (Soriano, Lim, & Rivera, 2015; Zainudeen, Iqbal, & Samarajiva, 2010). Men, on the other hand, used phones for purposes traditionally expected of them, such as work or business (Huyer, Hafkin, Ertl, & Dryburgh, 2006).

Third, ritualized interactions have emerged from the use of mobile phones (Ling, 2008, p. 167). For example, Ito, Okabe and Matsuda (2005) presented SMS—mediated ritualized interaction in a dating context in Japan, and Pertierra (2006) argued that ritualized greetings underlie the introduction of strangers in mobile chat lounges. Mobile devices also facilitate a ritual of 'connected presence' (Licoppe, 2004) and 'perpetual contact' (Katz & Aakhus, 2002) where small, regular messages and talks are exchanged to create an illusion of presence and continued connection between individuals.

The case of mobile phones in the Philippines demonstrates how a globally introduced technology interacts with local socio-cultural conditions (Pertierra, 2005, pp. 24–25). Filipinos are one of the most fervent adopters of mobile technologies as cheaper versions of phones found their way into the market and cellular networks began offering affordable schemes that fit the country's 'sachet culture' (i.e., prepaid, credit top-up, and "unlimited texting" promotions) (Mendes et al., 2007). As a testament to the ubiquity and extensive acceptance of this technology, studies have documented its importance in various realms of Philippine society. These include Filipinos' use of SMS in social movement formation and political protests (Rafael, 2003; Rheingold, 2002; Tilly, 2003), as well as in developmental applications such as m-government, mobile remittances, m-commerce, m-agriculture, and even m-education (Mendes et al., 2007). The overthrowing of President Estrada in 2001 via a 'coup d' text' (Pertierra, 2005) has made the Philippines a test case for assessing the political and community-building consequences of this technology (Tilly, 2003; Pertierra, 2005; Rafael, 2003; Rheingold, 2002). Mobile phones have also become more salient given their role in bridging transnational families in light of pervasive labor migration of Filipinos (Cabanes & Acedera, 2012; Madianou & Miller, 2011; Paragas, 2009; Uy-Tioco, 2007). As more than nine million Filipinos work in 135 different countries and territories as migrant workers (Philippine Overseas Employment Agency (POEA), 2012), the mobile phone keeps them connected to their loved ones at home.

The pervasiveness of the mobile phone and its social and political relevance must also be situated within the structural realities in Philippine society. Cell phone ownership is becoming a major index of modernity and the basis for a new form of inequality (Rafael, 2003). The increase in cell phone theft demonstrates that its possession has become an imperative (Pertierra, 2005). Mobile phone acquisition and use take up a significant portion of the Filipino household expense. In a study by LIRNEasia (Aguero, Da Silva, & Kang, 2011, p. 23), mobile telephone service expenditure figures show that the "bottom of the pyramid or BOP"[1] in the Philippines spends the highest on mobile phone services, at an average of US$9.50 per month or 57% of the personal monthly income, more than double the percentages for India (24.3%), Sri Lanka (27%), and Thailand (24.4%). The BOP is therefore a significant market for Philippine mobile networks, given the country's poverty incidence estimate of 26.5% in 2009 or an estimated 28 million people[2] (World Bank (WB), 2012). Thus it was imperative for the biggest telephone networks in the country, Globe Telecom and Smart Telecom, to create subsidiary brands that cater to the mass and lower income market, Touch Mobile and Talk n' Text, respectively. As will be shown later, the BOP figures prominently in the narratives of mobile network advertisements.

Recent studies exploring the intersections of mobile phones, families, and migration have shown that while the mobile phone can lead to increasing connections between migrant parents and their left-behind families, such mobile phone use has implications that are nuanced and complex (Madianou & Miller, 2011; Thomas & Lim, 2010). Furthermore, mobile relationships are becoming more common, and while many are advantageous, others have been found to be disruptive of certain cultural norms and social relations (Pertierra, 2005; Turkle, 2011). In light of these varied implications of mobile phone use in a developing society, this paper highlights the importance of culturally embedded rituals in shaping and understanding the mobile phone's place in society.

Methodology

We conducted a YouTube search of mobile and network television commercials from the Philippines from February to April 2011 using the combination of the following key words: advertisement, commercial, *patalastas* (local term for commercial), Smart Telecom, Smart Buddy, Globe Telecom, Globe Tattoo, Touch Mobile, Red Mobile, Sun Cellular (which pertain to the major network providers in the Philippines), Nokia, Samsung, Sony Ericsson, iPhone, Blackberry, and names of local brands such as Cherry mobile and MyPhone for the mobile phone advertisements. Obtaining commercial videos from YouTube allowed us to sample a range of advertisements from a broader time period, enabling us to analyze the changing patterns of mobile use across time. All videos YouTube suggested on the top right corner of the screen, carrying the network names in full or abbreviated form, were also reviewed. In all, over one hundred advertisements were reviewed. From this pool, we selected advertisements that were crafted specifically for the Philippine market and featured stories/narrative, as we wanted to explore the social embeddedness of the product or service being marketed. Advertisements that featured only a straightforward presentation of information on product prices and promotions were therefore excluded from consideration. A total of 60 advertisements were subjected to further semiotic analysis (Table 7.1). Most of the advertisements indicated the date created and aired on television (production range is 2002–2010) and ranged from 0.12 seconds to 1.2 minutes in length.

Table 7.1 Mobile advertisements reviewed by service provider and brand

Network Provider	No. of Advertisements	Mobile Phone Brand	No. of Advertisements
Globe Telecom	8	Nokia	5
Smart Telecom	13	Cherry Mobile	1
Sun	6	MyPhone	5
Touch Mobile (Globe)	7	Sony Ericsson	2
Red Mobile (Smart)	4		
Talk n' Text (Smart)	3		
Tattoo (Globe)	6		
Total (Network advertisements)	47	Total (mobile phone advertisements)	13
TOTAL			60

Findings: Rituals in Mobile Advertising: Depicting the Mobile Phone as Central in *Pakikipagkapwa*

The actualization of a collectivistic logic in a community's appropriation of new technologies has been overlooked in many studies of mobile phones (Sreekumar, 2011). Also, mobile advertisements in other countries have been found in previous studies to primarily represent individualistic values and aspirations (Ju, 2009). A few recent studies, however, have shown how the availability of mobile technologies has allowed for the amplification of collectivist cultures and enabled new modes of cooperation (Burrell, 2010; Campbell & Kwak, 2010; Sreekumar, 2011).

Consistent with these new directions, the advertisements in our corpus depicted mobile technologies as central in facilitating various forms of relating to the other (*pakikipagkapwa*): (a) nurturing familial bonds; (b) facilitating the maintenance of rituals of solidarity with the community (*bayanihan*); and (c) as contributor to rituals of 'People Power,' political mobilization, and nation-building. This concept of maintaining smooth interpersonal relationships (*pakikipagkapwa*, or *kapwa*) has been identified in previous studies of Filipino psychology as integral to the individual's belief systems and as an important means for maintaining social acceptance (Bulatao, 1992; Enriquez, 1978, 1994; Enriquez & Guanzon-Lapeña, 1985). The concept of *kapwa* is central in Filipinos' various relationships and actions—from nurturing familial ties and engaging in acts of solidarity with a neighbor to joining efforts towards broader goals, such as nation-building. In Filipino cultural psychology, *kapwa* implies other people connected to a person (me/other orientation) by virtue of a shared identity (Enriquez, 1978). Although the usual English translation for *kapwa* is 'other,' it is important to emphasize that the term *kapwa* regards other people as closely connected to oneself or even extensions of oneself, while the English term 'other' implies difference and separation from oneself (Sapitula & Soriano, this volume). Developed from the root word, *kapwa*, the term *pakikipagkapwa* is a verb that reflects the collectivistic logic running through Philippine society, where one's actions (i.e., use of the mobile phone) are conducted in consideration of one's *kapwa*, or in the process of acknowledging someone as a *kapwa*.

The notion of *kapwa* is an important lens through which to understand much mobile phone engagement in this particular locale. Through various forms of mobile communication, users are able to keep abreast of the goings-on in both the private and public spheres of their *kapwa*. As we discuss the findings in the succeeding sections, we explore the role of advertisements as 'media rituals,' which work both in articulating social values and affirming *pakikipagkapwa*, while promoting the essential role of consumer goods in their achievement.

Nurturing Familial Bonds

The most common theme in the advertisements is that of nurturing family and social relationships. These advertisements highlighted the use of the mobile phone for connecting with family and communicating familial responsibilities in light of increasing mobility. The family rituals these advertisements capture are those of children expressing their love for their parents, a renewal of ties with extended family through mobile calls, and family members communicating with one another while on the move. For example, Smart Telecommunications launched a series of advertisements focusing on stories about each family member: father, mother, son, and daughter. In multiple contexts, the mobile phone is represented as bringing the family together, sometimes even in death. Even as mobile communication services have evolved to facilitate diverse social and instrumental connections, this ritual of the family keeping in touch continues to be avidly used in advertisements.

This persistent representation by advertisers of the ritual of family connection is a reflection of the central role of the family in Philippine society (Cabanes & Acedera, 2012; Church, 1987; Quisumbing, 1963; Uy-Tioco, 2007). The Filipino family, believed to be the foundation of the nation, and the family—nuclear, extended, and transnational—is the cornerstone of Philippine culture. Among Filipinos, a strong sense of family solidarity exists regardless of its size. The importance of family and kin has been consistently emphasized as being the "highest value in Filipino culture" (Quisumbing, 1963, p. 135) and "the core of all social, cultural, and economic activity"

(Quisumbing, 1963, p. 137). The bilateral extended family provides emotional and economic security and support, and its functions in the economic, political, and religious realms are far-reaching. The advertisements that carried a central theme about the role of technology in mediating relationships—within or beyond the family, clearly disrupt individualistic assumptions about consumer culture and open avenues for conceptualizing advertising and technology use as undertaken in relational terms.

The maintenance of familial relationships is also depicted in light of the reality of increased migration of Filipinos. According to the Philippine Overseas Employment Agency (POEA), 1.47 million Filipinos left the country for employment overseas in 2010 (POEA, 2012). In these advertisements, Filipino migrants are shown to use cell phone technology to maintain relationships with their families in the Philippines. Communication technologies such as mobile phones allow people to imaginatively detach from their geographical locations and momentarily suspend their physical separation with loved ones (Uy-Tioco, 2007). Nurturing relationships, albeit virtual and mediated, can exist despite the separation of space and time. The advertisements also show how familial relationships are maintained through innovations in cell phone services (i.e., mobile-remittance, *pasaload,* or passing of phone credit from one account to another).

What is striking in some advertisements of mobile services is the positive depiction of overseas parenting, where overseas Filipinos are often depicted as professional workers who continue to actively parent their left-behind children despite their physical distance. Further, most of these advertisements depict the father as the overseas worker while the mother is rarely shown as based overseas. Notably, when the mother is overseas, the husband is not shown to receive the call at home. On the contrary, when the husband is based overseas, the wife/mother is always shown in the Philippine home to receive the husband's call and to pass on the call/mobile phone to her children. These depictions strike a discordant note with reality, where left-behind fathers performing the mother's role in the home is becoming a common phenomenon in light of increased migration of Philippine mothers (Cabanes & Acedera, 2012). The advertisements hide this real yet socially unacceptable scenario of mothers as breadwinners (possibly taking care of other people's children overseas) and fathers as homemakers. Instead, positive representations of mobile-mediated parenting in advertisements serve to create illusions of normalcy and efficient parenting, silencing the complicated realities faced by migrant families while setting unrealistic expectations (Soriano, et al. 2015). We argue that such depictions support particular social categories, positions, and expectations (i.e., gender roles in parenting) even when these do not necessarily match reality. Thus, the mobile phone is presented in the advertisement as successfully enabling the performance of such ritualized roles. Such depiction of technology's relevance through advertising can be construed as a 'media ritual' (Couldry, 2003). While highlighting the mobile phone's 'social centrality' through representations that affirm social order, family, and community, these also distort reality and hide issues of power that underlie consumption of mobile products and services.

Enacting *Bayanihan* (Solidarity with Community)

In Philippine culture, there is a specific exercise of *pakikipagkapwa* known as *bayanihan,* a traditional Filipino practice involving a community of Filipinos helping one's neighbor to (literally) move one's house (originally a *nipa* hut) from one location to another. *Bayanihan* is derived from the word *bayan*, referring to a nation, town, or community, and underscores a spirit of communal unity or joint effort to achieve a particular objective. Although *bayanihan* practiced in its original form is rare today, the word has come to mean any manifestation of the powerful spirit of communal unity that can make seemingly impossible feats possible through the cooperation of many people working toward a common goal.

Philippine communities' cultural practices of sharing resources as well as social bonding in an environment of struggle help explain the salience of this theme in the mobile advertisements reviewed. A significant number of advertisements in our corpus showed the use of mobile phones to promote a sense of *bayanihan* depicting culturally enhancing ways that facilitate community cooperation and solidarity, particularly in moments of struggle and hardship of economically marginalized communities. In one advertisement (Trevor Hone, 2010), the mobile phone is shown being used by a rural community of fisherfolk to keep a fellow fisherman driving a local *jeepney* (traditional mode of transportation) from falling off the cliff. Through the mobile phone, two fishermen in a threatened *jeepney* immediately send mass messages to other fisherfolk in the community, enabled of course by the low-cost mobile plans offered by the network. Showcasing the mobile phone's capability for micro-coordination and communal unity especially in rural contexts, the community of fisherfolk comes to the rescue, rapidly creating a magical bridge to save their peers. In another advertisement (Cerdian Gonzales, 2012), a poor student passes the entrance examination of the State University but does not have enough funds to enroll. The advertisement shows the student's friends mobilizing to form a dance group, using the mobile phone, to help the friend raise funds for his tuition. Both advertisements highlight the mobile network's capability for facilitating various moments of one's *pakikipagkapwa* and depictions of *bayanihan* (overcoming difficult situations through collective acts). Interestingly for some of the advertisements, mobile phones are not even used or shown at all, but the same themes are used as the company's slogan.

What is interesting in these depictions of the *bayanihan*, however, is the use of popular celebrities as leaders of the community movement. In mobile-mediated interpretations of *bayanihan* (silverballe, 2008; Trevor Hone, 2012) television celebrities star in the advertisement and are shown helping peasants carry their load (the first peasant is shown to carry seemingly heavy logs; the other peasant is shown to carry a heavy metal bucket of gravel). The heavy loads are marked with the mobile network logo, symbolizing the company's strong potential for empowering the masses. The masses are not shown to achieve empowerment on their own; they need the celebrities and the network, *Touch Mobile*, to be empowered. Couldry (2003) argued that the media ritual involving the juxtaposition of ordinary people with media celebrities is fundamentally a manifestation of symbolic power. In advertisements incorporating this media ritual, celebrities are seen walking ahead of peasants and are shown leading them or offering solace, subtly underlining the marginalized status of the consumer and the need to employ mobile communications for personal empowerment.

Nonetheless, these narratives of 'help' are applied in multiple and diverse contexts and a mobile-enabled environment where the cooperative use of new technology is highlighted. Thus, in contrast to the findings of mobile advertising in the Korean case (Ju, 2009), Philippine mobile advertisements frame progress as social cohesion and maintaining healthy and thriving community relationships. Such representations of the relevance of the mobile phone can be interpreted as exaggerating the role of mobile phones in community building and empowerment for purposes of persuasion, creating false aspirations that one's problems or hardship can automatically be alleviated through the connections enabled by mobile services. The very idea of new media as 'automatically transformative' in their social impact is perhaps the fashionable version of the myth that through media we can access our realities and our future.

However, in the midst of media and advertising messages that predominantly highlight individual material progress, such representations of the value and appropriation of technology in everyday life that is situated in local values of community shows how culture shapes the relevance of a consumer good in society. These also show the reflexivity by which technology producers and advertisers respond to cultural values.

Narratives of 'Empowering the Weak'

We also observed that many of the advertisements invoking the concept *bayanihan* represent the use of mobile phones by a broad range of users, including actors from the margins. This redefines the 'technological society'; beyond the middle and upper class as model of 'technology user,' and materialism as model of the 'good life.' A series of advertisements featured construction workers, farmers, fisherfolk, or street peddlers, who are not as prominently featured in the advertisements that we have reviewed for other countries (i.e., India and Indonesia). The Philippine mobile advertisements feature these users not as peripheral but as central actors and users of technology. The advertisement narratives revolve around them and how the mobile phone can be used as 'weapons of the weak' (Scott, 1985).

These advertisements reflect the attention given by mobile networks to a growing market, that is, the BOP. As mentioned earlier, the poorest of the poor, who spend over half of their monthly average income on mobile services, constitute a promising market for mobile companies in the aggregate. It is this market that has also driven innovative and effective marketing strategies attuned to the poor's 'sachet' culture in the country. A study by LIRNEasia (Aguero et al., 2011) found that the higher a person's income, the lower the relative importance of mobile telephony in his budget (i.e., 6.3% of average monthly income earners of USD$165). This can help explain the efforts by mobile networks to capture this market through well-targeted advertisements.

The use of ritual analysis in this regard is therefore appropriate, because the engagement of such advertising narratives targeting the poorer sectors of society show that consumption of the mobile phone has a 'consolatory function' in that "it enables people to carry on living in an imperfect world, believing that perfection can eventually be reached in a distant future" (Sassatelli, 2007, p. 111). The salience of communication for maintaining social and relational ties in Philippine society, in comparison to other Asian countries, can also be gleaned for the high spending on mobile services. However, over half of the monthly personal income spent on mobile services (or $9.50 out of $18.90) leaves a limited amount to be divided for food, transportation, water, electricity, education, and other basic needs. Future studies may explore the rationale behind this high percentage of mobile spending among the BOP in the Philippines, and the implications of such intensified mobile advertising to target the poor communities.

Mobilizing "People Power" for Nation-Building

Embedded in historically entrenched 'rituals of rebellion' in the country, the third trope of advertisements depict the mobile phone as providing the masses the collective power (symbolized by the mobile phone network) to form a concerted movement of aggrieved people. The mobile network Touch Mobile uses this theme of political mobilization prominently in its advertisements, with the tagline, "Power to the People."

Perhaps more than in any other Southeast Asian country, the ritual of revolution holds particular potency in the Philippines. The concept of "People Power" (denoting mass political mobilization), where "being with the other" is central to form a collective force, has been salient in the Filipinos' collective memory given important socio-political events in history: the revolutions of the masses during the Spanish, American, and Japanese occupations and during mass mobilizations against Philippine presidents. The role of the mobile phone in political mobilization had been especially salient in recent years. Notably, in 2001, the political protest demanding the resignation of President Joseph Estrada was catalyzed by the spread of text messages stating "Go 2EDSA, Wear Black." The viral exchange of this text message mobilized tens of thousands to troop to *Epifanio delos Santos* Avenue, (EDSA), which eventually led to the overthrow of President Estrada. In 1986, EDSA also hosted the "People Power Revolution" that led to the ouster and flight of then President Ferdinand Marcos and symbolized the reclaiming of Philippine democracy through collective efforts. Anthropologists have described such political occurrences as a 'ritual of rebellion' (Pertierra, 2005), or the 'messianic without the messiah' (Rafael, 2003, p. 41 invoking Derrida) characterized by the reclaiming of power, displays of community, and the momentary dissolution of difference (Pertierra, Ugarte, Pingol, Hernandez, & Dacanay, 2002; Rafael, 2003). Given the salience of the revolution theme to Filipinos and the assumed 'instrumental role' of the mobile phone in political mobilization, it is not surprising that the theme is used actively in mobile network advertisements.

In a Touch Mobile advertisement, peasants are shown to march together with their red flags (symbolizing the ritual of revolution) amidst a mountainous backdrop, accompanied by rousing music (eurasiaweb, 2009). The advertisements emphasize the power of communication technologies to transmit messages at a distance, thus emancipating the poor as they tap into that power. Such utopian visions portray the Filipino masses as believing they can utilize the power of the crowd to speak to the state, arising from epochal political revolutions in the collective memory. In these advertisements, the mobile network is portrayed as a benevolent enabler of People Power, empowering the masses with 'pro-poor' subscription plans for the BOP. The historical memory of revolutions past is thus engaged, even when these revolutions are not necessarily mass or peasant-led, and have even been criticized for their middle-class orientations (Tilly, 2003; Rafael, 2003). Moreover, the promises of such 'rituals of revolution' are still actively engaged despite popular resentment about the absence of concrete structural changes emanating from such revolutions, as well as the injustices left unanswered (Rafael, 2003).

The Triple Articulation of 'Ritual'

Advertisements as a representation and driver of culture draw from 'cultures of use,' which allow the brand and product to obtain greater resonance with the local market. Advertisements, like technology, are shaped by cultural values; this leads advertising to become a form of public communication for promoting a national history, culture, and values that further shape the construction and meaning-making of technology use in society. The use of rituals in advertising, where technology's role is highlighted in maintaining relationships and performance of rituals, communicates social order and affirms notions of community. However, this use of rituals in advertising is not free of power relations and asymmetries that are maintained through their regularity.

We argue that in these advertisements, rituals are triply articulated: First, advertisers appropriate traditional Philippine rituals as referential tools to communicate and resonate with consumers. The cultural representation of mobile technology use is rooted in a strong culture of communal connections denoted by the concept of *kapwa*: family ties, *bayanihan*, and mobilizations for social justice or 'People Power' that foreground Philippine history, culture, and politics. Thus, mobile advertising, in order to command legitimacy for consumption and promote the economic viability of mobile communication and the advertising industry, engages rituals that emphasize mobile communication's crucial role in social and political formation but also in reproducing category differences. Moreover, we saw narratives of technology use embedded in culturally dominant values such as nurturing relationships, cooperation, or political mobilization that contradict the values of human greed, competition, material progress, and control built into neoliberal and capitalist projects. While this could be seen as 'cultural objectification' or using culture to more effectively sell consumer goods, the use of such rituals and values in advertising plays a role in re-emphasizing the relevance of such values in the present age. It could be argued that this emphasis on particular cultural rituals enacts the societal importance of some values over others. This leads to our second argument that advertisers encourage the ritual consumption of mobile phones by showcasing communication rituals enabled by these devices, thereby setting normative ideals of communication for consumers. Advertising presents expectations on how mobile phones ought to be used and situates these uses within rituals of communication that also work to normalize the social centrality of mobile devices.

Third, advertising further entrenches the ritual of capitalist consumption through aspirational marketing campaigns that frame social reality through a ritualized system of symbolic production. It is important to see beyond these advertisements, recognizing which social values they highlight, and which social issues and realities they hide and dismiss. Through an analysis of advertisements as 'media rituals' it could be gleaned that advertisements carry a strong reflection of a consumer good's (mobile phone's) relevance in affirming and promoting social values, in highlighting important points in history as a source of solidarity, while distorting certain realities that are situated outside priced values and notions of acceptability. Thus, there is a need to reject not only the romanticism that sees media's consequences for society as automatically negative, but also the romanticism that sees these consequences as positive or at least isolated from questions of power. Similarly, it is imperative to question assumptions that society is a well-functioning unity and that mobile mediation works to maintain or solidify that unity. These romantic notions of technology and society captured by advertisements, while inspiring values, can keep us away from recognizing and acting upon the social issues it hides.

Our study is based solely on an analysis of advertising narratives. An extension of our work may include a mixed method design that will explore the logic of advertising agents—mobile companies, creative designers, or scriptwriters, in the crafting of mobile advertisements and the cultural meaning that they attach to these advertisements. Future research in this area should assess the impact of branding strategies reliant on representations of cultural rituals, in terms of both the commercial success of marketers and the social and cultural impact of these efforts.

Conclusion

The collectivist logic of *kapwa* as reflected in familial ties, *bayanihan* and 'People Power' is essential in the enactment of Philippine cultural rituals and evidently foreground the representation of mobile communication in the country. In turn, as mobile advertisements continually use these culturally relevant themes, the ideology that mobile technologies are crucial in the maintenance of cultural rituals and in promoting such collectivist logics is also solidified. Here we can argue that these concepts of *kapwa* and *bayanihan* have particular resonance in collectivistic societies and may even be extended to understanding the logics of the internet with its sharing economy and culture of reciprocity. It could be asserted that the concept of *kapwa* has particular resonance because it accords requisite weight to the affective dimensions of mobile communication. Finally, the trope of 'People Power' is an interesting one that can be usefully applied to the framing and popular understanding of the perceptions, utility, and impact of the recent wave of technologically facilitated Arab Spring and "Umbrella" revolutions.

Acknowledgment

We would like to thank Dr. Milagros Rivera-Sanchez whose insights and contributions in the early conceptualization of the study and during the screening of the advertisements were valuable. The research was supported by a grant from the De La Salle University-Science Foundation.

Notes

1. In said study, the Bottom of the Pyramid was defined as the socio-economic class E for the Philippines with average monthly personal income of US$18.9; n = 800, ages 15–60 (Aguero et al., 2011).
2. Poverty headcount ratio at $1.25 a day. Philippine population at 91.7M in 2009 and 93.3M in 2010 (WB, 2012).

References

Aguero, A., Da Silva, H., & Kang, J. (2011). Bottom of the pyramid expenditure patterns on mobile phone services in selected emerging Asian countries. *International Technologies for International Development, 7*(3): 19–32.

Appadurai, A. (1986). *The social life of things: Commodities in cultural perspective.* Cambridge, MA: Cambridge University Press.

Bulatao, J.C. (1992). Another look at Philippine values. In J.C. Bulatao (Ed.), *Phenomena and their interpretation: Landmark essays 1957–1989* (pp. 282–288). Quezon City, Philippines: Ateneo de Manila Press.

Burrell, J. (2010). Evaluating shared access: Social equality and the circulation of mobile phones in rural Uganda. *Journal of Computer-Mediated Communication* 15(2): 230–250.

Cabanes, J.V., & Acedera, K. (2012). Of mobile phones and mother-fathers: Calls, text messages, and conjugal power relations in mother-away Filipino families. *New Media and Society*, 14(6): 913–930.

Campbell, S.W., & Kwak, N. (2010). Mobile communication and social capital: An analysis of geographically differentiated usage patterns. *New Media & Society*, 12(3): 435–451.

Cerdian Gonzales. (Aug. 20, 2012). *Touch Mobile UPCAT – ANTHONY AXEL CORSAME* [video file]. Retrieved from: https://www.youtube.com/watch?v=gsCz9hVaUm4.

Chang, T.K., Jisu, H., McKinney, K., Sar, S., Wei, W., & Schneeweis, A. (2009). Culture and its influence on advertising: Misguided framework, inadequate comparative design and dubious knowledge claim. *International Communication Gazette*, 71(8), 671–692.

Church, T. (1987). Personality research in a non-Western culture: The Philippines. *Psychological Bulletin*, 102(2): 272–292.

Couldry, N. (2003). *Media rituals. A critical approach*. London: Routledge.

Couldry, N. (2012). Media as ritual and social form. *In Media, Society, World. Social Theory and Digital Media Practice* (pp. 59–83). Cambridge: Polity Press.

Dimacali, T. (2010). *Philippines still text messaging champ – US Study*. GMA New TV. Available from: http://www.gmanews.tv/story/198832/philippines-still-text-messaging-champ-us-study (accessed 10 July 2010).

Enriquez, V.G. (1978). Kapwa: A core concept in Filipino social psychology. *Philippine Social Sciences and Humanities Review*, 42: 1–4.

Enriquez, V.G. (1994). *Pagbabangong-dangal: Indigenous psychology & cultural empowerment*. Quezon City: Akademya ng Kultura at Sikolohiyang Pilipino.

Enriquez, V.G. & Guanzon-Lapeña, M.C. (1985). Towards the assessment of personality and culture: The Panukat ng Ugali at Pagkatao. *Philippine Journal of Educational Measurement*, 4(1): 15–54.

eurasiaweb [screen name] (Aug 21, 2009). TM Commercial—Dingdong Dantes & Cesar Montano [video file]. Retrieved from https://www.youtube.com/watch?v=biGSCrMKWc8.

Goggin G. (2006). *Cell phone culture: Mobile technology in everyday life*. London and New York, NY: Routledge.

Johnson R. (1986). What is cultural studies anyway? *Social Text*: 38–80.

Ju, H. (2009). Technology and social sensibility in South Korea: A case study of mobile phone advertising. *Communication, Culture and Critique*, 2(2): 201–220, doi:10.1111/j.1753-9137.2009.01035.x.

Huyer, S., Hafkin, N., Ertl, H., and Dryburgh, H. (2006). Women in the information society. In G. Sciadas (Ed.), *From the digital divide to igital opportunities: Measuring infostates for development*. Montreal: Orbicom.

Ito, M., Okabe, D., Matsuda, M. (Eds.) (2005). Personal, portable, pedestrian: Mobile phones in Japanese life. Cambridge, MA: MIT Press.

Katz, J., & Aakhus, M. (Eds.) (2002). *Perpetual contact: Mobile communication, private talk, public performance*. Cambridge, UK: Cambridge University Press.

Levy, S. & Zaltman, G. (1975). *Marketing, society, and conflict.* Englewood Cliffs, NJ: Prentice Hall.

Licoppe, C. (2004). 'Connected presence': The emergence of a new repertoire for managing social relationships in a changing communication technoscape. *Environment and Planning, 22*: 135–156.

Ling, R. (2007). Mobile communication and mediated ritual. In K. Nyiri (Ed.), *Communications in the 21st Century.* Budapest: Academic Press.

Ling, R. (2008). *New tech, new ties: How mobile communication is reshaping social culture.* Cambridge, MA: MIT Press.

Lury, C. (2011). *Consumer culture.* New Brunswick, NJ: Rutgers University Press.

Madianou M., & Miller, D. (2011). Mobile phone parenting: Reconfiguring relationships between Filipina migrant mothers and their left-behind children. *New Media & Society, 13*(3): 457–470.

McCracken, G. (1988). *Culture and consumption: New approaches to the symbolic character of consumer goods and activities.* Bloomington, IN: Indiana University Press.

Meijer, I. (1998). Advertising citizenship: An essay on the performative power of consumer culture. *Media Culture Society, 20*(2): 235–249.

Mendes, S., Alampay, E., Soriano, E., & Soriano, C. (2007). *Innovative mobile applications in the Philippines (Lessons for Africa).* A paper sponsored by the Swedish International Development Agency. Available from http://www.sida.se/shared/jsp/download.jsp?f=SIDA38306en_Phillippines+web.pdf&a=33306.

Otnes, C., & Scott, L. (1996). Something old, something new: Exploring the interaction between ritual and advertising. *Journal of Advertising, 25*(1): 33–50.

O'Reilly, D. (2005). Cultural brands/Branding cultures. *Journal of Marketing Management, 21*: 573–588.

Paragas, F. (2009). Migrant workers and mobile phones: Technological, temporal, and spatial simultaneity. In R. Ling and S. Campbell (Eds.), *The reconstruction of space and time: Mobile communication practices* (pp. 36–66). New Brunswick, NJ: Transaction.

Pertierra, R. (2005). Mobile phones, identity and discursive intimacy. Human Technology, *1*(1): 23–44.

Pertierra, R. (2006). *Transforming technologies, altered selves. Mobile phone and internet use in the Philippines.* Manila, Philippines: De La Salle University Press.

Pertierra, R., Ugarte, E. F., Pingol, A., Hernandez, J., & Dacanay, N. L. (2002). *TXT-ING selves: Cellphones and Philippine modernity.* Manila, the Philippines: De La Salle University Press.

Philippine Overseas Employment Agency (POEA) (2012). *OFW deployment statistics.* Available from www.poea.gov.ph.

Quisumbing, L. R. (1963). Characteristic features of Cebuano family life amidst a changing society. *Philippine Sociological Review, 11*: 135–141.

Rafael, V. (2003). The cell phone and the crowd: Messianic politics in the contemporary Philippines. *Public Culture, 15*(3): 399–425.

Rheingold H. (2002). *Smart mobs: The next social revolution.* Cambridge, MA: Basic Books.

Ritson, M., & Elliott, R. (1999). The social uses of advertising: An ethnographic study of adolescent advertising audiences. *Journal of Consumer Research, 26*(3): 260–277.

Rook, D. (1985). The ritual dimension of consumer behavior. *Journal of Consumer Research, 12*: 251–264.

Sapitula, M., & Soriano, C. (2015). My letter to heaven via e-mail. Translocal piety and mediated selves in urban Marian piety in the Philippines. In S.S. Lim & C.R. Soriano (Eds.), *Asian perspectives on digital culture: Emerging phenomena, enduring concepts.* London & New York, NY: Routledge.

Sassatelli, R. (2007). *Consumer culture. History, theory and politics.* London & New York, NY: Sage.

Scott, J. C. (1985). *Weapons of the weak: Everyday forms of peasant resistance.* New Haven, CT: Yale University Press.

silverballe [screen name] (Aug 10, 2008). *TM Kakampi* [video file]. Retrieved from: https://www.youtube.com/watch?v=Hw8tur7YMHE.

Soriano, C., Lim, S. S., & Rivera, M. (2015). The Virgin Mary with a mobile phone. Ideologies of mothering and technology consumption in Philippine television advertisements. *Communication, Culture and Critique, 8*(1): 1–19.

Sreekumar, T.T. (2011). Mobile phones and the cultural ecology of fishing in Kerala, India. *The Information Society, 27*: 172–180.

Thomas, M., & Lim, S. S. (2010). On maids and mobile phones: ICT use by female migrant workers in Singapore and its policy implications. In J. Katz (Ed.), *Mobile communication and social policy* (pp. 175–190). Piscataway, NJ: Transaction.

Tilly, C. (Oct 17–18, 2003). *Social movements enter the twenty-first century.* Prepared for the Conference on Contentious Politics and the Economic Opportunity Structure: Mediterranean Perspectives University of Crete. Retrieved from http://falcon.arts.cornell.edu/sgt2/pscp/documents/tilly2003-03.pdf.

Trevorhone [screen name] (April 1, 2010). *Tulay 30s Touch Mobile (Cesar Montano)* [video file]. Retrieved from: https://www.youtube.com/watch?v=7PtOYbSQTcg.

Turkle, S. (2011). *Alone together. Why we expect more from technology and less from each other.* Piladelphia, PA: Basic Books.

Uy-Tioco, C. (2007). Overseas Filipino workers and texting: Reinventing transnational mothering. *Continuum: Journal of Media and Cultural Studies, 21*(2): 253–265.

Wajcman, J., Bittman, M., and Brown, J. (2009). Intimate connections: The impact of the mobile phone on work life boundaries, In G. Goggin & L. Hjorth (Eds.), *Mobile technologies: From telecommunications to media* (pp. 9–22). New York, NY: Routledge.

World Bank (2012). Poverty headcount ratio at national poverty line (% of population). Available from http://data.worldbank.org/indicator/SI.POV.NAHC/countries.

Williams, R. (1980). Advertising the magic system. In *Problems in materialism and culture* (pp. 170–195). London: Verso & NLB.

Williamson, J. (1978). *Decoding advertisements: Ideology and meaning in advertising.* London: Myron Boyars.

Zainudeen, A., Iqbal, T., & Samarajiva, R. (2010). Who's got the phone? Gender and the use of the telephone at the bottom of the pyramid. *New Media and Society, 12*(4): 549–566.

Part IV

Discourses and Discursive Constructions of Meaning

8 What is Corporate Social Responsibility (CSR) in India? Discursive Constructions of CSR as *Sarva loka hitam* in Online Narratives of Companies in India

Ganga S. Dhanesh

The notion that businesses should be socially responsible can be traced back for many centuries and over multiple cultures and societies (Carroll, 1999). However, it was only in the last 60 years or so that the concept of corporate social responsibility (CSR) transformed into a topic for serious debate in both academia and business. Scholars such as Scherer and Palazzo (2008) and Chambers, Chapple, Moon, and Sullivan (2003) argued that globalization has played a crucial role in increasing the demand on businesses to be socially responsible. However, globalization has highlighted the ethnocentricity in research on CSR, which continues to be ensconced within Euro-American intellectual traditions of scholarship (Mohan, 2001). This enclave of CSR theorizing does not capture the broader gamut of the global phenomenon of CSR and thus presents an incomplete and imbalanced view of CSR.

Subsequently, scholars have called for more research on CSR in Asia. Asia has gripped the attention of the world, especially with China and India not only sharing almost half of the world's population but also clocking dramatic rates of economic growth, largely fueled by capitalist engines (Economist Intelligence Unit, India country report, 2013; China country report, 2013). Rapid economic growth led by corporations has resulted in massive adverse impacts on human and natural environments, exacerbating existing social disparities, which by themselves behoove the study of corporations' understandings of social responsibility in Asia. Further, research has found that Eastern philosophies such as Confucianism, Hinduism, Buddhism, and Zoroastrianism could have been influential in shaping notions of CSR in Asia (Pio, 2005; Whelan, 2007). Mohan (2001) argued that any variations in conceptualizing CSR around the world are deeply embedded within the system or superstructure. For instance, Western capitalism is based on the exclusivity of private property and individualism, as opposed to Eastern capitalism, which is based on the inclusivity of stakeholders innately oriented toward seeking consensus and harmony. Despite these compelling reasons to examine the phenomenon of CSR in Asia, research on CSR is still in its infancy and scholars such as Sriramesh, Ng, Soh, and Lou (2007) have called for more research on CSR from Asia. This study is a response to that call.

However, scholars have argued that Asia is not a homogenous entity. On the contrary, it is characterized by remarkable cultural, political, economic, social, and geographic diversity, and therefore research must be carried out within specific national contexts (Whelan, 2007). Although scholars have responded to this call, sparse research has been conducted on CSR in India despite compelling reasons that stem from India's specific social, economic, political and cultural contexts. Not only is India an emerging Asian economy, it also has an unbroken commercial tradition that dates back to its earliest recorded history (Mitra, 2007). Research has also documented India's deep traditions of social responsibilities in trade and commerce, particularly the work of the merchant guilds in social development, from as far back as the Vedic periods (circa 1500–600 B.C.E.). The guilds were guided by their proclaimed objective of *sarva loka hitam,* or the well-being of all. The guilds often engaged in social and political processes, meeting urgent societal requirements in the wake of the state's inability to extend aid (Sundar, 2000).

Further, Pio (2005) argued that in India, spirituality is an essential part of what it means to be Indian and that the religious life is not detached from public life. Indeed, Indian society has had an ethos of giving, instilled through cultural and religious traditions and practices, with concepts of charity, philanthropy, and sustainability ingrained in the collective social and cultural psyche of Indian commercial communities (Mitra, 2007; Pio, 2005; Sharma & Talwar, 2005).

Accordingly, framed by concepts from Vedic texts and ancient cultural traditions of India, this study aimed to analyze the discursive constructions of the meaning of corporate social responsibility in online narratives of 50 socially responsible corporations in India.

This study is significant for multiple reasons. First, it attempts to make a modest contribution to reduce the existing ethnocentricity of global CSR theorizing. Second, it offers an inside-out or emic view of CSR from the perspective of one of the largest and fastest growing emerging economies in the world with a long history of CSR. Third, it proposes relevant concepts from ancient Vedic and Indian cultural teachings to explain the discursive constructions of meanings of a concept that has immense significance in the world today, given the reach and impact of corporations in modern societies. Fourth, the rich, contextual data that will be generated from this research can help to enhance global understandings of the discursive constructions of CSR from the perspective of corporations in India. Fifth, the study is significant because it augments the nascent body of knowledge on CSR in Asia, specifically CSR in India.

Definitions of CSR

One of the basic problems in the field of corporate social responsibility is that there is no universally accepted definition of the concept. Broadly defined, CSR refers to responsibilities corporations have toward the society within which they are based and operate. However, the scope of CSR extends much beyond this conceptualization and is defined differently in different contexts.

Many early definitions of CSR generated in North America in the 1950s and 1960s encompassed corporations' obligations to society. Bowen (1953) offered one of the earliest definitions of CSR as the "obligations of business-men to pursue those policies, to make those decisions, or to follow those lines of action which are desirable in terms of the objectives and values of our society" (p. 6). Another related set of definitions reoriented the focus of CSR from responsibilities to a vague entity called society to responsibilities to specific stakeholders, as exemplified by Jones' (1980) definition of CSR: "the notion that corporations have an obligation to constituent groups in society other than stockholders and beyond that prescribed by law and union contract" (p. 59).

Yet another set of definitions falls within the rubric of the business case for CSR or strategic CSR that argues that corporations should be socially responsible because it brings mutual returns for business and society. For instance, consider Drucker's (1984) definition of CSR:

> The proper 'social responsibility' of business is to tame the dragon, that is, to turn a social problem into economic opportunity and economic benefit, into productive capacity, into human competence, into well-paid jobs, and into wealth. (p. 62)

Indeed, Lantos (2001) drew clear demarcations between strategic CSR and altruistic CSR and argued that only strategic CSR—CSR activities that could bring benefit to the organization—was legitimate, while altruistic CSR—CSR practices that did not secure any benefit for business—was not.

Carroll (1979, 1991) reconciled this apparently conflicting focus on shareholders and stakeholders and offered one of the most commonly accepted definitions of CSR. According to Carroll (1991), "the total corporate social responsibility of business entails the simultaneous fulfillment of the firm's economic, legal, ethical, and philanthropic responsibilities. Stated in more pragmatic and managerial terms, the CSR firm should strive to make a profit, obey the law, be ethical, and be a good corporate citizen" (p. 43).

Diversity in definitions of CSR also extends to the abundance of terms used to refer to the social responsibilities of corporations. Over a period of time, terms such as "corporate citizenship" and "triple bottom line" have come to denote various facets of the social responsibilities of businesses (Mohan, 2001). However, Carroll and Shabana (2010) argued that although terms such as corporate citizenship and sustainability are competing to become the most widespread term used to describe the field, the term 'corporate social responsibility' remains the most dominant term in academia and practice. This study uses the term CSR to refer to the social responsibilities of corporations.

CSR in India

Arora and Puranik (2004) compiled an overview of CSR in India and argued that community development plays a key role in the Indian CSR agenda and that the transition from philanthropy to CSR has not yet been achieved. Further, they questioned whether the CSR agenda as constituted in the West is appropriate to the needs and priorities of developing countries. Kumar, Murphy, and Balsari (2001) went a step further and proposed that four models of CSR are applicable to India. These are:

1 The ethical model based on Gandhi's trusteeship theory, which called for corporations' commitment to social welfare based on ethical awareness of broader social needs;
2 The statist model based on state-driven policies, pursued by Nehru, independent India's first Prime Minister;
3 The liberal model, based on Milton Friedman's view of CSR as primarily focused on economic responsibilities of corporations; and
4 The stakeholder model based on Freeman's concept of stakeholder responsiveness, which recognizes direct and indirect stakeholder interests.

Scholars have shown considerable interest in exploring the ethical model of CSR, especially Gandhi's trusteeship theory (Gopinath, 2005; Kumar et al., 2001). Gopinath (2005) explored Gandhi's concept of trusteeship as a foundation for conceptualizing CSR. According to the concept of trusteeship, the capitalist has the right to accumulate and maintain wealth and to use that wealth to benefit the larger society. Gopinath argued that this concept of trusteeship is based on the notion of *sarvodaya,* meaning universal uplift or welfare for all. He further argued that *sarvodaya* goes further than utilitarianism, which is founded on the welfare of the greatest number. Gopinath applied Gandhi's concept of individuals-as-trustees to organizations and argued that trusteeship requires running the organization in such a way that, in addition to its basic economic purpose, the organization acknowledges for itself a larger role in society aimed at bettering the welfare of those within the community.

In addition to these studies a few scholars have explored the influence of sociocultural aspects on diverse understandings of CSR. For instance, Pio (2005) identified nine core principles from ancient Indian literature such as the *Vedas, Upanishads, Puranas, Shastras,* and the *Bhagvadgita,* applied it in the context of CSR, and argued that Indian understandings of CSR are intricately influenced by ancient traditions and ethos such as those embodied in concepts such as *dharma, karma,* and the web of interconnectedness. The concept that has probably been most applied in the context of CSR in India is *dharma* (Muniappan & Raj, 2014). Although *dharma* has multiple meanings, the one that is most commonly employed in the context of CSR is that of *dharma* as righteous duty. More recently, Dhanesh (2014) found that the key driver of CSR in India is a delicate mix of moral and economic imperatives, elucidated by the complex construct of *dharma.*

The notion of the web of interconnectedness has been encapsulated in many similar constructs such as *sarva loka hitam* and the prayer *lokah samastah sukhino bhavanthu.* The web of interconnectedness refers to the interconnectedness of all living and non-living elements and mindful consciousness of one's larger responsibility to the universe (Pio, 2005). The concept of *sarva loka hitam* pushes the notion of the web of interconnectedness to posit the idea of the welfare of all beings in the world (Muniappan & Raj, 2014).

Although scholars have suggested that insights gleaned from ancient Indian scriptures can be used to shed light on Indian conceptualizations and understandings of CSR, hardly any empirical work has been carried out to apply these insights to corporate understandings of CSR and definitely not on how the concept of CSR is discursively constituted. Accordingly, the following research question was posited to guide the study: how are the meanings of CSR discursively constructed in online organizational narratives of social responsibilities of businesses in India?

Methodology

This study adopted a qualitative research strategy because the qualitative approach stresses the socially constructed nature of reality and is best suited to study phenomena in their natural settings and to understand them in the light of the meanings with which people imbue them. Qualitative research attempts to capture a holistic, situated perspective of the phenomenon under study and aims to give voice to the participants (Denzin & Lincoln, 2003). This helps to understand not just one version of reality but multiple realities (Lincoln & Guba, 1985).

The Information Sought and Sensitizing Concepts Used

This study sought both the socially constructed views of corporations on CSR in India and the extent of fit between these views of CSR and those in extant literature. In qualitative research, researchers are often encouraged to enter the field with a completely open mind, without any pre-conceived notions based on related literature. However, it is often not possible to practice this maxim because researchers usually conduct an extensive and thorough search of the literature before even arriving at the questions to study. In spite of this familiarity with the literature, researchers pursuing a qualitative study are not usually guided by a set of clearly defined variables. Instead, Blumer (1954) pointed out that qualitative studies are often guided by 'sensitizing concepts' that do not impose predetermined schemes on the social world, but instead provide "a general sense of reference and guidance in approaching empirical instances" (p. 7).

The sensitizing concepts that helped to scaffold the conceptual framework of this study included the four dimensions of CSR espoused by Carroll (1979) and concepts derived from India's social, economic, political, and cultural contexts such as inclusive growth, *dharma, karma, and sarva loka hitam* (Das, 2009; Pio, 2005). I was very conscious of the North American and European origins of some of the existing literature and therefore used these concepts only as a loose framework for organizing this study. While actively looking for similarities, I sought to uncover potential differences or dimensions of the social phenomenon that extant literature might have overlooked.

Sampling and Sampling Frame

This study employed a purposeful sampling strategy so as to access data sources that can generate rich, deep data that can throw light on the questions under study (Bryman, 2004). As it sought to understand the discursive construction of CSR in online narratives of corporations, the purposive sample had to include corporations in India that are recognized as socially responsible. Hence, I chose the Standard & Poor India ESG Index as a sampling frame. This index is a list of 50 companies selected from the first 500 Indian companies by total market capitalization listed on National Stock Exchange of India Ltd. (NSE) based on a company's environmental, social, and governance (ESG) practices. These parameters correspond with the dimensions of CSR expounded in the literature. The 50 companies in the index spanned both the service and manufacturing sectors representing a wide range of industries such as pharmaceuticals, steel, cement, power generation, information technology, banking, and telecom. Of these companies, an overwhelming majority were Indian private sector companies; some with operations in India and overseas such as Tata Steel Ltd. and Bharti Airtel; a handful of multinational companies such as ABB Ltd. and Hindustan Unilever Ltd; and a couple of public sector companies including Bharat Petroleum Corporation Ltd. and NTPC Ltd. The list also included companies that have long been an integral part of India's economic history such as Tata Steel Ltd. and Godrej Industries Ltd. and companies that are relatively new, especially in the sunrise information technology sector, such as Infosys Technologies. Overall, most of the companies were among the top companies in their respective industries, in terms of market capitalization.

Websites of these 50 companies were accessed and the pages relating to CSR were identified. These pages were usually listed under the "About Us" section or accessible from a link located on their homepage directing users to a separate section on CSR or in their Annual Reports uploaded online.

Qualitative Content Analysis

I chose to conduct a qualitative content analysis (QCA) of the online documents because QCA is one of the most prevalent forms of analysis of documents (Bryman, 2004). QCA entails a systematic analysis of the linguistic elements such as metaphors, exemplars, depictions, catchphrases, and images associated with each theme. The predominant goal of QCA is to bring a semblance of order to a large quantum of unstructured data and to generate ideas and thoughts about trends emerging from the data. This study used both etic and emic codes to capture recurring thematic motifs in the data. Etic codes such as 'ethical CSR,' 'stakeholder orientation,' and 'trusteeship reflected the sensitizing concepts of this study. Etic coding strategy helps to identify patterns in the data that reflect the existing conceptual framework and help to maintain focus on the research question. The study also employed emic or *in vivo* codes that are generated from the data such as 'interconnectedness' and 'collective future.' Emic coding strategy helps to generate new themes that reflect ideas that are important and relevant but have not yet been captured in the literature. This study used both kinds of coding strategies—one set of codes was drawn from the sensitizing concepts that guided this study, and the second set of codes was drawn from the data set.

Findings

The 50 companies had websites with pages relating to CSR that varied in terms of their navigability, information richness, design, and typography. Most of the websites presented their CSR pages fairly prominently, often dedicating a link to CSR or sustainability on the home page itself, while others had it under the "About Us" link. Only in very rare instances was navigability a challenge, with CSR information buried under the human resources or investor pages. Most of the websites also scored high on information richness with extensive coverage of their CSR or sustainability thinking, principles, policies, and practices. Again, a handful of sites lacked the breadth and depth of coverage of the majority, often uploading just a policy document on CSR. Finally, the websites differed in terms of design and typography with most websites opting for predominantly textual communication and some opting for a balance of textual and visual communication. The data for analysis was extracted mostly from these dedicated CSR pages found on the home pages or under the "About Us" link, in the absence of which content was drawn from the annual reports, the Chairman's speech, or other links such as the human resources page. The websites provided a mine of information on the articulation of CSR because a substantial portion of the pages was dedicated to propounding the companies' understanding of CSR and their enactment of CSR. The analysis presented in this paper focused specifically on the companies' articulation of what CSR means to them, as well as the vision and principles that guide their understanding of CSR.

The data analysis revealed one primary discourse that pervaded organizational narratives of CSR: a discourse of interconnectedness and welfare for all stakeholders. This discourse primarily invoked multiple CSR models including the ethical and stakeholder approaches to CSR and reflected concepts such as the web of interconnectedness, a keen awareness of one's larger responsibility to others around us, and welfare for all beings. According to the discourse of interconnectedness, corporations are an integral part of society with whom they share a 'collective future.' Hence, the goals of corporations have to be compatible with the goals of the societies into which they are embedded to ensure the long-term sustainability of intertwined social, economic, and environmental systems. For instance, the website of a leading corporation with presence in multiple industries said, "It (CSR) stems from the belief that corporations are socio-economic citizens and that their objectives have to be congruent with society's goals." Another organization in the pharmaceutical industry went so far as to declare, "It is not an expense, but an investment into our collective future." This expression of overarching belief in the interconnectedness of all elements of society was a leitmotif in the online narratives, amply demonstrated in the following quote:

> We believe that businesses exist to sub-serve larger societal goals. Therefore, their contribution is best measured by the value they create for the society at large, giving beyond traditional profit and loss statements.

The overarching discourses of interconnectedness and welfare for all were constituted through a set of two interrelated themes: (a) CSR as balanced and inclusive growth for the well-being of all stakeholders and (b) CSR as community development. In other words, congruence between corporations' and society's goals is achieved through (a) sustainable, balanced, and inclusive growth to ensure the well-being of all stakeholders—economic, social and environmental—especially (b) foregrounding the well-being and empowerment of one crucial stakeholder, the communities in and around corporations' sites of operations.

CSR as Sustainable Development

The concepts of sustainable development and inclusive growth ensure the well-being of all stakeholders of corporations—economic, social, and environmental. They highlight the importance of balancing multiple goals of corporations. For instance, one of the companies declared, "Corporate Social Responsibility (CSR) is the way to conduct business that achieves a balance or integration of economic, environmental and social imperatives, while at the same time addressing stakeholder expectations." The mindful management of today's resources for the benefit of future generations is an articulation of CSR as sustainability—a much broader concept than CSR. This is an interesting turn in corporate conceptualization of CSR and resonates with currently popular understandings of sustainability. A company can be sustainable only if it focuses concurrently on multiple aspects of performance, whether to do with management of human resources, sourcing, product development, quality control, or the development of local communities. Although the concept of CSR has been defined to have multiple dimensions, including economic, ethical, legal, and philanthropic (Carroll, 1979, 1991) prevalent understandings of CSR, especially in the context of developing countries, equate CSR with community development and social work (Lee, 2010; Visser, 2008), clearly situated within the philanthropic dimension. However, articulations of CSR as sustainability expand the definitional boundaries of CSR in tune with the primary discourse of the interconnectedness and harmony of all beings in the universe.

While most of the corporate online narratives focused on balancing multiple goals under the overarching umbrella of sustainability, some companies even went beyond and foregrounded the achievement of social goals as the engine to meet economic goals. The following illustrative quote is from the online annual sustainability report of an Indian conglomerate with diversified businesses in industries such as Fast Moving Consumer Goods and Information Technology. Its key highlight is not only the intense focus on balance and harmony amongst competing stakeholder claims on corporations' resources, but also the generation of economic value as a reward for the creation of social value:

> Business, as critical organs of society, cannot succeed in societies that fail. Therefore, they have to be an integral part of the solution. I am of the firm belief that corporates possess enormous capacity to create transformational change through innovative business models that deliver significant societal value even as they generate economic wealth. Shareholder value creation ought to be a reward for societal value creation. Responsible corporates create societal value by serving their consumers through competitively superior value propositions, by preserving and replenishing the environment and by innovating strategies that maximize sustainable livelihood creation.

CSR as Community Development

While the notion of sustainable development focuses on the well-being of all stakeholders, the stakeholder foregrounded most in organizational narratives in order to deliver sustainable development and inclusive growth is the community in and around corporations' sites of operation. Indeed, one of the founding fathers of Indian industry, JN Tata, the founder of the Tata group, was quoted as saying, "In a free enterprise, the community is not just another stakeholder in business but it is in fact the very purpose of its existence" (http://www.tatapower.com/sustainability/policies.aspx). Corporations partner with local communities to empower them. The online narratives portray corporations as creators of social engines of transformation within local communities, thus delivering not just a sustainable collective sustainable future for everyone, but also contributing to nation building in the process. Indeed, one of the corporations in the steel industry centered the local communities in its CSR Vision, "Empowered communities with sustainable livelihoods."

This notion of foregrounding one specific key stakeholder—local communities—within the broader conceptualization of CSR as sustainable development fits in well with the primary discourse of the interconnectedness and harmony of all elements in the universe by expanding the boundaries of corporations from being mere economic creations to being an integral part of society. This intense focus on the development and empowerment of local communities is not a new concept. Companies, especially those in the manufacturing sector who have often had immense impact on the lives and livelihoods of members of local communities, have traditionally practiced principles of community relations that aim to establish companies as good neighbors (Heath & Ni, 2010). The motives behind initiating and maintaining strong community relations have often been to garner legitimacy for the corporation and a 'license to operate' (Heath & Palenchar, 2009). While some companies articulated the notion of being a 'neighbor of choice' most of the online narratives articulated the harmony motive as the driver behind their community development efforts. For instance, a large Indian conglomerate in the *Fortune 500* with a long history in India asserted in its CSR policy document:

> Our community work is a way of telling the people among whom we operate that we care for you. The feeling that our Group is able to bring in a dramatic transformation of a people's life is uplifting. In all humility, we have been able to make a difference to more than 40 million lives.

Discussion and Conclusion

This study examines how socially responsible corporations in India discursively construct the meaning of CSR in online narratives. Framed by concepts from ancient Indian literature this study also examines how these narratives align with or reject extant conceptualizations of CSR. The data analysis revealed that the primary discourse of a web of interconnectedness amongst all elements in the societal system and the subsequent concern for the welfare of all the elements was constituted mostly through balanced, inclusive, and sustainable growth for the well-being of all stakeholders, especially centralizing on the well-being and empowerment of local communities in and around corporations' sites of operations.

Deep appreciation of the interconnections amongst all elements in the social system, whether social, economic, or environmental; an acute awareness of the shared future of all the elements in society; and the subsequent concern for the welfare for all are identified in this paper as the Vedic concept of *sarva loka hitam* or the well-being of all stakeholders and are invoked in the prayer *lokah samastah sukhino bhavanthu*. The prayer reminds us that all beings sharing the same universe ought to live in a state of peaceful unified coexistence. These are not new concepts. The finding that modern-day corporate online narratives of CSR in India are animated by notions of harmony and interconnections amongst all beings illustrates that CSR thinking appears to have very deep roots in India. Indeed, the notion of *sarva loka hitam* prompted merchant guilds in the Vedic periods (circa 1500–600 B.C.E.) to engage in social development. Mitra (2007) has documented that in ancient times, guilds, which were similar to modern-day trade unions, existed to ensure the well-being of their members. They set down principles and codes of conduct to guide apprentices in the practice of the trade. In times of need, the guilds went to the extent of helping families of members, their primary stakeholders. The guilds also engaged extensively with their secondary stakeholders by helping the community during crisis periods by contributing to the regular welfare of the community through building temples, shelters for the poor, etc. Similarly, Shah and Bhaskar (2008) reviewed literature on economic organizations in ancient India and contended that businessmen in ancient days were deeply aware of their social responsibilities and sought to advance the welfare of primary stakeholders as well as that of society. Interestingly, the notion of *sarva loka hitam* and other similar concepts that prompted merchant guilds and commercial communities in ancient ages to engage with the pressing problems of the time appears to be in congruence with the articulation of CSR even in the twenty-first century. One of the biggest contributions of this study is that although scholars have suggested that the principles of CSR inhered in ancient Indian traditions, customs, and practices (Mitra, 2007; Sundar, 2000), it is one of the few studies to have conducted an empirical analysis, especially on the discursive construction of CSR by corporations.

The discourse of coexistence and visions of a shared, collective future also reflect Gandhi's espousal of the trusteeship principle, which asserts that businesses are stewards of society's resources (Gopinath, 2005; Narayan, 1966). The trusteeship principle is built upon the concept of *sarvodaya* or welfare for all within which corporations assume a larger role, considering the well-being of all elements in their system (Gopinath, 2005). Narayan (1966) documented Gandhi's theory of trusteeship and wrote that according to Gandhi, the concept of trusteeship gave the capitalist the right to accumulate and maintain wealth, using it to benefit society. Renold (1994) noted that Gandhi believed that the wealthy should not be forced into sharing their wealth, but that they should do so voluntarily. Mitra (2007) posited that in formulating his concept of CSR as trusteeship Gandhi was influenced by both John Ruskin and Hindu philosophy. Gandhi wrote in his autobiography that by studying the *Gita,* a Hindu religious and philosophical text, and the rules of equity in English law, the concept of trustee became clear to him: Individual property is the rule in the West. Corporate property is the rule in the East.

This discourse of the interconnectedness of all elements in human and natural systems, the vision of a shared future, and the resultant notion of welfare for all resists the currently popular strategic perspective of CSR that privileges benefits to corporations over societies (Capelli, Singh, Singh, & Useem, 2010). Instead, it supports the more holistic construction of CSR as sustainability and as community relations, maintaining that a sense of interconnectedness of all beings and caring for the well-being of all, rather than foregrounding narrow corporate interests, constitute CSR in the Indian context. This conceptualization of CSR is eminently compatible with some of the earliest definitions of CSR generated in North America when Bowen (1953) stated that CSR refers to the "obligations of businessmen to pursue those policies, to make those decisions, or to follow those lines of action which are desirable in terms of the objectives and values of our society" (p. 6). It is also compatible with the ethical model of CSR (Kumar et al., 2001), the stakeholder model (Freeman, 2010), and the emerging concept of sustainability.

Although Carroll and Shabana (2010) suggested that the term 'corporate social responsibility' seems to have become the most popular term to refer to social responsibilities of corporations, findings from this study have revealed that in India, corporations are increasingly moving toward articulating their corporate social responsibilities as 'sustainability,' in recognition of the myriad ways in which all the elements of organizational subsystems and societal suprasystems are interlinked and share a common future. The World Business Council for Sustainable Development defines sustainability as "forms of progress that meet the needs of the present without compromising the ability of future generations to meet their needs." The idea of sustainability is rather complex, delicately managing a perceived paradox between social development and economic development, well-articulated in the cynical accusation that CSR is nothing but corporations' efforts to fix the very social and environmental ills that they have caused. But the findings of this study reveal that corporate narratives seamlessly melded these competing narratives under the broad overarching umbrella of sustainability.

In addition to the concept of sustainability, the companies' online narratives foregrounded the importance of community development as integral to delivering the vision of a shared future. The notion of CSR as community development in developing nations such as India has been confirmed by other studies as well (Arora & Puranik, 2004; Lee, 2010). The foregrounding of external publics in the CSR process in developing nations appeared to be a direct critique of some of the models of CSR developed primarily in the more developed countries of North America and Europe. The latter envisage CSR as encompassing internal and external aspects of social responsibility, often foregrounding the importance of internal aspects such as corporate governance. For example, Carroll's (1979, 1991) model of CSR considers economic, ethical, and legal CSR as the primary social responsibilities of a corporation, and philanthropic or discretionary responsibilities (within which community development would be included) as only the icing on the cake. However, in online corporate narratives in India, being socially responsible appears to be equated with contributing to community development, mostly external to the corporation. It appears to be the cake itself, not merely the icing. This intense focus on external stakeholders in corporations' CSR efforts could be construed as typical of a developing nation, where the highly visible dualistic existence of poverty and prosperity makes a compelling case for corporations to focus attention on community, societal, and national development as the key components of the concept of corporate social responsibility.

Although this study has thrown up some interesting findings it is not without its limitations. First, it only analyzed online narratives of corporations' articulations of the meanings of CSR. While this is probably sufficient to understand corporate conceptualizations and articulations of CSR, generating interview data on key corporate and organizational actors' understandings of CSR might enable a more in-depth exploration of the drivers of CSR. What are the thought processes that motivate these organizational actors to conceptualize CSR as sustainability or that motivate them to recognize the interconnections amongst various elements in society?

Second, this study examined the websites and online annual reports of only the top 50 companies that have been recognized as socially responsible in India. While this study enhances understandings of CSR, a larger study that includes companies from outside the top 50 list might help generate a more nuanced and complex palette of meanings of CSR in the Indian context.

Third, this study has only examined how corporations have articulated their understandings of CSR in the Indian context. Such CSR talk need not be matched by corresponding action. Such an analysis is beyond the scope of this study and needs more research, including a CSR program audit.

Finally, this study only examined the view of corporations in conceptualizing CSR. This could be just one perspective, albeit a very important one. Other key players such as the national and various state governments and NGOs might have diverse conceptualizations of CSR. Future studies could explore these alternative understandings of CSR from the viewpoint of other interpretive communities. Despite these limitations, this study has contributed to the literature on CSR in India by empirically applying concepts from Vedic literature and sociocultural traditions of India to analyze articulations of the meanings of CSR in online narratives of socially responsible companies in India.

Acknowledgment

I would like to thank Ms. Sujata Ramesh whose help during the data generation phase of this study was invaluable.

Appendix A

Table 8.1 Standard & Poor ESG India list of constituents, 2009

No.	Company	No.	Company
1	Dr. Reddy's Laboratories Ltd.	26	Financial Technologies (India) Ltd.
2	Infosys Technologies Ltd.	27	IndusInd Bank Ltd.
3	Jubilant Organosys Ltd.	28	KPIT Cummins Infosystem Ltd.
4	Aditya Birla Nuvo Ltd.	29	Jaiprakash Associates Ltd.
5	Wipro Ltd.	30	Bharti Airtel Ltd.
6	JSW Steel Ltd.	31	NTPC Ltd.
7	Mahindra & Mahindra Ltd.	32	Tata Power Co. Ltd.
8	I T C Ltd.	33	Axis Bank Ltd.
9	Reliance Infrastructure Ltd.	34	Divi's Laboratories Ltd.
10	Gujarat Alkalies & Chemicals Ltd.	35	GTL Infrastructure Ltd.
11	Tata Steel Ltd.	36	Ambuja Cements Ltd.
12	Tata Consultancy Services Ltd.	37	Sesa Goa Ltd.
13	Reliance Industries Ltd.	38	Moser Baer India Ltd.
14	Bongaigaon Refinery & Petrochemicals Ltd.	39	Hindustan Unilever Ltd.
15	Chambal Fertilizers & Chemicals Ltd.	40	United Phosphorous Ltd.
16	SRF Ltd.	41	Hero Honda Motors Ltd.
17	Panacea Biotec Ltd.	42	Jindal Steel & Power Ltd.
18	GTL Ltd.	43	Alok Industries Ltd.
19	Crompton Greaves Ltd.	44	ABB Ltd.
20	Gujarat NRE Coke Ltd.	45	HDFC Ltd.
21	HCL Infosystems Ltd.	46	Hindalco Industries Ltd.
22	Tata Tea Ltd.	47	Godrej Industries Ltd.
23	Titan Industries Ltd.	48	Andhra Bank
24	ACC Ltd.	49	Bharat Petroleum Corporation Ltd.
25	ICICI Bank Ltd.	50	Polaris Software Lab Ltd.

References

Arora, B., & Puranik, R. (2004). A review of corporate social responsibility in India. *Development, 47(3)*: 93–100.

Blumer, H. (1954). What is wrong with social theory? *American Sociological Review,* 19(1): 3–10.

Bowen, H. R. (1953). *Social responsibilities of the businessman.* New York, NY: Harper & Row.

Bryman, A. (2004). *Social research methods* (2nd ed.). New York, NY: Oxford University Press.

Capelli, P., Singh, H., Singh, J., & Useem, M. (2010). *The India way: How India's top business leaders are revolutionizing management.* Boston, MA: Harvard Business School Publishing.

Carroll, A. B. (1979). A three-dimensional conceptual model of corporate social performance. *Academy of Management Review, 4*(1): 497–505.

Carroll, A. B. (1991). The pyramid of corporate social responsibility: Toward the moral management of organizational stakeholders. *Business Horizons, 34*(4): 39–48.

Carroll, A. B. (1999). Corporate social responsibility: Evolution of a definitional construct. *Business and Society, 38*(3): 268–295.

Carroll, A. B., & Shabana, K. M. (2010). The business case for corporate social responsibility: A review of concepts, research and practice. *International Journal of Management Reviews, 12*(1): 85–105.

Chambers, E., Chapple, W., Moon, J., & Sullivan, M. (2003). *CSR in Asia: A seven country study of CSR website reporting.* Retrieved from http://www.nottingham.ac.uk/business/ICCSR/pdf/ResearchPdfs/09- 2003.PDF.

Das, G. (2009). *The difficulty of being good: On the subtle art of dharma.* New Delhi, India: Penguin Books.

Denzin, N. K., & Lincoln, Y. S. (Eds.) (2003). *The landscape of qualitative research: Theories and issues* (2nd ed.). London, UK: Sage Publications.

Dhanesh, G. S. (2014).Why corporate social responsibility? An analysis of drivers of CSR in India. *Management Communication Quarterly, 29*(1): 114–129.

Drucker, P. F. (1984). The new meaning of corporate social responsibility. *California Management Review, 26*(2): 53–63.

Economist Intelligence Unit (2013). China country report. Retrieved from http://www.eiu.com.libproxy1.nus.edu.sg/FileHandler.ashx?issue_id= 1919976776&mode=pdf.

Economist Intelligence Unit (2013). India country report. Retrieved from http://www.eiu.com.libproxy1.nus.edu.sg/FileHandler.ashx?issue_id= 1099997094&mode=pdf.

Freeman, E. (2010). *Strategic management: A stakeholder approach* (2nd ed.). New York, NY: Cambridge University Press.

Gopinath, C. (2005). Trusteeship as a moral foundation for business. *Business and Society Review, 110*(3): 331–344.

Heath, R. L., & Ni, L. (2010). Community relations and corporate social responsibility. In R.L. Heath (Ed.), *The SAGE handbook of public relations* (pp. 557–568). Thousand Oaks, CA: Sage Publications Inc.

Heath, R. L. & Palenchar, M. J. (2009). *Strategic issues management: Organizations and public policy challenges.* Thousand Oaks, CA: Sage Publications Inc.

Jones, T. M. (1980). Corporate social responsibility revisited, redefined. *California Management Review, 22*(3): 59–67.

Kumar, R., Murphy, D. F., & Balsari, V. (2001). Altered images, the 2001 state of corporate responsibility in India poll: Understanding and encouraging corporate responsibility in South Asia. Retrieved from http://www.terieurope.org/docs/CSR-India.pdf.

Lantos, G. P. (2001). The boundaries of strategic corporate social responsibility. *The Journal of Consumer Marketing, 18*(7): 595–639.

Lee, S. (2010). Corporate social responsibility in India: A case study for the Oxford-Achilles working group on corporate social responsibility. Retrieved from http://www.sbs.ox.ac.uk/achilles/downloads/research/India.pdf.

Lincoln, Y. S., & Guba, E. G. (1985). *Naturalistic inquiry.* Beverly Hills, CA: Sage Publications.

Mitra, M. (2007). *It's only business! India's corporate social responsiveness in a globalized world.* New Delhi, India: Oxford University Press.

Mohan, A. (2001). Corporate citizenship: Perspectives from India. *Journal of Corporate Citizenship*, (2): 107–117.

Muniappan, B., & Raj, S. J. (2014). Corporate social responsibility communication from the Vedantic, Dharmic and Karmic perspectives. In R. Tench, W. Sun, & B. Jones (Eds.), *Communicating corporate social responsibility: Perspectives and practice* (pp. 337–354). Bingley, United Kingdom: Emerald Group Publishing Limited.

Narayan, J. P. (1966). *Social responsibility of business.* Bombay: Manaktalas.

Pio, E. (2005). Eastern karma: Perspectives on corporate citizenship. *Journal of Corporate Citizenship, 19*: 65–78.

Renold, L. (1994). *Gandhi: Patron saint of the industrialist.* Retrieved from http://asnic.utexas.edu/asnic/sagar/spring.1994/leah.renold.art.html.

Scherer, A. G., & Palazzo, G. (2008). Globalization and corporate social responsibility. In A. Crane, A. McWilliams, D. Matten, J. Moon, & D. S. Siegel (Eds.), *The Oxford handbook of corporate social responsibility* (pp. 413–431). Oxford, UK: Oxford University Press.

Shah, S., & Bhaskar, A. S. (2008). Corporate stakeholder management: Western and Indian perspectives: An overview. *Journal of Human Values, 14*(1): 73–93.

Sharma, A. K., & Talwar, B. (2005). Corporate social responsibility: Modern vis-à-vis Vedic approach. *Measuring Business Excellence, 9*: 35–45.

Sriramesh, K., Ng, C. W., Soh, T. T., & Lou, W. (2007). Corporate social responsibility and public relations: Perceptions and practices in Singapore. In S. May, G. Cheney, & J. Roper (Eds.), *The debate over corporate social responsibility* (pp. 119–134). New York, NY: Oxford University Press.

Sundar, P. (2000). *Beyond business: From merchant charity to corporate citizenship: Indian business philanthropy through the ages.* New Delhi, India: Tata McGraw Hill.

Visser, W. (2008). Corporate social responsibility in developing countries. In A. Crane, A. McWilliams, D. Matten, J. Moon, & D. S. Siegel (Eds.), *The Oxford handbook of corporate social responsibility* (pp. 473–499). Oxford, UK: Oxford University Press.

Whelan, G. (2007). Corporate social responsibility in Asia: A Confucian context. In S. May, G. Cheney, & J. Roper (Eds.), *The debate over corporate social responsibility* (pp. 105–118). New York, NY: Oxford University Press.

9 Tweets in the Limelight

The Contested Relationship between (Dis)harmony and Newsworthiness

Yeon-Ok Lee

It is not uncommon around the world nowadays for individual tweets (messages of 140 characters or less posted on the social networking site Twitter) to become news items. In 2009, for example, the British Broadcasting Corporation (BBC) wrote an article about a "row" English actor and presenter Stephen Fry had on Twitter with a fellow user (BBC, 2009). In the Entertainment section of the online news outlet Huffington Post in 2012, there was an article attempting to interpret American pop singer Katy Perry's every activity on Twitter a month after her then husband, comedian Russell Brand, had filed for divorce (Huffington Post, 2012). The British Prime Minister David Cameron's tweet "I understand and support Barack Obama's position on Syria" was read by many journalists as an important move in international relations surrounding military intervention in Syria in 2013 (e.g., McGregor, Blitz, & Aglionby, 2013).

Against this backdrop, the present chapter was born out of a curiosity about whether, how, and to what extent such tweets are handled differently across varied cultural contexts. With that research question in mind, this study looks in particular at the Korean context, where what is happening on Twitter has been significantly reported in the news in recent years. In 2012 alone, at least 51,630 Korean news articles contained the word 'Twitter,' of which 1,777 contained 'Twitter' in their headlines. Based on a qualitative, in-depth analysis of these 1,777 articles, this study sheds light on the discursive mechanism through which certain tweets are selected and established as newsworthy by the South Korean mass media.

The remainder of the chapter first outlines its theoretical framework, which is a combination of three strands of theories. One is the notion of 'news values,' or the criteria used by media gatekeepers to determine if something is worthy of public attention. The second is the notion of 'Asian values,' representing a cultural relativist position that the nations of East and Southeast Asia, distinct from their Western counterparts, subscribe to a value system whereby social harmony is prioritized. Finally, in order to explore the intersection of the two aforementioned notions, the study draws on the literature on 'media logics,' i.e., the media grammars and content formats that are standardized and strategically employed by the news media and other institutions.

The chapter then discusses the steps taken to collect and analyze data to address the research question, the methodological rationale behind those steps, and the findings. The chapter concludes by discussing the implications of the findings for the overall theme of this volume, as well as proposing future avenues of research.

Literature Review

What Makes News News?

A substantial body of literature has explored what factors make an event or a story 'newsworthy.' Despite earlier contributions in this field (for example, see Lippmann, 1922/1997), Galtung and Ruge's 1965 study is regarded as one of the first to systematically consider the criteria for newsworthiness. By analyzing 1,262 foreign news stories in the Norwegian press concerning the crises in the Congo in 1960, Cuba in 1960, and Cyprus in 1964, Galtung and Ruge identified 12 factors at play as follows:

- Frequency (i.e., a current, timely, and frequent event is more likely to be selected);
- Threshold (i.e., an event of a high intensity or impact is more likely to be selected);
- Negativity (i.e., bad news is more likely to be selected);
- Unexpectedness (i.e., an event that is rare, unusual, or surprising is more likely to be selected);
- Unambiguity (i.e., an event that is easy to explain is more likely to be selected);
- Personalization (i.e., an event centering on a particular person or presenting a human-interest angle is more likely to be selected);
- Meaningfulness (i.e., an event that is culturally close to the audience is more likely to be selected);
- Reference to elite nations (i.e., an event involving powerful nations is more likely to be selected);
- Reference to elite people (i.e., an event involving famous and important people is more likely to be selected);
- Consonance (i.e., an event that fits news organizations' agenda and expectations is more likely to be selected);
- Continuity (i.e., an event that has already made it into the news is likely to remain in the news for a while); and
- Composition (i.e., an event that contributes to a balance in the overall coverage is more likely to be selected).

Galtung and Ruge's taxonomy of news values has been viewed as a landmark study (Watson, 2003) and has been further supported by subsequent studies (e.g., Peterson, 1979, 1981; Schwarz, 2006). However, it has also been criticized for its narrow scope and other inherent limitations. Harcup and O'Neill (2001) argue that Galtung and Ruge's work looked only at pre-selected and discrete 'events.' A problem with this approach, so their argument goes, is that it ignores implicit and mundane activities and, more importantly, the fact that journalists do not simply select and report but 'construct' news stories (see also Altheide, 2002; Herman & Chomsky, 1994; Van Dijk, 1988).

Numerous researchers have revisited and advanced Galtung and Ruge's study since, proposing updated or alternative criteria (e.g., Braun, 2008; Harcup & O'Neill, 2001; Shoemaker, Danielian, & Brendlinger, 1991). Researchers have also paid increasing attention to the fact that "news is a social construct [and] a commodity" (Shoemaker, 2006, p. 105), and the prominence with which events are covered is not necessarily a measure of the event's newsworthiness (Shoemaker, 2006, p. 111). Catenaccio et al. (2011), for example, state that previous studies have focused too much on the end products of news at the expense of the discursive processes that journalists adopt to shape them. According to the authors, "news values are in fact a product of the way in which events are written about" (p. 1845). Bednarek and Caple (2014) also share a constructivist stance toward the notion of news values. The two authors call for further attention to "the discursive construction of newsworthiness around a specific topic, event or news actor" (p. 135) and, to that end promote a multimodal and corpus-assisted discourse analysis of news values. The multimodality of news texts has indeed been increasingly researched—particularly the role that visual images play in the news construction processes (e.g., Bednarek & Caple, 2012; S. Hall, 1973; McCarthy, McPhail, & Smith 1996).

Cultural Dimensions of News-Making

This growing agreement on the constructivist nature of news values in the literature leads to our next question: To what extent does 'culture' account for choices that journalists and editors make during the news production process?

Hofstede, in his famous book *Culture's Consequences* (1980), presented a 'cultural dimensions' theory whereby he explains how a society's culture affects the values and behaviors of its members. Built on a large survey study within the global enterprise IBM that encompassed employees in more than 70 different countries in the 1960s and 1970s, the theory considers six dimensions of culture—i.e., members' acceptance of inequalities of power (Power Distance); members' social orientation (Individualism Versus Collectivism); members' attitude toward uncertainty and ambiguity (Uncertainty Avoidance); society's emphasis on competition and distinct gender roles (Masculinity Versus Femininity); members' interest in the future over the past (Long-Term Orientation); and society's stance on the gratification of needs (Indulgence Versus Restraint).

Once described as "more than a super classic" (Baskerville, 2003, p. 2), Hofstede's work has been cited and replicated in hundreds of studies since (for an analysis of citation and reference patterns of those studies, see Sondergaard, 1994; and Kirkman, Lowe, & Gibson, 2006). His postulations have generated much debate. Javidan, House, Dorfman, Hanges, and Sully de Luque (2006), for example, pointed out that the national characteristics Hofstede addressed were based on the data obtained more than 30 years ago and from employees of one particular company. Baskerville (2003) expressed her concern over the term culture and its indefinable nature. Hofstede was actively engaged in both debates and refuted the criticisms (Hofstede, 2006, for the former; Hofstede, 2003, for the latter).

Besides the Hofstedean framework and discussions around it, social orientation among the various aspects of culture has attracted particular attention in the literature contrasting behavioral differences between Western and Eastern societies. Coming from an anthropological point of view, E.T. Hall (1977) distinguished between high-context and low-context cultures. A 'high-context culture' is a society where much is left unsaid and relies instead on members' shared understanding of what to do and how to be in a given situation. In a 'low-context culture,' on the contrary, messages are communicated in a more explicit manner. East Asian culture is often cited as a typical example of the former, and Northern American culture is often cited as an example of the latter (e.g., Kayan, Fussell, & Setlock, 2006). Social psychologist Nisbett (2005; see also Masuda & Nisbett, 2001) also observed a measurable difference in the 'context sensitivity' of Japanese and American research participants and attributed it to the social orientation of the cultures from which they came. To put it more specifically, "cultures that endorse and afford interdependent social orientation [such as in East Asia] tend to emphasize harmony, relatedness, and connection" (Varnum, Grossmann, Kitayama, & Nisbett, 2010, p. 9). Consequently, members of such cultures display a more holistic cognitive tendency while those of independently oriented cultures show a more analytic pattern in their cognition (Varnum et al., 2010).

The emphasis placed on the importance of harmonious relationships with one's surroundings in East Asian societies has been understood as a Confucian influence and conceptualized as being central to 'Asian values.' The concept was first invoked to explain the 'miraculous' growth of some Asian economies between the 1960s and 1990s (until the 1997 financial crisis), but it was soon transformed into a political ideology promoted by some authoritarian leaders in the region (e.g., former Singaporean Minister Lee Kuan Yew, interviewed by Zakaria, 1994) in order to justify the relatively weak standards of democracy and human rights in their states and to bind their ethnically and religiously diverse constituencies while also maintaining the economic development drive (De Bary, 1998; D. J. Kim, 1994).

Echoing this cultural relativist stance, Xu (2005) stated that Asian societies look for an alternative model of journalism to "combat the dominance of Anglo-American cultures" (p. 6) and to serve values specific to the local context, despite the possibility that in that model the press might be required to operate "in close conformity with government regulations and expectations" (Kuo, as cited in Xu, 2005, p. 64). Massey and Chang (2002) quantitatively demonstrate, through a content analysis of 10 Asian online dailies, the strong presence of Asian values such as harmony and supportiveness in the journalism of the region as well as an indication of government prescriptions in the Southeast Asian sub-region. Borrowing the words of Singaporean journalist Chua (as cited in Massey & Chang, 2002, p. 999), the two authors add that the prevalence of Asian values in the journalism of Singapore, Malaysia, and Brunei is attributable to the fact that the political leadership promotes such values as beneficial to national development. Also, under an Asian model of socially responsible journalism, journalists see themselves as partners in the development endeavor.

Media Logic and Constellations of Values

The identification of various sets of norms and values at play in news-making leads to our next question about how journalists and news organizations engage with those values. Altheide and Snow (1979) argue that there exists a 'media logic,' the mass media's own way of seeing, interpreting, and presenting social affairs. Media organizations realize their media logics through conscious choices of formats, styles, languages (Altheide, 2004), and uses of different techniques such as framing (i.e., presenting information in a certain way with a view to steering the audience in one direction or another), agenda setting (i.e., placing emphasis on selected issues), and priming (i.e., offering the audience a prior context to set the stage for their opinion formation) (Scheufele & Tewksbury, 2007). With this toolkit of routines and strategies, the media increasingly subjects political communication and other aspects of social life to its logic or, in other words, "mediatizes" them (Mazzoleni, 1987; Mazzoleni & Schulz, 1999; for gauging the richness of the discussion surrounding the term mediatization, see also Couldry, 2012; Deacon & Stanyer, 2014; Marcinkowski, 2014).

Journalists and news organizations, especially in today's globalized and digitalized environment, face challenges of taking a complex array of factors into consideration when making professional decisions. To take an example, Balcytiene and Vinciuniene (2010, p. 153) describe journalists in Brussels (home of the EU headquarters) as constantly having to "cover issues and events of supranational importance while at the same time trying to 'domesticate' them by finding aspects of national relevance." Researchers have asked how decisions are made in such situations and which value takes priority if there are many competing ones. Such researchers include J.H. Lee et al. (2013), who attempted to map the news values addressed in the previous literature and identify hierarchical relationships among those values.

In more specific settings, Lin's (2010) survey of Chinese journalists shed light on the coexistence of three elements in contemporary Chinese journalism: Western professionalism, party journalism, and the literati tradition of the country. In a similar vein, Pintak (2014) conducted a survey of journalists in Muslim-majority countries and investigated how they align their professional and personal values and negotiate between global standards and local realities. Both Lin (2010) and Pintak (2014) drew on Reese's (2001) 'hierarchy of influences' model, which presumes that "journalistic norms are contextual" (Pintak, 2014, p. 482) and shaped by a hierarchy of influences including individual attitudes, professional routines, organizational goals and policies, and national and ideological systems.

This complex interplay between the journalistic understanding of newsworthiness and local values is where the present study hopes to contribute. Its contribution is grounded in an analysis of news reporting practices around Twitter activities in South Korea. The following section walks the reader through what the analysis entailed and how it was carried out.

Methodology

In order to build a corpus for analysis, the study relied on the Korean Integrated News Database System (KINDS, available at http://www.kinds.or.kr/). Operated by the Korea Press Foundation since 1990, it is the most comprehensive archive for Korean news, listing all articles from 64 sources at the time of data collection in April 2013: i.e., 44 regional, national, and specialist dailies, four terrestrial TV channels, 10 online news sites, one English-language newspaper, and five regional weeklies. From this database, all articles that appeared in 2012 and contained the word "Twitter" (in Korean) were first retrieved. There were 53,630 items, nearing 2.2% of the total number of articles in the database from that year. A large part of them, however, turned out to be of little relevance to this study. Many of them were included in the search results merely for the Twitter handles of the authors and owners of the articles to invite further inputs from the readers, which is an increasingly common practice both in and outside Korea.

The search was then limited to headlines only and yielded 1,777 articles with the word Twitter in their headlines. Those articles were subjected to analysis. They were spread over the year as in Table 9.1 and from across various sources as in Table 9.2.

Table 9.1 Sample articles across the period of study (Year 2012)

Jan	Feb	Mar	Apr	May	Jun	Jul	Aug	Sep	Oct	Nov	Dec
277	200	221	169	109	96	127	134	75	107	115	147

Table 9.2 Sample articles across the 64 listed sources

Type of Source	# of Articles	Type of Source	# of Articles
Business newspapers	996	Online news sites	65
National dailies	404	Current affairs magazines	12
Regional dailies	169	Regional weeklies	0
TV news	131	English-language newspaper	0 (excluded)

Next, the full texts of the 1,777 articles were retrieved and analyzed qualitatively. The articles were imported into NVivo 10 and Quirkos, both computer-assisted qualitative data analysis software (CAQDAS) programs, and were inductively coded, categorized, and organized into themes with a focus on the two following questions.

1 What are the common denominators, if any, of the tweets selected for news reporting?
2 What are the characteristics of the ways in which those tweets were discussed? Do any culture-specific values manifest?

In principle, the articles were examined in their digitized and archived form found in the KINDS database, although the original sources were consulted when necessary. How the articles were laid out and related to other pieces in the original publications was not considered in the analysis because it did not relate to the research questions guiding the present study.

Discussion of Findings

Whose Tweets Were Brought into the Limelight?

The most immediate finding of this study is that media attention was largely concentrated on national politicians, *chaebol* (재벌)[1] leaders, and K-pop stars—those whom Galtung and Ruge (1965) would have called 'elite people' or according to Harcup and O'Neill's (2001) updated taxonomy of news values 'the power elite' and 'celebrity.'

The significant amount of attention given to Korean national politicians was partly attributable to the fact that 2012 was a rare year when a parliamentary election and a presidential election coincided. With two major elections coming up, in April and December respectively, there was a constant stream of articles about existing legislators and presidential aspirants as well as their parties and campaign advisers, and that included their Twitter activities. Moreover, following a landmark court ruling in December 2011 that lifted restrictions on online electioneering, Twitter and other social networking sites became a strategically important battleground in the elections, which also explains the heightened attention (for a more detailed account of online campaign restrictions prior to the ruling, see Y.-O. Lee & Park, 2013).

Besides politicians, K-pop idols were another group whose Twitter activities unsurprisingly frequently made it into the news. K-pop signifies contemporary popular music of South Korea characterized by catchy tunes and meticulously synchronized choreography. Its global popularity in recent years is attributed to the intense training and management system of entertainment companies, the government's encouragement of cultural exports, and the prevalence of social media platforms, particularly YouTube and Twitter, around the world. In most cases in the data set, young pop stars' tweets were part of their explicit and implicit public relations (PR) efforts. Explicit efforts included having live chat sessions with fans on the Twitter platform. One source in particular, *Maeil Kyungjae*, was found to coordinate such sessions regularly with rising stars of the time, accounting for 143 articles in the data collected. More implicit PR efforts included their use of Twitter as a channel for unmediated communication with an 'imagined public' (see also Litt, 2012), examples of which ranged from posting their no-makeup 'selfies' to mitigating negative press coverage with their own voice. Whether calculatedly or spontaneously done, such 'authenticity appeals' play a central role in social media-based PR (Grow & Ward, 2013; Ott & Theunissen, 2014).

Meanwhile, two groups of Twitter users stood out among the recipients of media attention identified by this study. One was that of news presenters, reflecting the fact that they enjoy quasi-celebrity status in Korea. Eight news presenters were featured in 12 articles spread over the year. Five out of the eight were female presenters, and the reports about their tweets were more focused on their personal lives, marriages, and breakups.

The other group was that of Twitter users with a significantly large number of followers, popularly dubbed 'Power Twitterians' in Korean media jargon. While there are no agreed criteria, those who are called such in the media share the common characteristics of having a sizeable number of followers, posting prolifically, and supporting liberal politics. The Korean news media is not alone in writing about 'most followed Twitter accounts' and possible influences the owners of such accounts may have (e.g., Aral, 2013). The said identity label is, however, quite specific to the Korean context where one's Twitter followers are perceived as ideological supporters rather than mere subscribers. This perception was manifested on various occasions in the data collected, including five articles in July univocally celebrating Suzy (a member of a girl band) becoming "the first Korean woman with one million-follower breakthrough" (e.g., *Hankook Kyungjae*, July 9). Another example was 12 articles nicknaming Lee Oisoo (a renowned writer with 1.4 million followers at that time) 'Twitter president' or 'Twitter king' and even more articles speculating about his influence over voters in the upcoming elections.

Despite the absence of an agreed-upon definition of a 'Power Twitterian,' the data showed that this label was constantly and almost exclusively applied to the writer Lee Oisoo, another famous writer Gong Ji-Young, law professor Cho Kuk, and TV show host Kim Je-Dong. Interestingly, they were not the most followed users on Twitter in Korea, and there does not seem to be a threshold number of followers—half a million, for example—to have to be called a 'Power Twitterian' either. Besides some personal acquaintances among them, what binds Lee, Gong, Cho, and Kim into one category is their seemingly center-left political stance; they have openly expressed their support for the leading opposition Democratic Party at one point or another.

Moreover, Power Twitterians turned out to be a steady supply of news stories. In particular, Gong saw 21 of her tweets concerning 12 different topics cited by the mass media in the course of the year, accounting for 24 articles in the sample. Which aspects of her tweets attracted such media attention will be discussed in the following section.

What Attracted the Limelight?

As discussed earlier, the existence and extent of cultural and value differences between the East and West have long been considered in the literature. Asian values have been portrayed as rooted in Confucianism and its emphasis on the importance of knowing one's place and cultivating harmonious relationships with one's surroundings, natural and social. Discourses emerging from this value system therefore focus on social order and community consensus, and this emphasis is often seen as antithetical to Western perspectives that prioritize personal freedom and emancipation (Nisbett, 2005).

The coding results resonated with this notion of Asian values. The majority of the tweets picked up by the South Korean news media shared a common representation of 'disharmony.' To be more specific, such representation sometimes took place in forms of personal disputes between two individuals but more significantly in forms of unrefined language or socially frowned-upon behaviors. Twitter in general was illustrated by the mass media as an 'unreliable space,' and the reasons invoked were its propensity for rumor-mongering afforded by the anonymity and speed of the platform, as well as its incompatibility with the existing legal framework.

One such news item, covered in 28 articles, was the case of an army captain prosecuted in May for tweeting criticisms of then President Lee Myung-Bak and receiving in September a six-month sentence suspended for one year. The charge brought against him by the military prosecutors was 'defamation of one's superior,' and their rationale was that the president is the commander-in-chief of the country's armed forces and the tweets in question conflicted with hierarchical principles. In addition to this case, the army was featured in several other news reports, such as one about a soldier flagging up the inefficiency of the leave system at his unit directly to the Minister of National Defense on Twitter (January) and the Minister's tweet justifying some high-rank officers' reported censorship of soldiers' mobile apps (February).

Besides the military court case, three high-profile incidents were identified in terms of the media coverage generated. The first one was, as discussed in the previous section, about the female writer Gong Ji-Young. Her tweets were regularly picked up by the news media regardless of the topics or intended audiences, summarized in Table 9.3 below.

Table 9.3 The writer's tweets and the focus of subsequent news reports

What She Tweeted/Retweeted about	Where the Media Interest Lay
Her observation about some middle-class women on her flight expressing their support for the free trade agreement (Dec. 2011)	Her factually incorrect description of the flight; her use of emotive language (e.g., 'repulsion') (Feb. 2012)
Her disapproval of media *chaebol* and celebrities cooperating with them (Dec. 2011, Feb. 2012)	The fact that she expressed her dislike of specific individuals and productions (Feb. 2012)
Strongly worded complaints she received from angered fans of a political podcast that she had earlier criticized (Feb. 2012)	Her use of emotive language (e.g. 'suicide,' 'cyber bullies') (Feb. 2012)
Temporary closedown of her Twitter account (Feb. 2012)	Closedown as a dramatic response to criticisms (Feb. 2012)
Resumption of Twitter activity after 5 days (Feb. 2012)	Capriciousness of her actions (Feb. 2012)
Her disapproval of the naval base plan on Jeju Island (Mar. 2012)	Her use of emotive language (e.g. "no better than pirates") (Mar. 2012)
Her observation of the rich's voting patterns (Apr. 2012)	Incorrect statistics she cited (May, Jun., Aug. 2012)
Conversation with her son about her no-makeup look (May 2012)	Her passive-aggressive reference to a conservative pundit's recent ridicule of her and her no-makeup look (May 2012)
A supportive reply to a fellow user boycotting an upcoming international exposition in Yeosu for the mistreatment of animals (May 2012)	Her factually incorrect description of the exposition; her tendency to hasten (May, Jun., Aug. 2012)
Her support for the presidential candidate of the Democratic Party Moon Jae-In (Jun. 2012)	Her inconsiderate reference to the suicide of former President Roh Moo-Hyun (Jun. 2012)
Her support for the union of the newspaper *Kukmin Ilbo* (Jun. 2012)	Her mix-up of the words of the union and those of the head of the company (Jun. 2012)
The conservatives' victory in the December 2012 presidential election (Dec. 2012)	Her use of emotive language (e.g., "the period of Nazi rule") (Dec. 2012)

Her being a prolific Power Twitterian with a diverse range of interests and many followers does not sufficiently explain the disproportionate amount of media coverage that her tweets received during the period of study. Instead, perhaps what is more telling is the kind of news values that the media assigned to her tweets. Despite the seemingly unrelated topics about which she tweeted, the media focus was consistently on her emotive language and impulsivity. The media reinforced its frame by including references to prior incidents where she had wound up in trouble for her tweets. For example, the news reports on her tweets about the Yeosu International Exposition in May (9th row of the table) drew the reader's attention to her earlier retweet, although deleted by then, that had cited incorrect voter turnout rates in wealthy areas of Seoul on election day in April 2012 (7th row of the table).

The second incident involved a girl band called T-ara (pronounced tiara). Throughout July and August there were as many as 26 articles in the sample devoted to the band for alleged bullying of one new member by the remaining five. The whole allegation was initiated on Twitter where some users noticed that the original five members tweeted similar content simultaneously, alluding to an in-joke. The users suspected that those 'cryptic' tweets were intended to 'diss' the sixth member. This casual suspicion, however, turned into a serious social discussion on what is termed *wangtta*[2] in Korean slang. *Wangtta* refers to the act of a peer group isolating the weakest or least popular member and the rest ganging up to socially persecute that person—a particular type of bullying observed in Korea (see also Chee, 2006). Ten news outlets, including four business newspapers (*Etoday, Hankook Kyungjae, Herald Kyungjae,* and *Maeil Kyungjae*), started to monitor the unfolding of the issue closely and report it in real time. The 26 articles produced along the way paid attention to details as small as when the leader of the band 'unfollowed' (a Twitter term for unsubscribing from someone's feeds) the alleged victim of the bullying.

The third high-profile incident concerned a teenage girl singer with the stage name IU. As soon as she joined the Twitter platform in January 2012, she was already one of the recurrent celebrities in the data collected. However, the regular media attention on her was multiplied on November 10th when she accidentally made public a 'selfie' she took with a member of a boy band. The photo itself was not 'compromising' in any obvious way, other than the fact that in the eyes of fans the two young celebrities looked too 'comfortable' in it, with IU wearing what was believed to be pajamas. The data of the present study included seven articles from seven different news sources representing the intense media coverage at that time, four of them displaying the photo that the singer deleted immediately after the accidental leak. In fact, according to the KINDS archive, at least 139 articles were published between November and December 2012 with regard to this incident, although not all of them were included in the sample given the search parameters used for data collection.

In sum, the findings suggest that the South Korean mass media tends to pay attention to tweets that conflict with hierarchical norms (as seen in the incidents with regard to members of the military) or gendered expectations of conduct (as seen in the incidents about the female writer and singers).

Built on this, the following section will discuss the discursive mechanism through which the above incidents were presented in the news.

How Were Those Tweets Discussed and Presented?

When it comes to the languages and formats the South Korean mass media used for presenting certain tweets as news stories, what jumped out immediately was the use of overly sensationalizing headlines to preface the stories. The most frequently used expressions include 'controversy' (*non-ran*, in 101 headlines), 'coarse language' (*makmal*, in 32 headlines), 'issue' (*hwaje*, in 26 headlines), 'criticism' (*binan*, in 19 headlines), 'creating a stir' (*pamun*, in 15 headlines), 'verbal battle' (*seoljeon*, in 14 headlines), and 'shock' (*chunggyeok*, in 8 incidents). Added to that, many headlines were composed in the form of a tantalizing question, as opposed to Bell's (1991, p. 150) definition of a headline as 'an abstract of the abstract' aimed to provide concise information on the overall piece. That is partly a consequence of the news consumption patterns specific to the country in recent years; the vast majority of the population read news on one-stop web portals such as Naver and Daum, where news articles are aggregated and offered in a crowded display (see also S. Kim & Park, 2008). South Korean journalists and editors therefore have to compete for attention, resulting in the prevalence of 'click-bait.'

That said, headlines in this context were not only a desperate invitation to the reader to click through. More importantly, they were found to justify the journalists' and news organizations' decision to report the selected tweets. For example, in the aforementioned case of T-ara the headlines and the texts of the articles (e.g., "[Unfollowing,] how could a leader do that to a team member?" *Etoday*, July 29) suggested that the journalists were framing the story as an indicator for a broader social issue—such as the *wangtta* phenomenon and the diminution of team spirit—and not a mere triviality. In the case of IU's photo leak, the articles employed a noticeably judgmental tone and questioned the young singer's conduct (e.g., "Look at how the boy is [in the photo]. How can we think otherwise?" *Daejeon Ilbo*, November 10). In fact, during the period of study, such moral scrutiny led a few young celebrities to close down their Twitter accounts (so-called 'Twittercide').

While the news articles claimed that those highlighted tweets induced a 'public furor,' they did not furnish substantial evidence. Instead, the discursive device journalists relied on most was to attribute their claims to some unspecified online users. Occasionally, they also cited in their articles one or two tweets as representative of the voice of the public. The latter tactic is similar to the media practice identified by Anstead and O'Loughlin (2014) in the context of the 2010 UK general election, i.e., quoting a single tweet as representative of a strand in public opinion, comparable to a traditional 'vox pop interview.'

Concluding Remarks: Complex Interplay between Newsworthiness and Korean Values

On the basis of an in-depth, qualitative analysis of 1,777 articles sampled from the South Korean news archives, this chapter examined tweets that were picked up by the mass media as news stories in the course of 2012, their shared characteristics, and the culture-specific discourses constructed around them. Particularly noteworthy is that according to the cases discussed above a tweet is likely to attract media attention in the Korean context if it is perceived to disrupt social order and create disharmony. It was found that high-context protocols were at play in terms of public morality and gender-appropriate behavior. Furthermore, there was no either/or consensus on whether Twitter is a public space, but in the process of news-making, what was found to be in operation was a dual standard: If the user is a publicly known figure, his or her tweets are, regardless of the content or intended recipients, believed to be in the public domain and subject to a stricter application of the protocols. All these findings indicate a value system reflective of South Korean society, but that can possibly be extended to other societies influenced by the Confucian emphasis on social harmony.

The present study elucidates the significant degree to which a society's desire to maintain harmony and condemn sources of disharmony factors into how newsworthiness is determined. This is especially true of media in non-Western settings, where there has been a conscious effort to find an alternative model of journalism to "combat the dominance of Anglo-American cultures" (Xu, 2005, p. 6). The Asian concept of harmony can lend depth to our understanding of media logics and news-making processes.

By no means does this study argue that Asian values trump the news values identified by Western scholars like Galtung and Ruge (1965) and Harcup and O'Neil (2001). This chapter demonstrates the constructivist nature of media logics and the extent to which local values contribute to the construction and operation of such logics. News values like 'elite people,' 'unexpectedness,' and 'negativity' are all relevant. As seen throughout this chapter, however, what constitutes those values in the given Korean context is distinctly bound by the sociocultural protocols that come with the context. Power Twitterian, for example, is an 'artificial' category that did not exist previously in the South Korean media landscape and does not exist elsewhere. Nevertheless, South Korean news discourses arrogate considerable importance to them, reflecting the specific media logic at play. This realization highlights the need to denaturalize concepts such as newsworthiness and seek to further internationalize media studies. The present study and this edited volume inform that internationalization process empirically as well as theoretically.

This study acknowledges its own limitations, and the author invites colleagues to extend and build upon it by applying its methodology to other cultural contexts for comparison or by investigating how news reports about certain tweets are brought back on Twitter and consumed and played with, for a better understanding of the iterative relationship between mass and social media.

Acknowledgment

A preliminary report of this study was presented at the 8th *Media in Transition* conference at MIT, Boston, in May 2013.

Notes

1. Large business conglomerates in South Korea, typically owned and controlled by families. Literally meaning "money clans" in Korean, they are also known to be connected to the political elite, often by marriage alliances.
2. Korean slang for the act of a peer group isolating the weakest or least popular member and the rest ganging up to socially persecute that person. This specific type of bullying is a growing social problem in South Korea, most frequently observed in schools.

References

Altheide, D. L. (2002). *Creating fear: News and the construction of crisis*. New York, NY: Aldine de Gruyter.

Altheide, D. L. (2004). Media logic and political communication. *Political Communication, 21*(3): 293–296. doi:10.1080/10584600490481307.

Altheide, D. L., & Snow, R. P. (1979). *Media logic*. London: SAGE Publications.

Anstead, N., & O'Loughlin, B. (2014). Social media analysis and public opinion: The 2010 UK general election. *Journal of Computer-Mediated Communication* [early online view]. doi:10.1111/jcc4.12102.

Aral, S. (2013). What would Ashton do—and does it matter? *Harvard Business Review*, (May 2013). Retrieved from https://hbr.org/2013/05/what-would-ashton-do-and-does-it-matter.

Balcytiene, A., & Vinciuniene, A. (2010). Assessing conditions for the homogenisation of the European public sphere: How journalists report, and could report, on Europe. In C. Bee & E. Bozzini (Eds.), *Mapping the European public sphere: Institutions, media and civil society* (pp.141–158). Farnham: Ashgate.

Baskerville, R. F. (2003). Hofstede never studied culture. *Accounting, Organizations and Society, 28*(1): 1–14. doi:10.1016/S0361-3682(01)00048-4.

Bednarek, M., & Caple, H. (2012). "Value added": Language, image and news values. *Discourse, Context & Media, 1*(2–3): 103–113. doi:10.1016/j.dcm.2012.05.006.

Bednarek, M., & Caple, H. (2014). Why do news values matter? Towards a new methodological framework for analysing news discourse in Critical Discourse Analysis and beyond. *Discourse & Society, 25*(2): 135–158. doi:10.1177/0957926513516041.

Bell, A. (1991). *Language of news media*. Oxford: Wiley-Blackwell.

Braun, J. (December 17, 2008). *Rehashing the gate: News values, non-news spaces, and the future of gatekeeping* (Unpublished master's dissertation). Ithaca, NY: Cornell University. Retrieved from http://ecommons.library.cornell.edu/handle/1813/11652.

British Broadcasting Corporation (November 1, 2009). Fry ends row with Twitter critic. *BBC News*. Retrieved from http://news.bbc.co.uk/1/hi/entertainment/8336425.stm.

Catenaccio, P., Cotter, C., De Smedt, M., Garzone, G., Jacobs, G., Macgilchrist, F., ... Van Praet, E. (2011). Towards a linguistics of news production. *Journal of Pragmatics, 43*(7): 1843–1852. doi:10.1016/j.pragma.2010.09.022.

Chee, F. (2006). The games we play online and offline: Making Wang-tta in Korea. *Popular Communication, 4*(3): 225–239. doi:10.1207/s15405710pc0403_6.

Couldry, N. (2012). *Media, society, world: Social theory and digital media practice.* London: Polity.

De Bary, W. T. (1998). *Asian values and human rights: A Confucian communitarian perspective.* Cambridge, MA: Harvard University Press.

Deacon, D., & Stanyer, J. (2014). Mediatization: Key concept or conceptual bandwagon? *Media, Culture & Society* [early online view]. doi:10.1177/0163443714542218.

Galtung, J., & Ruge, M. H. (1965). The structure of foreign news. *Journal of Peace Research, 2*(1): 64–91.

Grow, G., & Ward, J. (2013). The role of authenticity in electoral social media campaigns. *First Monday, 18*(4). Retrieved from http://firstmonday.org/ojs/index.php/fm/article/view/4269.

Hall, E. T. (1977). *Beyond culture.* New York, NY: Anchor Books.

Hall, S. (1973). The determination of news photographs. In S. Cohen & J. Young (Eds.), *The manufacture of news: Social problems, deviance and the mass media* (pp.176–190). London: Constable.

Harcup, T., & O'Neill, D. (2001). What is news? Galtung and Ruge revisited. *Journalism Studies, 2*(2): 261–280. doi:10.1080/14616700118449.

Herman, E. S., & Chomsky, N. (1994). *Manufacturing consent: The political economy of the mass media.* London: Vintage.

Hofstede, G. (1980). *Culture's consequences: International differences in work-related values.* London: SAGE Publications.

Hofstede, G. (2003). What is culture? A reply to Baskerville. *Accounting, Organizations and Society, 28*(7–8): 811–813. doi:10.1016/S0361-3682(03)00018-7.

Hofstede, G. (2006). What did GLOBE really measure? Researchers' minds versus respondents' minds. *Journal of International Business Studies, 37*(6): 882–896. doi:10.1057/palgrave.jibs.8400233.

Huffington Post. (January 20, 2012). Katy Perry unfollows Russell Brand on Twitter. *The Huffington Post.* Retrieved from http://www.huffingtonpost.com/2012/01/20/katy-perry-and-russell-brand-divorce-katy-unfollows-russell-on-twitter_n_1219438.html.

Javidan, M., House, R. J., Dorfman, P. W., Hanges, P. J., & Sully de Luque, M. (2006). Conceptualizing and measuring cultures and their consequences: A comparative review of GLOBE's and Hofstede's approaches. *Journal of International Business Studies, 37*(6): 897–914. doi:10.1057/palgrave.jibs.8400234.

Kayan S., Fussell, S. R., & Setlock, L. D. (2006). Cultural differences in the use of instant messaging in Asia and North America. *CSCW '06 Proceedings*, 525–528. doi:10.1145/1180875.1180956.

Kim, D. J. (December 1994). Is culture destiny? The myth of Asia's anti-democratic values. *Foreign Affairs*, (November/December 1994). Retrieved from http://www.foreignaffairs.com/articles/50557/kim-dae-jung/is-culture-destiny-the-myth-of-asias-anti-democratic-values.

Kim, S., & Park, H. W. (2008). An analysis on portal journalism: Concerning news source sites' networks. *Informatization Policy, 15*(2): 25–42. [Korean].

Kirkman, B. L., Lowe, K. B., & Gibson, C. B. (2006). A quarter century of *Culture's Consequences*: A review of empirical research incorporating Hofstede's cultural values framework. *Journal of International Business Studies, 37*: 285–320. doi:10.1057/palgrave.jibs.8400202.

Lee, J. H., Gil, W. Y., Kang, S., & Choi, Y. J. (2013). A comprehensive and structural approach to news values in multimedia environment: Extraction of a structural model of news values. *Korean Journal of Broadcasting, 27*(1): 167–212. [Korean].

Lee, Y.-O., & Park, H. W. (2013). E-campaigning versus the Public Official Election Act in South Korea. *Aslib Proceedings, 65*(4): 388–405. doi:10.1108/AP-11-2011-0044.

Lin, F. (2010). Organizational construction or individual's deed? The literati tradition in the journalistic professionalization in China. *International Journal of Communication, 4*: 175–197.

Lippmann, W. (1922/1997). *Public opinion*. New York, NY: Free Press Paperbacks.

Litt, E. (2012). Knock, knock. Who's there? The imagined audience. *Journal of Broadcasting & Electronic Media, 56*(3): 330–345. doi:10.1080/08838151.2012.705195.

Marcinkowski, F. (2014). Mediatisation of politics: Reflections on the state of the concept. *Javnost – The Public, 21*(2). Retrieved from http://javnost-thepublic.org/article/2014/2/1/.

Massey, B. L., & Chang, L. A. (2002). Locating Asian values in Asian journalism: A content analysis of web newspapers. *Journal of Communication, 52*(4): 987–1003. doi:10.1111/j.1460-2466.2002.tb02585.x.

Masuda, T., & Nisbett, R. E. (2001). Attending holistically versus analytically: Comparing the context sensitivity of Japanese and Americans. *Journal of Personality and Social Psychology, 81*(5): 922–934.

Mazzoleni, G. (1987). Media logic and party logic in campaign coverage: The Italian general election of 1983. *European Journal of Communication, 2*(1): 81–103. doi:10.1177/0267323187002001005.

Mazzoleni, G., & Schulz, W. (1999). "Mediatization" of politics: A challenge for democracy? *Political Communication, 16*(3): 247–261. doi:10.1080/105846099198613.

McCarthy, J. D., McPhail, C., & Smith, J. (1996). Images of protest: Dimensions of selection bias in media coverage of Washington demonstrations, 1982 and 1991. *American Sociological Review, 61*(3): 478–499. doi:10.2307/2096360.

McGregor, R., Blitz, J. & Aglionby, J. (September 1, 2013). Barack Obama seeks congressional approval for strikes on Syria. *Financial Times*. Retrieved from http://www.ft.com/cms/s/0/481d2168-1279-11e3-9bcd-00144feabdc0.html#axzz3MYmuJEak.

Nisbett, R. E. (2005). *The geography of thought: How Asians and Westerners think differently – and why*. London: Nicholas Brealey Publishing.

Ott, L., & Theunissen, P. (2014). Reputations at risk: Engagement during social media crises. *Public Relations Review* [early online view]. doi:10.1016/j.pubrev.2014.10.015.

Peterson, S. (1979). Foreign news gatekeepers and criteria of newsworthiness. *Journalism Quarterly, 56*(1): 116–125.

Peterson, S. (1981). International news selection by the elite press: A case study. *Public Opinion Quarterly, 45*(2): 143–163. doi:10.1086/268647.

Pintak, L. (2014). Islam, identity and professional values: A study of journalists in three Muslim-majority regions. *Journalism, 15*(4): 482–503. doi:10.1177/1464884913490269.

Reese, S. D. (2001). Understanding the global journalist: A hierarchy-of-influences approach. *Journalism Studies*, 2(2): 173–187.

Scheufele, D. A., & Tewksbury, D. (2007). Framing, agenda setting, and priming: The evolution of three media effects models. *Journal of Communication*, 57(1): 9–20. doi:10.1111/j.0021-9916.2007.00326.x.

Schwarz, A. (2006). The theory of newsworthiness applied to Mexico's press: How the news factors influence foreign news coverage in a transitional country. *Communications*, 31(1): 45–64. doi:10.1515/COMMUN.2006.004.

Shoemaker, P. J. (2006). News and newsworthiness: A commentary. *Communications*, 31(1): 105–111. doi:10.1515/COMMUN.2006.007.

Shoemaker, P. J., Danielian, L. H., & Brendlinger, N. (1991). Deviant acts, risky business and U.S. interests: The newsworthiness of world events. *Journalism & Mass Communication Quarterly*, 68(4): 781–795. doi:10.1177/107769909106800419.

Sondergaard, M. (1994). Research note: Hofstede's consequences: A study of reviews, citations and replications. *Organization Studies*, 15(3): 447–456. doi:10.1177/017084069401500307.

Van Dijk, T. A. (1988). *News as discourse*. Hillsdale, NJ: Lawrence Erlbaum Associates.

Varnum, M. E. W., Grossmann, I., Kitayama, S., & Nisbett, R. E. (2010). The origin of cultural differences in cognition: The social orientation hypothesis. *Current Directions in Psychological Science*, 19(1): 9–13. doi:10.1177/0963721409359301.

Watson, J. (2003). *Media communication: An introduction to theory and process* (2nd ed.). Basingstoke: Palgrave Macmillan.

Xu, X. (2005). *Demystifying Asian values in journalism*. Singapore: Times Academic Press.

Zakaria, F. (April 1994). A conversation with Lee Kuan Yew. *Foreign Affairs* (March/April 1994). Retrieved from http://www.foreignaffairs.com/articles/49691/fareed-zakaria/a-conversation-with-lee-kuan-yew.

10 Shadow and Soul

Stereoscopic Phantasmagoria and Holographic Immortalization in Transnational Chinese Pop

Liew Kai Khiun

1980年，老爸買了收錄「你怎麼說」的鄧麗君專輯，送給交往未久的老媽當生日禮物；1984年，爸媽帶著三歲的我到中華體育館欣賞偶像的"15週年演唱會"，當晚，老爸帶著那張專輯讓鄧麗君在專輯封面簽了名；1995 年，鄧麗君過世了，無論旁人出了多高價碼要買下那張鄧麗君親筆親簽名的專輯，老爸始終不願意售出那張飽含無數甜蜜回憶的大碟。今年，爸媽到小巨蛋欣賞他們 兒子的偶像--杰倫的演唱會。那曲你怎麼說，勾起兩老從初次相遇到結婚生子的種種點滴；那晚，老爸聽到全場年輕人唱著當年的流行金曲，眼眶泛淚了，而老媽 在鄧麗君出現時流下感動的眼淚，彷彿，偶像復活了！！這是向一代巨星致意的極致表現，也是串起兩代情感的絕佳橋樑，杰倫，謝謝你！！！ elvis8087

In 1980, my dad bought a record of Teresa Teng's album "How Do You Say" and gave it to my mother as her birthday present. In 1984, when I was three, they took me to the Chung Hwa Sports Stadium to watch their idol Teng's "15th Anniversary Concert" and brought that particular album along for her to autograph. In 1995, Teng passed away, and no matter how much people offered my dad, he refused to part with the autographed album that has brought him sweet memories. Tonight, my parents went to the Taipei Arena (Mini-Big Egg) to watch their son's idol, Jay Chou, in concert. The songs brought a rush of memories of their married lives. That night, my father was immensely touched, and tears rimmed his eyes when he heard the entire stadium sing the popular songs of his youthful days. My mother cried when she saw the holographic apparition of Teng, as if their idol had returned to life!! This was an extraordinary performance paying tribute to a generation of stars and served as a great bridge to two generations. Jay Chou: Thank you.

(Audience member elvis8087's comments on a YouTube video featuring the holographic projection of the late Teresa Teng in Jay Chou's concert on 6 September 2013 [Author's translation])

Introduction: The Idol Has Returned to Life!

Known as "Little Teng" who dominated the night with her uniquely melodious songs while "Big Deng," Deng Xiaoping, ruled the day, Taiwanese songstress Teresa Teng (1952–1995) was the personification of the transnational circulation of popular culture in Asia. Two decades after her sudden death in 1995, with her songs continuously replayed and reproduced on both traditional and social media, the legacy of Teng continues to be a significant part of popular musical memories (Liew, 2014). The astounding impression created by this holographic staging of a lifelike virtual Teng singing one of Jay Chou's latest songs, "The Red Tavern" (紅塵客棧) signaled a new dimension of aesthetic presentation, cognitive affectivity, and an engendering of cultural memories from intergenerational dialogues. From the advances and convergence of techno-media platforms that have integrated stereoscopic projections with Computer Generated Images (CGI) and Performance Capture emerges animated, three-dimensional virtual resurrections of departed celebrities such as Teng.

With characters seemingly emerging from screens, holographic projections have become part of the larger practices of popular culture rememberings, presences, and intimacies, particularly with the digital resurrections of departed celebrities "live" on stage. In the transnational Chinese pop scene, prominent stereoscopic exhibitions include those of the late Wong Kar Kui (1962–1993) from the band Beyond in 2003 and both Bruce Lee (1940–1973) and Teresa Teng in 2013. With these artistes as case studies, using the concept of *ying hun,* this chapter seeks to explore the performative re-"present"-ing and re-enchantment of the past with the latest innovations in digitally sculptured holographic technologies.

Techno-Sentimentality

Dating back to the eighteenth century, holography was first used in "lantern shows." By the 1960s, this technique of three-dimensional imaging had evolved into more animated wavefront reconstructions of images with more complex parallax (the ability to look around). With the advancement of mainly digital and laser technologies, holographic projections have attained an unprecedented level of animation, interactivity, and liveliness through the fusion of stereoscopic imaging and computer animation (Johnston, 2004). Since its commercialization in the 1970s, laser-generated three-dimensional holographic imaging has been hailed as a futuristic tool in its ability to transcend optical and spatial boundaries (Schroter, 2011; Sherlock, 2013). Besides the functional purpose of replicating images, holographic projections have served to surface buried fantasies and memories. From such holographic resurrections of these artistes, the presence of the past continues to occupy the audiences' imagination. While the discourses of reproducibility and simulacrum around these projections constitute the production of phantasmagoria (a word deriving from *phantasma* or 'apparition' and *agoreo* or 'I speak'), the digital resurrection of departed celebrities serves as a guide to understanding the metaphors of haunting in the evolving mediascapes (Ross, 2013). It was perhaps in the sharply lifelike holographic projection of the late Tupac Shakur (1972–1996) in the Coachella concert in 2012 that a more vivid intensity of phantasmagoria was projected. Such new technologies have in turn added new dimensions to a celebrity who has been undergoing perpetual resurrections since his death (Prestholdt, 2009) and are part of the consumer fetishism of emotional investments in imagined relations (Harris, 2013; Stacy & Suchman, 2012). The increasing usage of such imageries points toward the engendering of an ephemeral and translucent stereoscopic visual and media culture.

The trends in holographic technologies are also evident in the East Asian entertainment industries. In the case of South Korea, together with KT Communications, the YG entertainment group has set up the Klive Hologram Hall in the culturally vibrant Dongdaemon district of Seoul that features highly animated stereoscopic projections of Korean pop idols in programmatic performances. While the Hall is projecting holograms of actual Korean celebrities like Psy, 2NE1, and Big Bang, Hatsune Miku of Japan became a sensation as a wholly holographic image through the design of Crypton Future Media, Sega, Toyota, and Google. Unlike the desires of life-like imageries that match the actual person, Hatsune takes the form of a cartoonish manga character that is marketed more as a roboticized 'singing voice synthesizer.' As can be seen, as either replicas or independently designed characters, holographic personas are increasingly prominent.

Compared to the emphasis on the replication of the contemporary and the envisioning of the future in the South Korean and Japanese markets, the holographic projections of Wong, Lee, and Teng, the transnational Chinese market based in Hong Kong and Taiwan (popularly termed as *Gangtai* (港臺)), tend to emphasize the past. Understanding the enduring collectivity of *Gangtai* popular cultural products after the spotlight fades on deceased celebrities entails awareness of the politics of nostalgia and memory within the rapidly changing physical and political landscapes that have turned popular texts into cognitive markers of disruptive macro sociohistorical milestones. Located within the meta-historical trajectory is the persistent presence of otherwise dated media texts, not only television reruns and radio broadcasts of old programs. Intersecting with the evolution of popular culture productions and recordings are broader political transformations that have marked such public memories.

For the transnational Chinese world of entertainment, the popularity of Bruce Lee, Teresa Teng, and Wong Kar Kui in the 1960s to the early 1990s were simultaneous with the decades of the Cold War that saw Hong Kong and Taiwan separated from Mainland Communist China. At the same time, significant transformations were witnessed in these two places, from growing prosperity following the post-Maoist riots in Hong Kong in 1967 to the loosening of martial law in Taiwan in 1984, as well as the Tiananmen Massacre of 1989. As Mao's China was consumed in the Cultural Revolution, the otherwise politically peripheral Chinese societies of Hong Kong and Taiwan became centers for modern Chinese entertainment cultures in the areas of film, television, and popular music. In this respect, all three artistes have been significant players in the projection of Chinese/Asian based films and popular music, first to the Chinese diaspora and subsequently to the rest of the world. Lee's death in 1973 did not reduce the flow as Hong Kong prepared for the rising popularity of Hong Kong cinema or Cantonese-based Canto-pop in the 1980s and 1990s. Intimately linked through the sharing of common platforms of artistes in Hong Kong and Taiwan, the burgeoning media productions were also evident in Taiwan where the newfound spirit of liberalization with the end of the martial law in 1987 created an entire generation of popular stars in Taiwan.

At around the same time, the popular culture productions of Hong Kong and Taiwan started making inroads into post-Mao Mainland China as the first symbols of Western-styled cultural modernity. The glamour, aesthetics, and subtleties of *Gangtai* entertainment cultures contrasted starkly with the rigid Soviet-inspired, Maoist-themed, and antiquated official folk offerings in the People's Republic of China in the early 1980s. As such, both culturally and commercially, the decades of the 1980s and '90s could be regarded as the Golden Age of *Gangtai*. With the growing independence of the domestic Mainland Chinese market, as well as aggressive competition from the recent "Korean Wave" and in particular, K-pop, that has made unprecedented inroads into regional markets, the 1970s and '80s are now viewed with increasingly nostalgic fondness by *Gangtai* devotees.

Through publicly accessible materials that are repeatedly and continuously broadcast on various media platforms to audiences in rapidly changing temporalscapes, popular culture icons have become more recognizable memory markers of different decades. For the area of transnational Chinese entertainment, the marketing of memory becomes as important as newness. The world of Chinese popular music often commemorates its departed stars with a mixture of television documentaries, live tributes, and replays of productions, songs, and films associated with these personalities. Usually, the staging of these commemorative events involves the showcasing of archival materials and recordings to evoke and reaffirm the collective sense of loss and memories shared by fans and the larger public. Increasingly, by erecting statues of departed singers like popular Hong Kong singer Anita Mui (1963–2003) and Bruce Lee in the city where their cultural bases were formed, there has been more official recognition of celebrities as part of the place's cultural identity. Here, the internet and social media have provided new cyber-platforms of cultural remembrances for fans by allowing them to share their personal recollections on individual and fan pages.

Elaborately packaged CD and DVD sets with complete collections of scores of album releases, photo illustrations, and artiste signatures signal that the icons of yesteryear are evergreen and classic, rather than dated and residual. Advances in stereoscopic and holographic technologies have provided a new layer of meaning for the *Gangtai* entertainment scene. Unlike the Japanese approach of using completely computer-generated virtual artistes and Korean efforts in holographically multiplying the presence of their existing K-pop stars, transnational Chinese pop has moved toward the "resurrection" of its departed celebrities.

Unlike the distinct binaries of modernity, there is an increasing appreciation of the amorphous and fluid cosmopolitan cultural sensibilities of the boundaries between the sacred and the profane in non-Western contexts. Such fluidities are also extended into the everyday practices and performances of popular culture and media where meanings, fetishes, and memories in objects and performances are inflected with semi-divine connotations. In the case of the cultural remembrances of departed celebrities in the transnational Chinese entertainment scene, the innovations in holographic technologies have offered a phenomenological presence that seems to amount to resurrection. Even as they are conscious of such simulacra, these projections can nevertheless be captivating for live audiences. Here, I would like to frame the holographic experiences not merely as a visual spectacle, but as a manifestation of the Chinese theological concept of *ying hun*, loosely translated as 'shadow and soul.' The contemporary reception of these digital-stereoscopic projections can be understood in the context of earlier historical and phenomenological notions of imaging that have been associated with traditional shadow theater that was prominent in Asia prior to the advent of the modern mechanical image. As part of either the animation of religious mythologies or the re-conjuring of departed souls, from the *Wayang Kulit* or 'shadow puppets' in the Malay Archipelago to the *Piying (皮影)* or 'skin theatre' in China, the culture of shadow theaters has been familiar in the region (Fan, 2003). Suggestive of the mythical and the distant, the shadow then becomes the manifestation of narratives and memories. While the shadow can be understood as the optical aspect of the stereoscopic projection, it is the "soul" that brings out the more complex notions of phantasmagoria in the digital resurrection of departed celebrities. Here, the soul does not just encompass the spirit of the dead. It carries the transient and affective memories that were accumulated during the celebrities' lifetimes. With the advent of analogue audio-visual technologies since the nineteenth century, the preservation and rebroadcast of their performances have become possible. With the latest innovation in stereoscopic holography, the process of remembering is no longer confined to the acts of repeating but extends to resurrection and re-witnessing. The three case studies featured here serve to juxtapose the temporal-spatial dynamics in the holographic re-imaging of these celebrities that resurface to give new meanings to old sentiments.

Beyond: Continue "Fighting for 20 Years"

In the transnational Chinese market, one of the more memorable attempts of a stereoscopic resurrection came from the move by the Hong Kong rock band, Beyond, to commemorate the accidental death of its lead vocalist Wong Kar Kui during their concert in 2003. Forming Beyond together with his brother Wong Kar Keung, Paul Wong, and Yip Sai Wing in 1983, Wong Kar Kui suffered a fatal fall during his performance in Japan on June 24, 1993, while promoting their Japanese songs. A decade later, in their twentieth anniversary concert, a new song "Fighting for twenty years" (抗戰二十年) was introduced.

On the stage was a transparent glass panel that projected a faint image of a red-suited man strumming the guitar and humming a tune alone. In less than a minute, the stage brightened and the chorus of the other band members joined this image of the late Wong. As the song proceeded, it became evident that the image could only perform a singular repetitive mode, and it was left to the group members to continuously reference this image as a signifier of the symbolic completeness of Beyond.

Figure 10.1 Beyond's Concert in 2003 (CCHO, 2010).

More than a decade after it was featured, this segment of the concert was uploaded repeatedly on YouTube and still attracts comments years after these clips were shared online. The affective pull of this particular holographic projection can be reflected in a comment from "Kateoh" in 2013 on one of the videos uploaded on a YouTube clip:

真係喺咗我地當中。
　　當年我也在場，見到家駒出場，我都眼濕濕，氣氛真係好感人，我感覺到家駒真係喺咗我地當中。　呢首歌有句歌詞好正：那怕再去抗戰二十年，去到多遠，我也銘記我起點，不會變！ 希望 Beyond 真係銘記家駒，銘記 Beyond 嘅起點！

> I was at the concert where Kar Kui appeared. My eyes were teary, and the mood was very touching. I felt like Kar Kui was in our midst. The lyrics of this song say it well: "not afraid to fight for another 20 years, no matter how far, I will still remember our starting point, never change." Hope that Beyond will still remember Kar Kui, remember its starting point.
>
> (CCHO, 12 December 2006) [Author's translation]

Successful as it had been in getting audiences to feel the presence of a singer who had been gone for a decade, this effort would be remembered as part of the early history of cultural stereoscopy. It would be another decade before new developments in holographic imagery could bring more deceased personalities back to time and to life, with icons such as Bruce Lee and Teresa Teng.

Johnnie Walker's Bruce Lee: Game Changer

With his influence spanning martial arts, music, and philosophy, Bruce Lee is a veritable icon of contemporary popular culture. In the aftermath of his sudden death in 1973, efforts were made to complete his ongoing productions; also, his son, Brandon Lee, tried to carry on his father's legacy until he himself met a similar fate in an accident during filming in 1994. Lee's surviving family has been involved in preserving his legacy by commissioning museums and memorials. Added to these commemorations, a plethora of films, songs, video games, and even an art installation has been produced as tributes. Whisky company Johnnie Walker's Game Changer advertisement sought to bring out Bruce Lee in his most lifelike form through a mixture of performance capture and CGI in time for the commemoration of his untimely death in July 1973.

Released in July 2013 on television and YouTube, the film was an instant international sensation. The opening scene showed a commanding view of the spread of Hong Kong's iconic evening skyline, after which the camera switched to a close-up of the rear view of a man in a smartly tailored black suit. Taking the perspective of the subject, the image then moved to the scene of the lit-up skyscrapers fronting Victoria Harbor, before cutting away to a photograph of Lee. The scene switched back to feature the top rear view of the same man in a commanding position at a balcony of the high floor of a spacious apartment with a clear sight of the postcolonial city's urban landscape. The man looked to the side of a black and white archived motion image of Bruce Lee that is enlarged and projected onto the wall of an adjacent building. Hearing the last sentence from the image, "Water can flow or crash. Be water my friend," audiences familiar with the legacy of Bruce Lee would immediately be reminded of a quote from his short-lived television series "Long Street" (1971) and a similar line from his interview on the Pierre Burton show earlier that same year.

Turning his head from the ghostly image and distant voice of the projection, the subject was none other than the "same" Lee, as he affirms his presence with his opening line, "Dragons will never die, because dragons draw power from water. It's like instincts" (Figure 10.2 below). The dragon allegory has probably not been uttered by Lee himself, but his followers would immediately recognize the reference to his blockbuster, "Enter the Dragon" (1973), that was filmed in Hong Kong. With this, the audiences were brought into the experience of an ever-present and immortalized Bruce Lee.

Figure 10.2 Bruce Lee revealed in Johnnie Walker's Game Changer (Johnnie Walker, 2013).

Alone in a dimly lit but spacious room, Lee went on to explain his concept of instinct, which is:

> Shapeless … formless … fluid … you cannot grasp hold of it. But let it flow and it has the power to change the world. I believe in instincts. Everyone possesses this unlimited power. It tells you to never follow the rules but to make them. That, it isn't enough just to think, but to feel. This is what helped me change everything. This is how legends are made. Follow your instincts. It's the most honest path. Don't just seek the path to success, but to exceptional success.

While not articulated by Lee himself during his life, the emphasis on "instincts" here evidently defined his legacy as an originator not just of his particular style of Juk-Kun-Do, but as subsequent inspiration for popular urban and street cultures through his films and other productions. Lee's character then moved from reflecting on his own legacy to addressing the audiences, challenging them to emulate the spirit of his path:

Do you have the guts to follow your guts?
Do you have the courage to express who are?
Be water, my friend.
Because someday you'll be more than a success.
You'll be a game changer.

This quote was accompanied by swift thrusts of his palms elegantly scooping up water from a small, crystal clear illuminated pool in the apartment. From the hand movements pointing at the viewers to the extreme close-up of the intensely gripping stare from his eyes, the postures and intonations, as well as the facial features, were synonymous with none other than Bruce Lee himself.

Figure 10.3 Eyes of Bruce Lee in Game Changer (Johnnie Walker, 2013).

Figure 10.4 Bruce Lee executing Kungfu moves in Game Changer (Johnnie Walker, 2013).

What distinguished this character from either the archived footage or human re-enactment was his unusually pale blue, unbreathing facial features amidst the more animated moving body. Being an amalgamated product of both Performance Capture and CGI, the semi-digitized character is designed to marry the spontaneity of biomechanical movement with the minute accuracy of digital facial mapping. Pouring through voluminous archival footages and experimenting with varying combinations of movements and layers, the film crew was instrumental in creating the most naturalized resurrection, to date, of Bruce Lee.

Alone in a hauntingly quiet apartment above the hustle and bustle of the city, the Bruce Lee in the 2013 Johnnie Walker advertisement watched over the Hong Kong that was an intimate part of his cultural and artistic heritage. Although the human version had departed four decades before, the reconstituted Lee seemed to be in tune with the times, while delivering timely philosophical lessons. By speaking to a seemingly empty apartment instead of the usual crowds in his films, Lee drew out the memories of this legacy from the recesses of the individual viewer's memories in a highly personalized manner. As the final scene faded away, the viewer was left with the impression of the continued presence of Lee watching over the daily lives of the city that might have forgotten him.

Game Changer was commissioned by whisky label Johnnie Walker as part of its "Keep Walking" series featuring the philosophies behind inspirational characters (Lych, 2013). Receiving the blessings and active participation of Shannon Lee, the daughter of Bruce Lee, this production was overseen by BBH China's Creative Director (Campaignbrief.com, 2013), Johnny Tan. Supporting the CGI efforts were London Base, The Mill that worked with cinematographic director Joseph Kahn to digitally sharpen the movements of the actor, Danny Chan Kwok Kwan, in line with the mannerisms modelled after voluminous archival footage of Bruce Lee. With the location shoot on the top floors of the Crown Plaza Hotel that provided a commanding view of Hong Kong (Artinfo, 2013), the production entailed the fusion between traditional filmmaking and the newer modes of performance capture with 250 different expressions from the grid of Chan, with the computer-generated model of Lee (Johnnie Walker, 2013). Emphasizing the humanness of the production, Tan stated that "they are not seeing the wireframes, but Bruce Lee the man. They feel that they are seeing the Master talking to them" (Ibid).

Figure 10.5 Bruce Lee behind the scenes (Johnnie Walker, 2013).

In what he terms "Bruceploitation," Hu (2008) details the continuous recycling of Lee's cinematic persona by both Hong Kong and Hollywood long after his death, in a cultural ecology that is no longer underpinned by ownership but replicates by extensibility (p. 124). Evidently sensitized to the clichéd imitative versions of the past in terms of narrative and screenplay, with the assistance of performance capture technologies, the producers have sought to present a resurrected and contemporized Bruce Lee. Stoic, restrained, and reflexive and more importantly backed by the Lee family, the persona opens a new dimension in the four decades of "Bruceploitation." Based on social media attention, his resurrection was dwarfed by that of the Taiwanese songstress Teresa Teng two months later.

Teresa Teng at the Red Tavern

Reputed as an outstanding songwriter and singer, the otherwise unassuming and meek-looking Jay Chou can be considered as having defined the Taiwanese and transnational Chinese music industry for the past 10 years. Debuting at the beginning of the twenty-first century, Chou has given the genre a more sophisticatedly subtle lyrical and musical layering with more sublime poetic expressions and more diverse sampling. Nonetheless, Chou has been consistently keen in combining his performances with those by singers from previous generations. In his concert on September 6, 2003, at the "Mini-Great Egg" of the Taipei Arena, the premium venue for concerts in the city, Chou sang the late Teresa Teng's 1980 song, "What Do You Have to Say?" (你怎麼說) to a fully packed venue.

Before he started, Chou told audience members that the older generation would love this song. Pushing the microphone out to the crowd to get them to continue singing the song, Chou demonstrated the power of Teng's legacy when he received a unified response from the thousands of attendees. During the interlude, a blue-colored message in Chinese flashed on the stage and stated, "I thought that if I could go back in time to 30 years ago to

Figure 10.6 Holographic appearance of Teng (JVR International, 2013).

sing this song together with her, it would be such a great honour." As the message faded away, Chou announced softly, "Welcome Teng Li Jun." At the center of the stage was the façade of a traditional Chinese styled house with bamboo roof and intricately carved wood frames, with a board bearing the words "Red Tavern" (紅塵客棧) hung on top of the entrance, the hologram of Teng appeared and took over the singing from Chou. Fans familiar with Jay Chou knew instantly that this was the title track of a popular historical television drama.

Figure 10.7 Holographic Teng with Jay Chou (JVR International, 2013).

Dressed in an elegant and shapely white Chinese *qipao* with a pattern of stemmed red flowers spreading gracefully from the shoulder, the holographic Teng looked surreally slender and rejuvenated. With the yellowish illuminated window panels at both sides of the house, Teng was projected as if standing behind the dimmer entrance in the center and made visible only by the reflections from her gleaming milky *qipao*. Going for a simpler and less lavish contemporary tone, Luo Liang, the designer of virtual Teng's gown, was the only person in the production team who had witnessed the actual Teng's dressing. The choice of the *qipao* here was meant to remind the audience of Teng's enthusiasm for showcasing Chinese culture with such styles during her own performances outside of Taiwan (Nanfang Media, September 9, 2013). Just as the audience expected a playback of her songs, the holographic Teng began to sing in her own voice, Chou's "Red Tavern" as well as his "Thousand Miles Away" (千里之外).

Organizers did not reveal the 'secret' behind Teng's ability to sing songs that had emerged after her death. Populist media analysts speculated that the voice behind this holographic Teng had originated from a female teenager from Teng's ancestral home in Hubei who was able to mimic her accent closely (CTI TV, 2013). Performing the excerpts of these two songs together as duets, on stage, Chou was seen to be carefully keeping his distance from the holographic Teng. On the small screen however, their distance was bridged by a gradual dissolve that brought the two images more closely together.

As with Bruce Lee's Game Changer, the stereoscopic projection of Teng was brought about with innovations in holographic technologies. In early 2013, as part of the commemoration of what would have been the 60th birthday of the songstress, the Teresa Teng Foundation staged a four-month exhibition from January 26 to April 21 at the stately Chiang Kai Shek Memorial Hall in the heart of Taipei. The highlight of the exhibition was a hologram of her singing her songs. Compared to its counterpart in Chou's version, this image was significantly less sharply defined and animated (WantChinaTimes, 2013). With the endorsement of the Teresa Teng Foundation and Teng's family members, Digital Domain 3.0 led the project in creating a virtual 'comeback' for the late singer. A subsidiary of the Hong Kong-based Sun Innovation Group, the enterprise was also responsible for holographic projections or Virtual Image Effect (VFX) like the Tupac Shakur Coachella music festival in 2012 (Cinecore, 2013). This was effectively the first major project that Digital Domain 3.0 embarked on for the Asian market after being acquired by the Sun Innovation Group in July 2013 (Yahoofinance, 2013).

Through close interactions with the Teresa Teng Foundation, the project team took about three months to construct the holographic image after going through about 7,000 audio and visual archival footages of Teng during her lifetime and deliberating on the identification of her imagery along the different stages of her life. The group claimed that the biggest challenges in modeling the virtual Teng were digitally sculpting her hair and eyes, as well as finding the appropriate voice to match that of the departed singer (Nanfang Media, 2013). Speculations were rife that preparations were made for a fully holographic 'live' concert at the end of 2014 featuring a virtual Teng in Macau, Hong Kong, Southeast Asia, and most importantly, mainland China (CTI TV, 2013), which she had never had the opportunity to visit in her lifetime. In the meantime, similar attempts to create the virtual Teng to commemorate her legacy have been seen at a museum devoted to her at her ancestral hometown in Hubei, China (Xinhua, 2014).

The global impact of Bruce Lee may far exceed that of the more regionally oriented Teng. However, in terms of YouTube records, compared to the relatively lackluster reception to Game Changer, the "virtual Teng" garnered close to half a million views and thirty thousand shares within 24 hours of the official upload of that segment of the performance (Nanfang Media, 2013). As of August 26, 2014, the JVR Music International account that hosted the site registered nearly four million views with about three thousand comments (JVR International, 2013). In contrast, the Bruce Lee's Game Changer video on YouTube registered slightly above thirty thousand views with 40 comments and 155 shares (Johnnie Walker, 2013). For a person who consciously abstained from alcohol, the production was criticized for manipulating the icon of Bruce Lee toward endorsing a whisky brand. In addition, there was unhappiness from netizens over the holographic Lee's articulation in Mandarin or *Putonghua* (普通話), with which the English- and Cantonese-speaking Lee was never acquainted during his lifetime. On a broader front, the contrast in the reception of virtual Teng and Lee could be attributed to the relatively more affective draw of music over that of visuals in the anchoring of collective memories in the region.

Within the same year, in 2013, the stereoscopic resurrection of the two departed celebrities revealed the measurement of affective sentimentality of audiences gauged in terms of social media views and commentaries. Just as Teng captured the intimate soundscapes of the region in her living years, her holographically resurrected presence continues to dominate the memory-scapes of the transnational Chinese audiences across generations. Echoing Amy Holdsworth's (2008) concept of 'medium specific-interrogation of memory,' Paul Grainge argued that "in the world of archival and semiotic abundance, memory has become subject to renewable configurations and articulations within the cultural terrain" (2010, p. 58). However, even as considerable archival research into the footages of the two personalities was carried out by the producers, the emphasis of newness in terms of not just appearance but also performance, offered audiences the imagination of continuity from living personas rather than archival footage.

Conclusion

Writing about the use of laser and holographic projections on building facades in aesthetic installations or 'light show,' however temporary their effects, Bakowska sees these illuminating images collectively "activating the silent monumentality of buildings" (2007, p. 61). Departing from the predictable reruns of recorded productions, the three examples of highly original and animated stereoscopic projections of the virtual personas of Wong Kar Kui in 2003 and Bruce Lee and Teresa Teng in 2013 have opened up new cognitive-spatial imaginations and reinterpretations of these departed celebrities. Working closely with the endorsement of custodians of the departed artistes and a range of digital engineers and artistic directors, the holographic projections are the result of extensive archival research, digital sculpturing, and performance capture of substitute characters behind the wireframes.

These holographic projections can be framed more along the Chinese concept of 'shadow and soul' or *ying hun*. Like the 'red dust' in Chou's song and 'water' in Bruce Lee's analogy, the otherwise amorphous, scattered, and fluid individual subjectivities encompassed in the soul can be remediated digitally and projected stereoscopically to form a shadowy presence. Even as the projections have been carefully pre-programmed and meticulously staged, the innovations in media technologies, specifically in performance capture, have permitted new levels of movements and interpretations. Effectively breathing life and soul into otherwise departed artistes in new spatial dimensions, the *ying hun* provide the sensation of immanence that is not alien to Sinitic religious cultures accustomed to marking the presence of departed relatives and venerated ancestors returning as 'ghosts' during festive periods. However, the intensity in the reception of the emerging stereoscopic and media technologies seems to be felt more as a live rather than mediated televisual and cinematic moment. Comparing the effects of the projection of Wong Kar Kui and Teresa Teng to a live concert audience, the reception of Lee's Game Changer television commercial seems relatively muted. It is therefore in the actual witnessing of the *ying hun* of the two singers that audiences can collectively draw on and express years of affective memories.

Defined by the electric light bulb, Western modernity has valorized light instrumentally, in terms of its production and illumination, over that of the sensory and shadowy (Billie & Sorensen, 2007). The rationalization of luminosity supersedes earlier classical Greco-Roman notions of the illusionary as encapsulated in the concept of "Plato's Cave." But, it has in the process other-ed non-Western notions of light as irrelevantly primordial. Framing the concept of *ying hun* here is not meant to create a binary of Asian "spirituality" and Western "rationality." Manovich (2006) theorizes that the "new information aesthetics" of CGI is based more on "reality sampling" in approximating the actual physics involved in the construction of the image.

In many respects, the principles behind the new technological convergence in the concept of performance capture discussed in this chapter are similar to those of traditional skin and shadow theater prior to the advent of modern cinema. However, in the case studies presented here, the departure from Manovich's algorithmic constructions' 'image future' comes in the form of the resurrected 'past images.' While technological developments have engendered new visual dimensions in these vividly sharpened apparitions, the more amorphous discourses of *ying* (shadow) and *hun* (soul) still apply to how cognitive-cultural memories are being shaped by more familiar narratives of departure, momentary return, and reappearance of the spirit in these performances. As they become more popular in not just re-projecting holograms of living artistes, but resurrecting departed celebrities to evoke old memories and create new ones in the region, one should perhaps delve into more geo-culturally grounded epistemologies and vocabularies to understand such changes and their effects on audiences.

References

Artinfo, B. (2013). How Johnnie Walker resurrected Bruce Lee. July 15, 2013. Retrieved August 24, 2014, from http://www.blouinartinfo.com/news/story/929643/how-johnnie-walker-resurrected-bruce-lee.

Bakowska, M. (2007). Image in architecture—from murals to illuminating projections. *Town Planning and Architecture*, 30: 54–61.

Billie, M., & Sorensen, T. (2007). An anthropology of luminosity: The agency of light. *Journal of Material Culture*, 12: 263–284.

Campaignbrief.com (2013). BBH China brings Legend Bruce Lee back to life in gamechanging campaign for Johnnie Walker. July 10, 2013. Retrieved August 26, 2014, from http://www.campaignbrief.com/asia/2013/07/bbh-china-brings-legend-bruce.html.

CCHO. (2010 August 7). *Beyond 10: Sharing* + 抗戰二十年. Retrieved from: http://www.youtube.com/watch?v=QI0XnsImYNQ.

Cinecore (2013). Digital domain creates virtual Teresa Teng for Taiwanese concert. September 9. Retrieved August 25, 2014, from http://www.btlnews.com/crafts/visual-fx/digital-domain-creates-virtual-teresa-teng-for-taiwanese-concert/.

CTI TV (2013 October 11). *10/11*新聞龍捲風 *part1* 揭密！鄧麗君復活 *210*秒 周董、小鄧美聲之謎. Retrieved from: http://www.youtube.com/watch?v=3GA97jKA4wQ.

Fan. P.C. (2003). Shadow theatres of the world. *Asian Folklore Studies*, 62: 25–64.

Grainge, P. (2010). Elvis sings for the BBC: Broadcast branding and digital media design. *Media, Culture & Society*, 32: 45–61.

Harris, M. (2013). The hologram of Tupac at Coachella and saints: The value of relics for devotees. *Celebrities Studies*, 4: 238–240.

Holdsworth, A. (2008). Television resurrection: Television and memory. *Cinema Journal*, 47: 137–144.

Hu, B. (2008). 'Bruce Lee' after Bruce Lee: A life in conjectures. *Journal of Chinese Cinemas*, 2: 123–135.

Johnnie Walker (July 11, 2013). Bruce Lee | Hail to game changers | Behind the scenes. Retrieved from: http://www.youtube.com/watch?v=wB52JyeN-LQ.

Johnston, S. (2004). Telling tales: George Stroke and the historiography of holography. *History and Technology*, 20: 29–51.

JVR International. (September 6, 2013). "2013周杰倫魔天倫台北小巨蛋演唱會與鄧麗君合唱「你怎麼說」「紅塵客棧」「千里之外」Retrieved from: http://www.youtube.com/watch?v=TixHYua3XCI.

Liew, K.K. (2014). Rewind and recollect: Activating dormant memories and politics in Teresa Teng's music videos uploaded on YouTube. *International Journal of Cultural Studies*, 17: 503–515.

Lych, N. (2013). Johnnie Walker launches new global 'Keep Walking' integrated campaign spearheaded by 'From the Future' TV spot via BBH London, *Campaignbrief.com*. 26 September. Retrieved August 24, 2014, from http://www.campaignbrief.com/2013/09/johnnie-walker-launches-new-gl.html.

Manovich, L (2006). Image Future. *Animation*, 1: 25–44.

Nanfang Media. (2013). '邓丽君"复活"210秒 幕后团队大揭秘' 9 September. Retrieved August 26, 2014, from http://ent.sina.com.cn/y/2013-09-10/03294005294.shtml.

Prestholdt, J. (2009). The after lives of 2Pac: Imagery and alienation in Sierra Leone and beyond. *Journal of African Cultural Studies*, 21(2), 197–218.

Ross, I. (2013). Digital ghosts in the history museum: The haunting of today's mediascape. *Continuum: Journal of Media and Cultural Studies*, 27: 825–836.

Schroter, J. (2011). Technologies beyond still and the moving image. The case of the multiplex hologram. *History of Photography*, 35: 23–32.

Sherlock, A. (2013). Larger than life: Digital resurrection and the re-enchantment of society. *The Information Society: An International Journal*, 29: 164–176.

Stacy, J., & Suchman, L. (2012). Animation and automation: The liveliness of labour of bodies and machines. *Body & Society*, 18: 1–46.

WantChinaTimes (2013). Teresa Teng hologram to headline 60th birthday celebrations. February 1. Retrieved August 25, 2014, from http://www.wantchinatimes.com/news-subclass-cnt.aspx?id=20130102000076&cid=1803.

Xinhua. (2014). "湖北省博物馆举办《邓丽君特展》 3D浮空投影再现歌后人生" May 9. Retrieved August 26, 2014, from http://news.xinhuanet.com/local/2014-05/09/c_1110613670.htm.

Yahoofinance (2013). Jay Chou concert showcases Sun Innovation's VFX production enjoys highly positive reception. September 23. Retrieved August 25, 2014, from https://sg.finance.yahoo.com/news/jay-chou-concert-showcases-sun-122200973.html.

Part V

Conclusions and Ruminations

11 Asian Modernity and the Post-Human Future

Some Reflections

T. T. Sreekumar

Introduction

In his comprehensive analysis of the critique of modern reason and the project of the Enlightenment, Habermas (1987) uses a variety of assumptions about modernity to prove that the discourse of modernity is not obsolete and nowhere near ready to give way to postmodernity. He acknowledges that it was with the attempt to develop a universal rational foundation for democratic institutions that the modern age began. He considers this attempt unsuccessful, mainly because of an adherence to the tradition of the philosophy of the subject, which was fundamental in every Western philosophical enquiry about modernity. The notion of a subject as autonomous and essential, and as one that creates its own normativity, is central to the prevalent Western tradition of the philosophy of the subject Habermas scrutinized in his works. Building on the intersubjective focus in Hegel's 'world spirit' and Marx's 'working class,' Habermas theorizes 'communicative rationality' as a means of overcoming "subjectively based views in favor of a rationally motivated agreement" (Habermas, 1987, p. 315). However, the Western adherence to reason as the primary paradigm is recognized and projected by Habermas as an important ground to sustain the Enlightenment project of modernity. Reason, here in a predominantly Western perspective, is the alternative for any state of contextualism, relativism, and nihilism. Habermas' project is centered on a revisiting of the given concepts of modernity as well as seminal arguments to adjourn postmodernity as an antithesis to it. The arguments against postmodernity that Habermas advanced resonate in the critiques of many theorists like Giddens, Beck, and Bauman who argued against a postmodern era *per se*.

Giddens (1991) observes that contemporary social forms are deeply linked to conditions of modernity and are in effect in a "a post-traditional order, but not one in which the sureties of tradition and habit have been replaced by the certitude of rational knowledge" (pp. 2–3). It is a risk culture, as Beck (1992) would have argued, in which risk as a concept underlies the organization of the social world by both lay actors and technical specialists. The extent of risk is such that it goes beyond the unpredictable to become imponderable and has widespread and unavoidable impacts on day-to-day life. This condition of pervasive risk leads to "reflexively organised life-planning" (Giddens, 1991, p. 5). According to Giddens (1991, p. 15), modernity has four dimensions: industrialism (the social relations implied in the widespread use of material power and machinery in production processes), capitalism (a system of commodity production involving both competitive product markets and the commodification of labor power), surveillance (the supervisory control of subject populations), and total war (the immense potential of the destructive power of weaponry).

The nation-state features prominently in Giddens's map of the contours of modernity as a product—a socio-political entity that "contrasts in a fundamental way with most types of traditional order" (1991, p. 15). He points out the covert nature of the equation that positions the nation-state as the entity that sociological theory posits as 'society.' The practice of according a status of agency rather than structure to the nation-state justifies the reification of modernity as a concept, for it mirrors the rise of the organization—another general feature of modernity. Giddens (1991) examines modern states as reflexively organized systems that are deeply affected by the dynamism of modernity. This dynamism springs from three main elements: the separation of time and space, the disembedding of social institutions, and institutional reflexivity.

The theory of reflexive modernity (Beck, 1992) on which Giddens builds has been described as a "seemingly dystopian outcome of rationalization" (Lash & Wynne, 1992, p. 2), because it runs counter to the "utopic evolutionism" (ibid) of thinkers such as Habermas, Marx, and Parsons. So we have a set of theories that envisages modernity as being characterized as reflexive and random on the one hand and another set of theories that understands modernity as a utopian evolution from some pre-existing randomness on the other. Although both orders have specific limitations, the project of reflexive modernization in particular can let social actors free themselves from structures in response to structural change. The problem with a theorization of modernity based on reflexivity and individual identity projects is that it assumes, in a categorically Western pattern, a level playing field of selves that are not relational but individual. Adams (2003) problematizes the construct of unbounded reflexivity, critiquing Giddens, Beck, and Castells in particular for propounding this thesis. Unbounded reflexivity, Adams asserts, "overlooks many crucial factors in identity formation, and misjudges somewhat the nature of the current age" (2003, p. 224). Here, Adams also emphasizes the social embeddedness of identity formation. While the individual self might be disembedded, the reflexivity is not only very much embedded, but inevitably socialized as well. Reflexivity in itself, Adams argues, could be a concept that is shaped by a "neo-modernist take on culture, which values rationality, teleology, voluntarism and instrumentalism" (ibid, p. 225) when in fact what we need to be aware of is that this is only one way of understanding identity and therefore can only ever be partial. Thus, when we see "traditional" and "modern" in terms of some chronology, it implies that even in current time and across space, any society that is not structured along rational capitalist lines is deemed not global, and hence culturally naive.

There have been substantial oppositions to the theories of reflexivity that find that individualization and reflexivity are largely absent—or if present, are in very shallow forms that do not allow for the transcendence of class structures in the reflexive worker (Atkinson, 2011). Lash and Wynne (1992) argued in resonance with this position emphasizing the need for maintaining a sociological focus on any project of criticism that attempts to disrupt the assumptions of the Enlightenment:

> With a few exceptions, sociologists have been timid and complacent in the face of this pervasive apologia for the (always temporary but incessantly extended) repair of modernity. Whilst from the well-pad- ded armchairs of the seminar rooms of Paris, modernity may appear dead and nearly buried, and reflexivity may be thriving as a collective form of discourse, the conditions of ordinary life for many may call this into question, both as a general account of the present and as a model of the future by diffusion outwards and (it seems) downwards from the vanguard intelligentsia.
>
> (Lash & Wynne, 1992, p. 5)

The work of Bauman perhaps presents the most striking reflection of the con- tradictions and uncertainties inherent in reconceptualizing modernity and looking beyond the Enlightenment project. In *Modernity and Ambivalence,* Bauman (1991) deals with the allure of the unfamiliar as well as the negative aspect of this strangeness. In *Modernity and the Holocaust* (1989), he argues that the catastrophic event of the holocaust, far from being a throwback to a premodern, barbaric time, was in fact a direct result of modernity. With his conceptualization of modernity as existing in 'solid' and 'liquid' states Bauman (2000) captures the ambivalence of the postmodernity debate.

Over and above these critiques of the prevalently European readings and understandings of modernity, there is an ironic and hence very significant aspect that modernity, as a European phenomenon, is one "constituted in a dialectical relation with a non-European alterity that is its ultimate content" (Dussel, 1993, p. 65). Eurocentrism is not only a fallacy in the understand- ing of modernity held by major contemporary thinkers, but as Dussel points out, the very idea of modern reason and its emancipatory project conceals an irrational myth that connects Eurocentrism with developmentalism— another fallacy:

> The fallacy of developmentalism consists in thinking that the path of Europe's modern development must be followed unilaterally by every other culture. Development is taken here as an ontological, and not simply a sociological or economic, category.
>
> (Dussel, 1993, p. 68)

Dussel is scathing of Hegel's perspective on modernity, pointing to his comments on Africa as being particularly illustrative of European prejudice and superiority and interpreting Hegel's position on the re-establishment of Christian freedom leading to the rise of the consciousness of the self-justification of the spirit, as an assertion that "modern Christian Europe has nothing to learn from other worlds, other cultures" (Dussel, 1993, p. 72). Deconstructing Hegel's analysis of World History, Dussel highlights its Eurocentrism and critiques its conceptualization of colonization as occupation of 'free space,' when in reality this meant seizing land from other people. Habermas is similarly criticized for being "in this Hegelian mode" (ibid, p. 74) when Dussel identifies the Reformation, the Enlightenment, and the French Revolution as being "decisive for the implantation of the principle of [modern] subjectivity." Arguing that there is a need to consider the Latin American role in the constitution of European modernity, Dussel concludes that the realization of modernity is no longer in the passage from any abstract potential to a real European embodiment, but rather in a process where both the European modernity and its negated alterity co-realize into a mutual creative fertilization. This postcolonial position on modernity attempts to reclaim from classical theories of modernity a role for the alterity in the project that would mitigate its Eurocentrism. Langston (2009) also refers to the abstract European ideal of modernity as a myth and asks whether it can be sustained. Specifically, he harkens back to Marx's vision of technological advancement and notes that it is premised upon a limitless supply of energy and requires a reorganization of society to meet its demands. The myth Langston refers to is that of an infinite supply of natural resources for driving modernity that evidently was non-European.

It is pertinent in this context to note that in her chapter on Philosophy in *A Critique of Postcolonial Reason* (1999), Gayatri Spivak provides a critique of Hegel's discussion of the *Bhagavt Gita* and notices a "structural complicity of dominant texts from two different cultural inscriptions," which has to be understood primarily as a "gesture against some of the too-easy West-and-the-rest polarizations sometimes rampant in colonial and postcolonial discourse studies" (Spivak, 1999, p. 39). Such a polarization, she argues, will be "too much a legitimation-by-reversal of the colonial attitude itself" (ibid, p. 39). Westphal's critique of Hegel's views on *Gita* and Hinduism can be seen as an example of the kind of polarization and legitimation-by-reversal that Spivak criticizes (Westphal, 1992). This takes us directly to an interesting discussion on East-West modernity that has emerged in the context of understanding Eurocentrism as well as deciphering the changing meaning of modernity in specific Asian conditions of social and economic transformation and political change, including democratic transitions, aspirations, and social movements in Asia. Referring to East-West modernity as "the heart of twenty-first century globalization" (Ma, 2012, p. 6) sets up a case for examining the concept of Asian modernity as a necessary intertwining of two perspectives, each constructing the other. In Ma's conceptualization,

Asian modernity is not an empowering concept that evens out the balance and makes modernity less Eurocentric as a construct. On the contrary, the idea of alternative modernities appears as an awareness of inequality, as "modern colonialism lays waste much of the East, it quickens not only the awakening of life's futility but also new sprouts of human consciousness— such as alternative modernities—from the charred earth" (Ma, 2012, p. 2). While this may seem like a resistance to Eurocentrism and a new confidence in an alternate identity, recent literature on Asian modernity has highlighted the inherent and persistent inequality that not only limits but in fact constitutes this alternate modernity.

The paradox of Asian modernity is perhaps most visible through the lens of information and communication technology (ICT)—technologies that arguably have had the greatest impact on social transformation in recent times. This paper will trace some of the key issues relating to this complex concept of Asian modernity, as well as its emergence and contestations. If the acceptance of an Asian modernity is in itself contingent upon the acceptance of the multiplicity of modernity, it also presupposes the existence of a coherent Asian region. A common question that runs through modernities, but one that is often ignored is: What is it that makes a society modern if not all modernities are the same? Multiple modernities, East-West modernities, and postcolonial perspectives have all come up as antitheses to the monolithic Western idea of an evolution from pre-supposed social conditions. But as we see it today in the Asian context, these paradigms do not sufficiently explicate the experience of modernity. This is not only because modern Asian identity is colonially structured or because of the incoherent plurality of Asiatic region. Perhaps, this is more so because of new forms of colonialism that are emerging. This chapter attempts to conceptualize technology as one of the several global and local inequalities associated with twenty-first century modernity, Asian or otherwise. Ultimately, it is argued that the uneven landscape of Asian modernity may be implicated in the development of technological identities, as citizens are interpellated as technological subjects, albeit in varied and culturally specific ways.

A Multiplicity of Modernities

Multiple modernities as a concept come into the purview of the modernity debate predominantly due to the need to frame a non-monolithic understanding of not only the rest of the world, but even what we have come to view as 'Western.' Eisenstadt (2000), in proposing the term 'multiple modernities,' identifies the first anomaly to the idea of a monolithic modernity in the West that emerged with the plurality of Soviet nation-states. Despite their embeddedness in the cultural program of Enlightenment, the plurality of Soviet states brought in a confrontation between the universalistic and the particular within the Western paradigm of modernity. Thus the notion of diverse perspectives on modernity has been framed as one that carries the connotation that Westernization and modernity are not identical. Eisenstadt (2000) notes that

> The actual developments in modernizing societies have refuted the homogenizing and hegemonic assumptions of this Western program of modernity. While a general trend toward structural differentiation developed across a wide range of institutions in most of these societies … the ways in which these arenas were defined and organized varied greatly, in different periods of their development, giving rise to multiple institutional and ideological patterns (p. 2).

Within this framework, however, the original Western project is seen as constituting the crucial reference point, and Eisenstadt asserts that a common core constitutes modernity, however many varied forms it takes. Referencing Weber's assertion that modernity is defined by "an intensive reflexivity [that] developed around the basic ontological premises of structures of social and political authority" (Eisendtadt, 2000, p. 3), Eisendtadt points to, among other things, "the inherently modern tension between an emphasis on human autonomy and the restrictive controls inherent in the institutional realization of modern life" (ibid, p. 8). Analyzing the ways in which this tension played out in Western countries, he makes a case for viewing the various empirically specific trajectories of modernity as evidence of multiplicity. Through this lens, colonialism is seen as a vehicle by which other parts of the world were drawn into the Western project and also as the means by which colonizer and colonized influenced each other's perceptions and trajectories of modernity. In addition, even new social movements—which are often held up as evidence of completely divergent trajectories—are in Eisenstadt's analysis, linked to Western modernity, which serves as their "major frame of reference" (2000, p. 20). In fact, every project of building alternative collective identities bears resemblance to earlier revolutions and movements that constituted Western modernity. While countering and contesting the hegemonic narrative of Western modernity, what the empirical trajectories toward multiple modernities sought to transcend was the model of the nation-state. Ultimately, for Eisenstadt, the term 'multiple modernities' is not an admission of difference as much as a reinforcement of similarity, especially as all modernities share the ontological premises of the Western logic. They are "multiple interpretations of modernity" (Eisenstadt, 2000, p. 24). Different cultural positions are no more than resources to draw upon while regions coped with new social problems.

  Schmidt (2006) is also skeptical about the notion of multiple modernities and argues that scholarly explorations using this lens have invariably limited themselves to cultural factors, rather than taking a holistic structural approach of modernization theory. The result, according to Schmidt, is that while "modernization theorists have a tendency to *underrate* existing differences" (Schmidt, 2006, p. 81, emphasis in original), proponents of multiple modernities may be in danger of overrating cultural differences. Rather than making a case for modernity itself as multiplicitous, Schmidt suggests that the empirical differences between modern societies be seen, insofar as they exist at all beyond vague notions of culture, as varieties of modernity, given that they are all fundamentally united by their existence within a common mode of societal organization—modern capitalism. Particularly problematic in the multiple modernities discourse, in Schmidt's view, is the conflation of nation and culture because there are similarities that cut across sub-national groups at transnational levels. With this political economy approach, it is no surprise perhaps that the concept of multiple modernities holds little weight. Yet, Schmidt does not discount (or underrate) the cultural differences. Rather, he proposes going beyond cultural, political, and economic differences to embrace a higher level of abstraction that examines "the entire structure of society, all aspects of modern life and all institutional sectors differentiated out of embeddedness in the religiously sanctioned moral economy and the stratification-based social order of the pre-modern past" (Schmidt, 2006, p. 88). Ultimately, the notion of multiplicity suggests homogeneity within civilizations, which is again deeply problematic.

This complexity is clearly visible in many debates related to Asian modernity. In a paper that examines modernization theory more closely in light of critiques by the proponents of multiple modernities, Schmidt (2010) finds that any diversity is amply accounted for by modernization theory. Conversely, the concept of multiple modernities is unable to account for similarities across civilizational units, even assuming such units could be unproblematically identified. Zooming in on the East Asian Region, Schmidt compares it against the West and finds that while degree of convergence varies, "the *lived experience* of a typical middle- (or upper-, or lower-) class person in almost all respects resembles that of his or her counterpart in the other region" (Schmidt, 2010, p. 526, italics in original). At the same time, he does not dismiss multiple modernists offhand, suggesting that they could "help overcome some of modernization theory's biases and parochialisms" (ibid, p. 529).

Asian Modernity: Asian Values and Development

The theme of Asian modernity, despite skepticism about multiple modernities, is persistent. Echoing the viewpoint that this new modernity is manifested by the phenomenon of localization as the specific unique feature of globalization (Wischermann, 2004), Raud (2007) points to Japan's apparent success in adopting Western technologies in the broadest possible sense of the word, while retaining its own distinct cultural identity. An Asian modernity is seen as emerging out of the dialogue between Western values and cultural practices on the one hand and indigenous traditions (both genuine and constructed) on the other, with attendant successes and perils encountered by most modernizing Asian countries. Japanese modernity, Raud suggests, has made an impact on East and Southeast Asian countries both as a model to be imitated and a force to be reckoned with. Raud also cautiously points to the multiple dimensions of the multiplicitousness of Asian modernity by citing the interestingly similar instances of cultural particularism evident in the local narratives of modernity from exponents in India and Japan. In order to overcome the imperialist discourses of Western modernity, the local exponents invariably overemphasized their distinctiveness to counter any overarching explanations of uniform development. However, it is indeed true, as Clammer (1995) points out, that the incapacity to see the exclusivities of particular societies stems from the limitations of Western social theory that imagined them as monolithic. A similar blindness is evident in discussions about the economically developed regions like the United Arab Emirates (UAE), where economic modernity does not coexist with the institutional and social modernity of the Enlightenment order but essentially reflects an undemocratic and authoritarian political order clubbed with crony capitalism. There is a strong implication that the very concept of 'multiplicitousness' of Asian modernities has evolved corresponding to the myth of a homogeneous modernity, provided by the Western project, that posits uniform change and development existing side by side with deep structural changes toward a democratic society.

Asian modernity as a new consciousness has come to frame the technocratic rhetoric of some Asian economies that have enjoyed relative economic success. In this context, Asian modernity is seen as one that does not use the West as its sole reference point and is not seen as an inferior type of modernity because it does not match Western realities step for step. For Aihwa Ong (1999), Asian nation-states are engaged in "critical modes of ideological repositioning," where

> new narratives of Asian modernity, spun from the self-confidence of vibrant economies, cannot be reduced to a pale imitation of some Western standard (for instance, full-fledged democracy combined with modern capitalism). Ascendant regions of the world such as the Asia Pacific region are articulating their own modernities as distinctive formations. The historical facts of Western colonialism, ongoing geopolitical domination, and ideological and cultural influences are *never* discounted (only minimized) in these narratives, but they should nevertheless be considered alternative constructions of modernity in the sense of moral-political projects that seek to control their own present and future.
>
> (Ong, 1999, p. 23, emphasis in original)

Contrary to modernization theory, by which former Asian and African colonies have to supplant elements of cultural context with Western programs in order to achieve social and economic progress, narratives of Asian modernity are built on the claim that progress has been achieved through these local cultural elements (L. Wee, 2003). Yet Ong (1999) cautions that such a claim of alternative modernities does not necessarily imply any critique of capital, but

> suggests the kinds of modernity that are (1) constituted by different sets of relations between the developmental or post-developmental state, its population and global capital; and (2) constructed by political and social elites who appropriate 'western' knowledge and re-represent them as truth-claims about their own countries.
>
> (Ong, 1999, p. 35)

This results in a form of cultural globalization, which

> creates both the universalization of western values and cultural patterns, and at the same time the revitalization of local values and traditions, paving the way to the universalization of western modernity and the emergence of alternative modernities.
>
> (Keyman & Koyuncu, 2005, p. 111)

Keyman and Koyuncu (2005) use the framework of alternative modernities as explicated by Ong (1999) and highlight the key role played by new economic and civil society actors in repositioning the discourses of modernity within the Turkish state. They identify varieties of modernity discourses like liberal modernity, Islamic modernity, and conservative modernity that are specific to Turkey in its socio-political positioning as a tail end of Europe with Muslim majority. Alternative modernities, in non-Western empirical studies, thus becomes a concept to gather up the different approaches to modernities specific to the Asian locale rather than as any alternative to the predominant Western model.

   Yet this sort of analysis once again falls within the 'culture-biased under-theorization' with which skeptics of multiple modernities take issue. One debate in particular has garnered a great deal of scathing scholarly critique. Quite apart from a general critique of the concept of multiple modernities, Kessler (1999) criticizes the framing of Asian modernity in terms of Asian values—a notion that Kessler seems to have come up with as a narrow project to equate East Asia's economic boom of the '80s and '90s to some arbitrary idea of cultural values. It only helped to lose any tight focus on the developmental trajectory of Asian societies, distinct from the Western idea of modernity. Needless to say, the idea of contemporary Asian modernities is one that requires unpacking and scrutiny of its composite terms: In particular, neither 'Asian' nor 'modernity' may be taken for granted as having widely acceptable conceptualizations (Chu & Man, 2010). East Asian modernity discourse might also function "as a successor to earlier anti-imperial and nationalist discourses" (C. J. W. L. Wee, 1996, p. 211). Thus while popular national discourses in non-Western states build on the concept of Asian modernity as one that signals economic progress delinked from hegemonic geopolitical conditions, scholarly work on this view of an alternative modernity has pointed to its complex relationship with the West.

There have been attempts to look beyond "prevalent but outmoded exclusive dichotomies: the traditional/modern, the West/rest, and the local/global" (Tu, 1996, p. 196) by anthologizing the various influences of Confucianism in East Asian modernity. This attempt to use a regional framework and Confucian concepts such as self-cultivation, regulation of the family, social civility, moral education, well-being of the people, governance of the state, and universal peace, do certainly scrutinize the presence of Confucian ethics as a common discourse in industrial East Asia. However, no unified answer is reached in this edited volume, itself indicative of the controversial nature of such a position. The question itself is problematic because of the assumption of cultural homogeneity across the East Asian region. As the debates on multiple modernities reveal, culture plays a part in shaping the trajectory of societal development, although there can be no satisfying conclusion that Confucianism or any other specific framework forms a homogenizing cultural umbrella under which all the East Asian countries comfortably gather. Other factors would have to be considered, especially in light of more recent developments such as economic setbacks and political change. Furthermore, there are differences in the rates and time-frames of development among East Asian countries. Rather than refuting Weber's claim about the economically debilitating effects of Confucianism, recent developments may actually be seen as validating Weber's conceptualization of legal-rational authority and bureaucratic organization (Schmidt, 2011).

The 'Asian values' argument is one that has been particularly problematic in its use as a defining characteristic of and justification for Asian modernity as qualitatively separate from the Western project of modernity. Thompson (2001) suggests that economic crisis forms an effective critique for ideology in light of the collapse of the Asian values argument following the financial bust of 1997–1998. Yet he warns against summarily dismissing the impact of the argument. While it may have failed as a rationale for Asian economic success, it still has traction at the domestic level:

> Asian critiques of liberal democracy had been invoked not only in the name of good governance needed to achieve rapid economic growth in poor countries but also in defence of a paternalistic state after high living standards had been attained. Where 'Asian values' had been defended from a developmental perspective (above all in Indonesia), the economic crisis was devastating. But in countries that were already economically advanced, such as Singapore and Malaysia, claims about distinctive 'Asian values' are likely to continue in the postcrisis period.
> (Thompson, 2001, p. 154)

This apparent paradox is underscored by the rise of a large middle class in Singapore and Malaysia, where the coexistence of high living standards and illiberal politics seems to disprove the rule that democracy follows economic development. The Asian values argument is one that has not only been dismissed by Western scholars, but by local scholars as well. Chong (2005) evinces strong critique of the notion of "Asian values" as any sort of factor in an Asian modernity. In fact, what may be safely assumed in the line of Thompson, who looks to the Imperial German critique of Western civilization, could be that "the real issue involved is not 'Asia' versus the 'West,' but rather authoritarian versus democratic modernity" (Thompson, 2001, p. 159). Instead of a dichotomy of West and East, what might be required is a similar paradigmatic shift toward the understanding of modernity in terms of its authoritarian and democratic agendas. On a wider scale of such an agenda the cultural plurality questions may not be overplayed, and a distinct pattern to include the existing dichotomies of West/East, local/global etc. could also be proposed.

The Postcolonial Perspective

Challenging the idea that notions of modernity and colonialism are mere imports from the West, Barlow (1997) shows how colonial modernity has evolved from and into unique forms throughout Asia. He spots a wide consensus reached on colonialism and the discourses of modernity relating to the need to acknowledge (a) the context of political economy that frames modernity; (b) the inseparability of modernity and colonialism; and (c) the indisputability of both the modernity of non-European colonies and the colonial core of European modernity. However, the East Asian region, Barlow argues, has always been wrongly seen as existing outside of this colonial framework due to its mistaken perception as a culturally and historically homogeneous regional bloc. Laying the blame on scholarly epistemological blindness, Barlow asserts the value of the term 'colonial modernity' as a useful innovation given the current geopolitical remapping of regions. This historiographic formulation allows for discursive re-examination of previously hegemonic Eurocentric epistemologies.

In this context other attempts have been made to problematize the notion of the Asian region by analyzing the historical nature of its construction. For instance, Duara (2010) argues that parallel to the historic attempts of the British and Japanese empires to create autarkic, interdependent regions to sustain their imperial power in Asia, the emergent anti-imperialist nationalist discourse in the region sought to build an alternative conception of an 'Other Asia' evoking "earlier linkages between their societies, but it should be noted that their conceptualization of Asia was itself premised and enabled by contemporary imperialist technologies and modes of regional integration" (Duara, 2010, p. 969). Tracing the development of the Asian region through decolonization to World War II, the Cold War, and post-Cold War globalization, Duara argues for the existence of an Asian modernity, but one that is defined as a space in which there are "significant continuities and novelties" (Duara, 2010, p. 980).

Oommen (1999) argues that plurality of modernity is a fact, based on four different conceptualizations of modernity all originating in the West. Whether it is Durkheim's structural differentiation, Weber's rationalization, Marx's history-making project, or Simmel's modern life, modernity cannot be singular because each articulation so far has been inherently and necessarily incomplete. This, asserts Oommen, accounts for the persistence of conflicts based on identity all around the world:

> All the four classical thinkers recognized the discontents of modernity. Durkheim recognized increasing individuation, Weber warned about depersonalization, Marx alerted about alienation and Simmel noted the loss of intrinsic worth. Through these processes the community is sentenced to death by modernity, individualism is celebrated and a homogeneity based on similarity in behaviour and attitudes emerge which has no organic base, but is merely aggregative. That is social actors are apparently similar viewed in terms of their lifestyle but actually they are different in terms of their deeper values. This explains why individuals and groups who share the same life styles enter into persisting conflicts based on race, religion or language.
>
> (Oommen, 1999, p. 5)

Significantly, Oommen goes so far as to suggest that accepting the verity of multiple modernities necessitates the acceptance of multiple globality as well, on the basis that "the point of departure inevitably influences the point of destination even when the process of displacement is the same" (Oommen, 1999, p. 6).

There is something tautological about this argument because the varied local empirical contexts—or 'destinations'—of modernity lead to claims for the notion of multiplicity. It appears to argue that these societies are moving toward multiple globalities due to the differences, and modernization is the only common yardstick to tie them, forgetting how different regions have responded differently to the process. Also inherent in it is the danger of stressing the parochial differences as unrelated to the trajectories of the collective history of colonial modernity. Yet at a conceptual level, Oommen's contribution here is the analytic separation of globalization into the process of displacement and its ultimate manifestations, because globalization is often characterized as a process of standardization. Yet empirical cases highlight the very different ways in which societies respond to it.

For Dirlik (2003), the current period of modernity is better characterized as "global modernity," because this term not only highlights the essential singularity of modernity around the world while accounting for localized differences. It also asserts the decoupling of modernity today from its earlier Eurocentric avatar. Thus the opposite of Eurocentric modernity is not multiple modernities, but a new global form of modernity that has power centers distributed around the world because of global capitalism. Pointing

to the significance of the fall of socialism for the creation of a singular conception of capitalist modernity, Dirlik notes that in a post-socialist world,
resistance to capitalism "finds expression now in revivals of native traditions as alternative modernities" (Dirlik, 2003, p. 282). He draws upon the
example of how Confucianism was co-opted and resurrected by opponents
of Eurocentrism to highlight the paradoxical nature of this use of the very
tradition that modernity discourse posits as overridden by the trajectory of
development. Thus postcolonial intellectuals draw upon native pasts in pro-
claiming cultures and knowledges, but the use to which these resources are
put is only possible because of a globality as construed through Eurocentric
perspectives. Ultimately, Dirlik argues, "'Multiple modernities' suggests a
global multiculturalism, that reifies cultures in order to render manageable
cultural and political incoherence" (Dirlik, 2003, p. 284), and the very entities, such as nations and cultures, around which arguments for multiple
modernities are structured are themselves products of modernization and its
thinking. Embedded in Dirlik's argument is a critique not just of postcolonial positions on modernity, but postcolonial scholars themselves who argue
against the tenets of modernity from intellectual locations made possible
by modern thought. The danger in this epistemological paradox is its equal
vulnerability to use by reactionary as well as progressive politics. Additional
complexity resides in the lack of a real binding force between cultures and
nations and in the depoliticizing nature of culturalism, especially when culture acts as a euphemism for ethnicity and religion. Dirlik concludes with
the warning that the concept of multiple modernities is not as democratiz-
ing as it appears, due to the real dominance of the United States as well as
the creation of an elite that, cutting across regional distinctions, embraces
economic globalization even as it proclaims particular cultural identities.
For these reasons, he concludes, postcolonial critics of modernity cannot
afford to "wallow in identity politics" (Dirlik, 2003, p. 289). The notion of
global modernity, he proposes, both takes into account the European origins of modernity and is "less bound to those origins than such concepts as
postmodernity or globalization" (Dirlik, 2003, p. 289). What we find here
is an interesting imbroglio of arguments that revolves around culture and
modernity as if these are antithetical to each other as far as the Asian regions
are concerned. Traditions and cultures appear to need to be evoked in order
to substantiate claims about alterities, thereby rendering them as mere tools
in the ontological revamping that ensued after major epistemic shifts. Other
paradigms that were instrumental in the seismic shifts of the time are merely
accounted to as already inherent in the modernization project.

Postmodernity and the Cyborg Future: Complex Inequalities

It can be observed that the technological aspect of development is often
either sidelined in debates about modernity or given much too prominent
a position such that its interaction with other factors is ignored in favor

of technological fetishism. Discourses about technology, whether they are located in the field of science, education, development, governance, or even politics, are often based on the assumption that technology is neutral. Yet studies show that the political is embedded in the technological because it is developed under ideological conditions (see for example Barbrook & Cameron, 1996), and it is introduced into situations where there are pre-existing political and social conditions (see, for example, Nolan & Lenski, 1996; Harrison & Huntington, 2000). Critical positions on technology are numerous. From Heidegger's (2009) characterization of modern technology as "challenging forth" and Marcuse's (2009) notion of instrumental rationality, to Ellul's (2009) position that technology is ultimately dehumanizing as it eliminates the natural order, the picture that emerges is that of an entity that ultimately depoliticizes and therefore disengages from the political itself. Within this picture, there is no space to talk of the politics of technology. Ultimately, technology does not matter in the sense that there is nothing that can be done in the face of its relentless march toward a post-human future (Lyotard, 1991; Cecchetto, 2011; Chiew, 2014). Hence, debates over whether technology is a positive or negative paradigm within the project of modernization have become highly redundant. So, too, debates that delink technology from culture and politics or those that argue for its embedded political nature seem to be of no use. What we need to summarize is a context where technology can hardly be dissociated from anything else. Within the discourse of modernity, technology has been treated mostly as a pervasive element, sometimes even overlooked and understood as its imperative. The theoretical orientations of the two disciplinary terrains have also been very distinct, and the macro-level modernity theories and the micro-level technology studies could rarely intersect (Brey, 2003). The politics of technology was never separated from the process of modernity, as technological advancement was the requisite for the condition called modernity. Even the ethics of 'good' and 'bad' informed by the modernity rationale swept into the discourse of technology, just as access to technology became the norm of empowerment and sole ground by which to measure modernity.

There are also scholars who have viewed technologization of the social order as an opportunity for new forms of political action. Andrew Barry (2001) writes of technological societies where interactivity, for example, may be tapped as a mode of learning that empowers citizens to discover for themselves their place in the social order, and he positions this empowerment as a contrast to Foucauldian docile bodies that are disciplined into following orders. The notion of technological citizenship is also taken up by Frankenfeld (1992), who argues that the central role of technology in human life makes it urgent to draw decisions related to technology into the political sphere such that well-informed citizens can participate in the making of these decisions. Amid all the critique of technology to the point of removing the human and the absorption of technology to the point of removing the political, Feenberg's (2009) 'democratic rationalization of technology' and Winner's (1980) 'political technology' address the politics of technology from the dual perspective of the technological and the social. These conceptualizations are important because they allow for the agency of technological artifacts to be taken into consideration. Latour's (1999) notion of nonhuman agents, for example, is controversial, but only if, as McMaster and Wastell (2005) argue, symmetry within the human and the non-human is confused with equivalence. Continuing this theme of socio-technically constructed agency, Castells (2001) suggests that the dangers of technologies of control may be countered by technologies of freedom. Escobar (1994, p. 214) makes reference to a 'regime of technosociality' and invests this with the potential for agency when he suggests that "other worlds are (already) possible" because of this regime (Escobar, 2004).

All of these scenarios presuppose a level playing field. The argument has even been put forward by Hughes (2004) that we are entering the age of transhumanism, when technologies are available to improve our lives by making us more than human, and hence there is a need for new forms of citizenship that go beyond current humanist assumptions. However, no theory about the cyborg citizen can be put forward with any claim of universality in light of the inequalities between the developed and developing worlds and even within the developed world. Proponents of cyborg citizenship, transhumanism, and even technological citizenship in the context of a postmodern framework have to account for problems that are very much located within the realm of modernity, especially its multiplicity and its ontological foundations that we had summarized in the early sections of this essay. The inequalities in the realm of technological modernity in Asian regions, if they were only related to access, would have been easily resolved. Eubanks (2011), however, puts forward the argument that the resonance of the digital divide in policy discourse is due mainly to the fact that it fits in with the neoliberal solutions. Access does not serve as a solution when the given technology is instrumental in fulfilling the authoritative agendas and constricted ideas of development. When the real problem is one of social injustice, neither neoliberalism nor transhumanism can provide an answer.

Examples of inequalities are many. Examining the asymmetries of internet infrastructure between the developed and developing world, Main (2001) concludes that the closing of this North-South divide requires more than a transfer of technology. In fact, she goes so far as to accuse the United States of neo-imperialism in its domination over the regulation and governance of ICTs. Chib and Chen (2011) study the introduction of mobile phones among midwives in Aceh, and find—perhaps unsurprisingly—that while there is potential for many lives to be saved by access to timely information, existing gender norms make it difficult for the midwives to avail themselves of the empowering possibilities of the new technology. In a similar vein, the complex ways in which technology gets overlaid on existing divides, exacerbating them and creating new ones, have been dealt with in relation to several other aspects of India's rural network society. It has been found that the social enterprises of rural cyber-kiosks that claim to reduce gender inequalities and mitigate caste oppression "are not inclusive enough, and the social factors that perpetuate inequalities in rural areas are in fact reinforced by the projects—rather than eliminating them" (Sreekumar, 2011, p. 123).

The cyborg future is thus not a universal one, and if current trends are an indicator, marching toward a future of transhuman elites will certainly create even more and deeper inequalities in a world where modernity is differently experienced. Goh (2010) critiques the cyborg concept as a totalizing mechanism, imposing one worldview globally that co-opts all other visions of modernity. This, he argues, is done via Eurocentric paradigms of science. The result is that while the Western world's concept of the cyborg is seen through the lens of human superiority, the rest of the world is seen as dehumanized by technology. The project of Asian modernity, he seems to argue, is for Asian countries to rescue for themselves the humanizing and human face of the cyborg, rather than be relegated to the electronic trash heap of global capitalism. For Goh, the development of technological identities that are associated with an empowered, humanized version of the cyborg is arguably the new face of Asian modernity. Deeply seated in this view, again, is the dichotomy of East and West and a necessarily nobler East that can possibly redeem the technological evil projected as Western.

Conclusion

I have tried to argue out the complicated dynamics of perspectivizing the concept of Asian Modernity in the wake of the technological paradigm. The differences that are made to our understanding of everyday life in Asian societies owe much to both the Western ontology of modernity and colonial modernities. The cultural logic of existence and the negotiations and articulation conducted and performed in the living contexts of these societies are also being increasingly defined through technology. The uniqueness of modernity in Asian societies has been enabled at once by contesting and denouncing the sequencing logic of Western rationality and modernization theory, and this in itself was a political project that has charted its course in search of an alternative modernity. The acceptance of an Asian modernity is contingent upon the acceptance of the multiplicity of modernity, as well as of the existence of a coherent Asian region. It is undeniable that Asian modernity as an ontological theme has its origin in the universalistic and Eurocentric restrictions of Western rationality. In the complex domain in which it situates itself, Asian modernity can neither be the result of the apposed multiplicities nor the outcome of a singularity imposed on the region in the wake of a technological drive. The claims for multiplicity that were juxtaposed in the evolution of its theme were mainly to delay any uncritical jump toward postmodernity and to oppose the flaws and limitations of the Eurocentric precepts of modernity. Those claims in themselves do not frame a sufficient ontological premise to espouse a singular response toward the various aspects of modernization that Asiatic regions encountered. The non-consensus within the empirical studies about Asian modernity, the absence of any sustaining singular paradigm to comprehend modernization, thus leads us to think of technology as one such paradigm that can cut across the existing binaries about the West and the rest. For this, what we may perhaps need is a framework to connect the theoretical paths of modernity and technology.

One may question the common thread that runs through all modernities. What is it that makes a society modern if all modernities are not the same? In the wake of such a question, the evolving conceptualizations of cyborg and post-human futures may also need to be scrutinized as concepts that essentially carry over the fallacies of a monolithic Western modernity to subtler and newer premises. Given that the modern Asian identity is a colonially structured one, the division between Asian modernity and the rest point to new and continuing forms of colonialism. These new forms of colonialism cannot be explicated within the relatively uncritical binaries of West/East, global/local etc. Technology could be viewed as embedded with the regional and material inequalities that the history of modernity also embodied. This overview of technology could show how the conceptualization of the post-human in the context of global and local inequalities associated with twenty-first century modernity, Asian or otherwise, is becoming increasingly problematic. Ultimately, the uneven landscape of Asian modernity may be implicated in the development of technological identities as citizens are interpellated as technological subjects, albeit in varied and culturally specific ways. Perspectivizing the concept of Asian Modernity is thus a complex exercise. To solve the tension among different terms like Western modernity, European modernity, Post-colonial modernity, Global modernity, and Asian modernity, we need to bring these terms to correspond to the specific economic processes, technological regimes, labor relations, cultural logic, and social structures. The politics of technology and the role of technology in development are important aspects of modernity to consider in building toward a position on a uniquely Asian modernity, however much diversity this position allows for within that entity.

References

Adams, M. (2003). The reflexive self and culture: A critique. *British Journal of Sociology, 54*(2): 221–238.

Atkinson, W. (2011). Class, individualization and late modernity: In search of the reflexive worker. New York, NY: Palgrave Macmillan.

Barbrook, R., & Cameron, A. (1996). The Californian ideology. *Science as Culture, 6*(1): 44–72.

Barlow, T. E. (1997). *Formations of colonial modernity in East Asia*. Durham, NC: Duke University Press.

Barry, A. (2001). *Political machines: Governing a technological society*. London & New York, NY: Athlone Press.

Bauman, Z. (1989). *Modernity and the Holocaust.* Ithaca, NY: Cornell University Press.

Bauman, Z. (1991). *Modernity and ambivalence.* Cambridge: Polity Press.

Bauman, Z. (2000). *Liquid Modernity.* Cambridge: Polity Press.

Beck, U. (1992). Risk society: Towards a new modernity (M. Ritter, Trans.). London: Sage Publications.

Brey, P. (2003). Theorizing technology and modernity. In Thomas Misa, Philip Brey, and Andrew Feenberg (Eds.), *Modernity and technology* (pp. 33–73). Cambridge, MA: MIT Press.

Castells. M. (2001). *The Internet galaxy: Reflections on the internet, business and society.* New York, NY: Oxford University Press.

Cecchetto, D. (2011). Deconstructing affect: Posthumanism and Mark Hansen's media theory. *Theory, Culture & Society, 28*(5): 3–33.

Chib, A., & Chen, V.H.H. (2011). Midwives with mobiles: A dialectical perspective on gender arising from technology introduction in rural Indonesia. *New Media and Society, 13*(3): 486–501.

Chiew, F. (2014). Posthuman ethics with Cary Wolfe and Karen Barad: Animal compassion as trans-species entanglement. *Theory, Culture & Society, 31*(4): 51–69.

Chong, T. (2005). *Modernization trends in Southeast Asia.* Singapore: ISEAS.

Chu, Y.-W., & Man, E.K.-W. (Eds.) (2010). *Contemporary Asian Modernities: Transnationality, Interculturality, and Hybridity* (Vol. 16). Berlin, Germany: Peter Lang.

Clammer, J.R. (1995). *Difference and modernity: Social theory and contemporary Japanese society.* London & New York, NY: Kegan Paul International.

Dirlik, A. (2003). Global modernity? Modernity in an age of global capitalism. *European Journal of Social Theory, 6*(3): 275–292.

Duara, P. (2010). Asia redux: Conceptualizing a region for our times. *The Journal of Asian Studies, 69*(4): 963–983.

Dussel, E. (1993). Eurocentrism and modernity (Introduction to the Frankfurt Lectures). *Boundary 2, 20*(3): 65–76.

Eisenstadt, S.N. (2000). Multiple modernities. *Daedalus, 120:* 1–29.

Ellul, J. (2009). The autonomy of technology. In C. Hanks (Ed.). *Technology and values: Essential readings* (pp. 67–75). Chichester, U.K. & Malden, MA: Wiley-Blackwell.

Escobar, A. (2004). Other worlds are (already) possible. In J. Sen & P. Waterman (Eds.), *World social forum: Challenging empires* (pp. 393–404). Montreal: Black Rose Books.

Escobar, A. (1994). Welcome to Cyberia: Notes on the anthropology of cyberculture. *Current Anthropology, 35*(3): 211–223.

Eubanks, V. (2011). *Digital dead end: Fighting for social justice in the information age.* Boston, MA: MIT Press.

Feenberg, A. (2009). Democratic rationalization: Technology, power and freedom. In D.M. Kaplan (Ed.), *Readings in the philosophy of technology* (pp. 139–155). Lanham, MD: Rowman and Littlefield.

Frankenfeld, P. (1992). Technological citizenship: A normative framework for risk studies. *Science, Technology and Human Values, 17*(4): 459–484.

Giddens, A. (1991). Modernity and self-identity: Self and society in the late modern age. Stanford, CA: Stanford University Press.

Goh, R.B.H. (2010). Cyberasian: Science, hybridity, modernity, and the Asian body. In Y.-W. Chu & E.K.-W. Man (Eds.), *Contemporary Asian Modernities: Transnationality, Interculturality, and Hybridity* (247–270). Berlin, Germany: Peter Lang.

Habermas, J. (1987). The philosophical discourse of modernity: Twelve lectures (F. Lawrence, Trans.). Cambridge, MA: MIT Press.

Harrison, L.E., & Huntington, S.P. (Eds.) (2000). *Culture matters: How values shape human progress*. New York, NY: Basic Books.

Heidegger, M. (2009). The question concerning technology. In C. Hanks (Ed.). *Technology and values: Essential readings* (pp. 99–113). Chichester, U.K. & Malden, MA: Wiley-Blackwell.

Hughes, J. H. (2004). *Citizen cyborg: Why democratic societies must respond to the redesigned human of the future*. Boulder, CO: Westview Press.

Kessler, C. S. (1999). The abdication of the intellectuals: Sociology, anthropology and the Asian values debate – or, What everybody needed to know about 'Asian Values' that social scientists failed to point out. *Sojourn: Journal of Social Issues in Southeast Asia, 14*(2): 295–312.

Keyman, E. F. & Koyuncu, B. (2005). Globalization, alternative modernities and the political economy of Turkey. *Review of International Political Economy, 12*(1): 105–128.

Langston, D.L. (2009). Is modernity sustainable? One hundred and fifty years of the myth of modernity. *The Mind's Eye*. Retrieved from https://www.mcla.edu/Assets/uploads/MCLA/import/www.mcla.edu/Academics/uploads/text Widget/4506.00017/documents/Minds_Eye_2009.pdf#page=6.

Lash, S., & Wynne, B. (1992). Introduction. In U. Beck (Ed.), *Risk society: Towards a new modernity* (M. Ritter, Trans.) (pp. 1–8). London: Sage Publications.

Latour, B. (1999). *Pandora's hope*. Cambridge, MA: Harvard University Press.

Lyotard, J. F. (1991). *The Inhuman: Reflections on time*. Stanford, CA: Stanford University Press.

Ma, S.M. (2012). *Asian diaspora and East-West modernity*. West Lafayette, IN: Purdue University Press.

Main, L. (2001). The global information infrastructure: Empowerment or imperialism? *Third World Quarterly, 22*(1): 83–97.

Marcuse, H. (2009). The new forms of control. In C. Hanks (Ed.), *Technology and values: Essential readings* (pp. 159–168). Chichester, U.K. & Malden, MA: Wiley-Blackwell.

McMaster, T. & Wastell, D. (2005). The agency of hybrids: Overcoming the symmetrophobic block. *Scandinavian Journal of Information Systems, 17*(1): 175–182.

Nolan, P. & Lenski, G. (1996). Technology, ideology, and societal development. *Sociological Perspectives, 39*(1): 23–38.

Ong, A. (1999). *Flexible citizenship: The cultural logics of transnationality*. Durham, NC: Duke University Press.

Oommen, T. (1999). Recognizing multiple modernities: A prelude to understanding globalization. New Delhi: Jawaharlal Nehru University. Retrieved from http://social-theory.eu/texts/oommen-1999_modernities.pdf.

Raud, R. (Ed.). (2007). *Japan and Asian modernities*. London: Kegan Paul Limited.

Schmidt, V. H. (2006). Multiple modernities or varieties of modernity? *Current Sociology, 54*(1): 77–97.

Schmidt, V. H. (2010). Modernity and diversity: Reflections on the controversy between modernization theory and multiple modernists. *Social Science Information, 49*(4): 511–538.

Schmidt, V. H. (2011). Max Weber in light of East Asian development. *Max Weber Studies, 11*(1): 13–34.

Spivak, G.C. (1999). *A critique of postcolonial reason: Toward a history of the vanishing present.* Cambridge, MA: Harvard University Press.

Sreekumar, T. T. (2011). *ICTs and development in India: Perspectives on the rural network society.* London & New York, NY: Anthem Press.

Thompson, M.R. (2001). Whatever happened to "Asian Values"? *Journal of Democracy, 12*(4): 154–165.

Tu, W.M. (Ed.) (1996). *Confucian traditions in East Asian modernity: Moral education and economic culture in Japan and the four mini-dragons.* Cambridge, MA: Harvard University Press.

Wee, C.J.W.L. (1996). The 'clash' of civilisations? Or an emerging 'East Asian Modernity'? *Sojourn: Journal of Social Issues in Southeast Asia, 11*(2): 211–230.

Wee, L. (2003). Linguistic instrumentalism in Singapore. *Journal of Multilingual and Multicultural Development, 24*(3): 211–224.

Westphal, M. (1992). *Hegel, freedom, and modernity.* Albany, NY: State University of New York Press.

Winner, L. (1980). Do artifacts have politics? *Daedalus, 109*(1): 121–136.

Wischermann, J. (Ed.). (2004). *Asian modernity—Globalization processes and their cultural and political localization.* Berlin: Heinrich-Boll-Stiftung.

12 Re-orienting Global Digital Cultures

Gerard Goggin

It is a longstanding paradox of technology, especially the digital, networked technology that emerged from the 1970s onward, that it has supported an extraordinary growth and intensity of global communication—yet the importance of local, regional, national, and other contexts, locations, and frames of reference has remained decisive. With the rise of globalization as a key concept and field of study, much research was preoccupied with the salience and novelty of transborder communication and the mixing up of domestic, local, and subcultures with global cultural and media forms—believed to be evident in the rise of digital technologies such as the internet, mobile media, digital broadcasting, new audiovisual economies, digital music, online advertising, and new forms of digital popular cultures. Globalization, narrowly construed, blindsided us to the actual complexity of understanding global digital cultures. Hence there is a stubbornly resistant contradiction that still governs research: On the one hand, digital cultures rely upon global networks, supply chains, trade and economy, transnational communications giants (notably the new social media titans), and international users, producers, and audiences; on the other hand, global digital cultures are profoundly emplaced in particular cultural, social, and political settings and contexts. Research has so far largely failed to join these two parts of the digital cultures puzzle.

To understand what is happening in even a quotidian interaction among users or among users, technology, media formats, and cultural representations, on a social media platform, one needs to understand the layering and shaping of this digital 'assemblage.' We are beginning to appreciate that there are considerable differences among, say, QQ, WeChat, and Baidu, in a Chinese context, that do not simply map onto, or are amenable to being deducted from, Facebook, Twitter, or, even WeChat, in a U.S. context. Even the exportation of platforms like Facebook, or more recently Alibaba, across the globe should cause us to pause and question the cultural terms of trade, so to speak. How, for instance, is Facebook introduced into particular markets? How does it relate to, or displace, early social networking systems—Friendster, for instance, in Indonesia, or the Philippines, Mixi in Japan, or Cyworld, in Korea? (Goggin, McLelland, & Yu, 2016; Hjorth & Arnold, 2013).

As this rich, timely, and rigorous volume shows us, the path to under-standing contemporary media and communication, especially the leading and privileged case of digital cultures, involves a profound re-orientation, so to speak, of our stances, positions, theories, concepts, frameworks, and methods as researchers (Lim & Soriano, this volume). As many scholars have argued, the time has long passed the point where we can assume and apply a shared general approach to media and culture that is based on the worldview, ideas, and experience of one particular group—even a very large and, actually, heterogeneous group that constitutes a "Western" approach to the study of how the "rest of the world" communicates (Curran & Park, 2000; Miike, 2006; Wang, 2011). The proponents of such cross-cultural, intercultural, subaltern, non-Western, cosmopolitan paradigm shifts bring with them distinct suppositions about how the world works, how we should take it, and what the cardinal norms and coordinating values should be. One tendency I have subscribed to is the loose coalition of scholars arguing for an internationalization of media studies (Abbas & Erni, 2005; Goggin & McLelland, 2009, 2016; Thussu, 2009), but the antecedents and new responses are multifarious indeed, including, for instance, those arguing for a need to understand new regional powers and blocs (Nordenstreng & Thussu, 2015) or the "geo-linguistic" constitution of the world's regions (Sinclair, 1999).

Expressed in these terms, of course, the call for internationalization runs the risk of not doing justice to the complexity of research. When one exam-ines the body of research in a particular area, such as digital cultures, it is hard not to come to the conclusion that we have a long way to go to genuinely, evenly, rigorously, and comprehensively understand the global picture. Further, two major stumbling blocks are: 1) a lack of research on many of the world's media and communication systems; and 2) a lack of recognition that media and communication everywhere is shaped by specific local and regional histories, conditions, infrastructures, policies, meanings, and projects. If we were to unpack these difficulties further, we find some important starting points to change the worlds of research—to achieve a necessary, and belated, re-orientation toward the international dimension.

The dominance of English as the language of international scholarship and research, especially in the fields of media and communication, has its mixed blessings. Researchers are enjoined to publish in English-language journals and books, and, increasingly, participate in international confer-ences in the field in English. English does provide a *lingua franca* for a global communications research community, increasingly diverse in character yet wishing to find common ground and build bridges across its different groups and preoccupations. The status of English as a default language, however, means that a significant amount of research and the meaning-laden tradi-tions of communication, its conceptions, and practices around the world are missing—not only in translation, but indeed stranded across geopolitical divides as well as gulfs of difference (Lim & Soriano, this volume). One only has to look at the local terminologies for the mobile phone or metaphors by which the internet is imagined to be reminded how much language matters to thought processes and so too to research. In recognition of its importance, some conferences attempt bi-lingualism, or tri-linguism—for instance, the International Association for Media and Communication Research (IAMCR) and regional communication conferences will feature some presentations in two or more languages (with translation options). For its part, the International Communication Association (ICA), having long been based on, and hence shaped by, North American traditions and interests, has for some time been intensively engaging in an internationalization strategy, with some success (especially through regional conferences). In the case of Asian communication, there are regional journals (such as *Media Asia*, or the *Asian Journal of Communication*) and now well-established research groupings and conferences, such as the annual *Chinese Internet Research Conference*, or various Asian conferences and edited volumes on mobile communication (Chu, Fortunati, Law, & Yang, 2012). Yet there remains an obvious gap between the knowledge and research on digital cultures in non-Anglophone research communities, and the apprehension of, and reflection upon, this literature in the Anglophone academic discourse; it is not simply an oversight, of course; it is bound up with the asymmetric power relations of knowledge production and distribution and regimes of value (Chen, 2010; Dissanayake, 2009). This is something I have discovered in a collaborative project on histories of the internet in the Asia-Pacific. There are, in fact, substantial histories of the internet and associated digital cultures in countries such as Japan and Korea, in particular. Yet the customary, taken-for-granted understanding of East Asian internet histories contains myths and preconceptions unalloyed by the existence of research that contests them (see, for instance: Goggin et al., 2016; McLelland, 2016).

Language is a major factor to address, but it also is an index of the complexity, different scales, institutional shifts, resources, and priorities required. There are long-standing concentrations and inequities in the resources available for knowledge, as embodied in educational and research systems, especially universities. Universities take sustained investment—increasingly from private sources—and especially need to attract students and faculty in conditions of increasing (if constrained) global mobility and competition. Universities also need to attract governmental support and funding. So, it is not surprising that there are areas of the world where digital cultures have been intensively studied and research reported and circulated—precisely because countries that provide training, development, and support for advanced research remain relatively few. In the case of Asia, countries such as Japan and Korea were in the vanguard of conceptions of the 'information society,' and early investment in computerization, communication networks, and digital networks, in which technology research capacity was key. It is no surprise that we also see substantial research on these countries—from researchers based overseas, local counterparts, and custodians of cultural to media, and communication traditions. Now leading investors in universities, teaching, and research are countries such as China, Hong Kong, Taiwan, Singapore, and Malaysia, as well as India, each with considerable investments in information and communication technology, as well as domestic, household, social, political, educational, and cultural take-up of digital technology. This kind of marked shift in both technology infrastructures and diffusion, as well as universities, provides a pre-condition, as well as major impetus, for a groundswell of change in how we conceive and research digital cultures globally. As T.T. Sreekumar lays out in his magisterial chapter, these issues of technology are woven into accounts and visions of Asian modernities (Sreekumar, this volume). Reflecting on these changes, we may draw attention to the way in which some countries receive a good deal of attention, and often figure as the 'reference' cases for understanding general considerations of digital technology (and indeed associated cultural formations), where other countries receive little attention and remain overlooked, unremarked, and lacking in prestige or relevance.

What Asian Perspectives Tell Us about Global Digital Cultures

Against this backdrop, the central concern of this book is that Asian perspectives provide important insights concerning digital cultures. As such, we can locate this volume and its research alongside the growing body of work on Asian digital technologies and cultures. The research literature contains many studies of digital technology in specific Asian countries. It also contains a body of work that takes up the gambit of offering a broader *Asian* perspective or at least discussion on what an *Asian* perspective might constitute (for instance, Dissanayake, 2009; Donald, Anderson, & Spry, 2010; Erni & Chua, 2005; Ho, Kluver, & Yang, 2003; Han & Nasir, 2015; Pertierra, 2008). So, for me, this volume enters the heartland of thinking about media, communication, and digital culture. What is particular to this book is its contention that at the heart of such Asian perspectives are 'enduring concepts' that we might then use to interpret "emerging phenomena" such as new media. This is a very interesting and extremely ambitious undertaking and proves very fruitful indeed.

The book contains a number of studies that tackle resonant and apparently well-known 'Asian' concepts, thinking them through in relation to digital cultures in the region and potentially globally. Sun Sun Lim and Iccha Basnyat's nuanced study of online social networking takes up one of the categories of Asian thought best known globally—face. What I found especially suggestive about their discussion of face is that they go well beyond recourse to the Chinese or even Japanese understanding of face and produce a cross-cultural Asian account—including India/Pakistan, Thailand, and Vietnam. This provides them with a nuanced and precise Asian account of face that they can then parlay back into the center of Western (especially

North American-influenced) communication studies, via a reading of Goffman's work. As they argue:

> A central trope across the different Asian conceptions of face is "social face" that reflects a stronger relational dimension of self than in the Western conception. This pronounced social dimension lends itself particularly well to online social networks that are designed to be deeply social, while allowing for individual introspection. ... The Asian concept of face thus sensitizes researchers to different dimensions of social, cultural, and possibly economic capital that individuals can derive while giving, saving, and gaining face via their online network interactions.
>
> (Lim & Basynat, this volume, pp. 28–29)

This is an especially interesting balance of theoretical considerations across local and regional cultures and global communications that typify the studies collected here.

Other contributions to the volume also take up major, widely invoked Asian concepts and use them to theorize media and communication: Jun Liu looks at the Chinese notion of *guanxi* in explaining mobile communication in recent protests; Cheryll Soriano and Sun Sun Lim take up a number of important, lesser known Filipino concepts, alongside the widely known 'People Power,' to elucidate ritual and community in mobile phone communication; Ganga S. Ganesh offers an especially interesting, long historical view of the traditions of corporate social responsibility in contemporary Indian companies, drawing on the resources of ancient philosophical, religious, and social thought. Other contributions discuss notable cultural phenomena, now reconfigured in digital forms. Manuel Victor J. Sapitula joins Soriano in an examination of the online, 'translocal' forms of piety found in the highly popular *Perpetual Help Devotion*. Liew Kai Khiun uses the Chinese cosmological concept of *ying hun*, translated literally as shadow and soul, to discuss the luminous uses of holographic technologies in the posthumous projects of Hong Kong and Taiwan transnational Chinese celebrities.

It is important to emphasize that major implications for how we approach media studies arise from the studies in this collection. This is explicit especially in two chapters that engage the 'super' or 'classic' theories of culture, communication, and media in Asia. A major challenge in research on global communication, and culture in media studies in particular, has been making headway in the face of 'macro-level' theories about societies and how they differ—across the West and East. Thus the sweeping accounts of Geert Hofstede, in particular, still hold sway, offering comparative accounts at scales that characterize cultures as 'high-context' or 'low-context,' more or less collectivist (Hofstede, 1980, 1991), or by particular configurations of gender (such as the 'masculinity dimension' (Hofstede, 1998). Despite their popularity, it can be contended that at this conjuncture especially these are at best grand accounts that offer little purchase for understanding the cultural dynamics and social functions of media and communication in actually existing societies. The kind of reification of culture to be found in Hofstede and other theorists of relatively 'undifferentiated' culture is only matched, in an odd way, by more garden-variety, and yet still common, invocations of 'Asian culture' or 'cultural values,' as a handy weapon in concrete political and cultural contests (Avonius & Kingsbury, 2008; Barr, 2002). Such accounts of culture fly in the face of the work undertaken in the area of Asian cultural studies (e.g., Chen, 2005; Iwabuchi, Muecke, & Thomas, 2004), as well as—for the most part—the body of research on Asian media and communications already alluded to here. Indeed, these debates about the nature of culture and technology have been a feature of internet studies and mobile communication studies as newer fields, and there is a rich heritage to be acknowledged and drawn upon here—as, for instance, the Cultural Attitudes toward Technology and Communication conference series (see Ess, 2016).

These still influential Western theories of communication undergird the dense and contentious arena deftly negotiated by Yeon-Ok Lee in her thoughtful study of the highly constructed and mediating melding of 'news values' and 'Asian values,' evident in how the new, culturally salient, and valorized category of 'Power Twitterians' play a pivotal role in South Korean new discourses. In her chapter, Lee makes the subtle and powerful argument that:

> By no means does this study argue that Asian values trump the news values identified by Western scholars like Galtung and Ruge (1965) and Harcup and O'Neil (2001). This chapter demonstrates the constructivist nature of media logics and the extent to which local values contribute to the construction and operation of such logics.
>
> (Lee, this volume, p. 147)

In carefully considering and rejecting the still dominant theories of Hofstede, as stepping through the minefields of the ever-green 'Asian values' (or in this case, 'Korean values'), Lee's chapter helpfully points the way to more productive avenues for future inquiry and conceptualization of digital cultures. In a quite different treatment, Michael Prieler engages these overarching theories of global communication. Prieler examines "face-ism" (that is, the presentation and prominence of face and its implications for gender) in relation to online dating sites across two Western sites (U.S., Sweden) and two Eastern sites (Japan, South Korea). In doing so, he plumps for the conceptual yield of Confucianism over Hofstede's 'masculinity index.'

As is hopefully evident from this brief discussion, this is an important volume at this point of time in the field. The studies collected genuinely offer fresh and challenging perspectives on digital cultures—not just as we find such emergent media and social practices in 'Asia'; however, we approach and define this resonant, handy, and strategically useful concept. Rather, the volume provokes us to rethink how we approach global digital cultures—not just as objects of study but in terms of the fundamental ways we frame, conceptualize, and theorize such deeply cultural, social, and political phenomena. As such, it is important to consider the Asian histories of technology, raised by Sreekumar, but to a large extent not so well canvassed here. Given the contribution of science and technology studies to media and communication studies, more future work on Asian theories of technologies could be helpful to take the agenda of re-orienting global digital culture research in new directions.

Finally, the volume builds purposely, creatively, and tellingly on the last two decades of work toward Asian theories of communication and media, as an integral part of de-Westernizing, decolonizing, and internationalizing the field. It turns out that this is a worthwhile endeavor not simply for communication and media scholars. If we take seriously this latest Asian turn, as part of a global re-orientation, there is a real prospect we can at last re-frame the fundamental coordinates of how we see communication—and finally dislodge the distorting and profoundly problematic accounts of communication that still govern popular, policy, and scholarly conceptions.

References

Abbas, A., & Erni, J. N. (Eds.) (2005). *Internationalizing cultural studies*. Malden, MA: Blackwell.

Avonius, L., & Kingsbury, D. (Eds.) (2008). *Human rights in Asia: A reassessment of the Asia values debate*. New York, NY: Palgrave.

Barr, M.D. (2002). *Cultural politics and Asian values: The tepid war*. London: Routledge.

Chen, K-H. (Ed.) (2005). *Trajectories: Inter-asia cultural studies*. London and New York, NY: Routledge.

Chen, K.-H. (2010). *Asia as method: Towards deimperialization*. Durham, NC: Duke University Press.

Chu, R. W.-c., Fortunati, L., Law, P.-l, & Yang, S. (Eds.) (2012). *Mobile communication and greater China*. London and New York, NY: Routledge.

Curran, J., & Park, M-J. (Eds.) (2000). *De-westernizing media studies*. London and New York, NY: Routledge.

Dissanayake, W. (2009). The production of Asian theories of communication: Contexts and challenges. *Asian Journal of Communication, 19*(4): 453–468.

Donald, S. H., Anderson, T. D., & Spry, D. (Eds.) (2010). *Youth, society, and mobile media in Asia*. London and New York, NY: Routledge.

Erni, J. N., & Chua, S. K. (Eds.) (2005). Introduction: Our Asian media studies? In J. N. Erni & S. K. Chua (Eds.), *Asia media studies: Politics of subjectivities* (pp. 1–15). Malden, MA: Blackwell.

Ess, C. (2016). What's "culture" got to do with it? A (personal) review of CATaC (Cultural Attitudes towards Technology and Communication), 1998–2014. In G. Goggin, G., & McLelland, M. (Eds.) (2016). *Routledge companion to global Internet histories*. New York, NY: Routledge.

Goggin, G., & McLelland, M. (Eds.). (2016). *Routledge companion to global Internet histories*. New York: Routledge.

Goggin, G., & McLelland, M. (Eds.) (2009). *Internationalizing Internet studies: Beyond anglophone paradigms.* New York, NY: Routledge.

Goggin, G., McLelland, M., & Yu, H. (2016). Alternative social media histories. In *Sage Handbook of Social Media*, edited by Jean Burgess, Thomas Poell, and Alice Marwick. Los Angeles, CA: Sage, 2016.

Goggin, G., McLelland, M., Yu, H., Lee, K., Takanori, T., Hamada, T., & Albarrán-Torres, C. (2016). *Imagining the web in the Asia Pacific: Regional histories shaping a global technology.* Forthcoming.

Han, S., & Nasir, K. M. (2015). *Digital culture and religion in Asia.* London and New York, NY: Routledge.

Hjorth, L., & Arnold, M. (2013). *Online @ Asia Pacific: Mobile, social, and locative media in the Asia-Pacific.* London and New York, NY: Routledge.

Ho, K. C., Kluver, R., & Yang, C. C. (Eds.) (2003). Asia.com: Asia encounters the Internet. London and New York, NY: Routledge.

Hofstede, G. (1980). *Culture's consequences: International differences in work-related values.* Los Angeles, CA: Sage.

Hofstede, G. (1991). *Cultures and organizations: Software of the mind.* London and New York, NY: McGraw-Hill.

Hofstede, G. (1998). *Masculinity and feminity: The taboo dimension of national cultures.* Thousand Oaks, CA: Sage.

Iwabuchi, K., Muecke, S., & Thomas, M. (Eds.) (2004). *Rogue flows: Trans-Asian cultural traffic.* Hong Kong: University of Hong Kong Press.

Lee, Y.-O. (2016). Tweets in the limelight: The contested relationship between (dis) harmony and newsworthiness. In S. S. Lim & C. Soriano (Eds.), *Asian perspectives on digital culture: Emerging phenomena, enduring concepts* (pp. 135–151). New York, NY: Routledge.

Lim, S.S., & Basynat, I. (2016). Face and online social networking. In S. S. Lim & C. Soriano (Eds.), *Asian perspectives on digital culture: Emerging phenomena, enduring concepts* (pp. 17–32). New York, NY: Routledge.

Lim, S.S., & Soriano, C. (2016). A (digital) giant awakens—Invigorating media studies with Asian perspectives. In S. S. Lim & C. Soriano (Eds.), *Asian perspectives on digital culture: Emerging phenomena, enduring concepts* (pp. 3–14). New York, NY: Routledge.

McLelland, M. (2016). Early computer networks in Japan, 1984–1994. In G. Goggin & M. McLelland (Eds.), *Routledge companion to global internet histories.* New York, NY: Routledge.

Miike, Y. (2006). Non-western theory in Western research? An Asiacentric agenda for Asian communication studies. *Review of Communication*, 6(1–2): 4–31.

Nordenstreng, K., & Thussu, D. (Eds.) (2015). *Mapping BRICS media.* London and New York, NY: Routledge.

Pertierra, R. (Ed.) (2008). *The social construction and usage of communication technologies: Asian and European experiences.* Manilla: University of Philippines Press.

Sinclair, J. (1999). *Latin American television: A global view.* Oxford: Oxford University Press.

Sreekumar, T. T. (2016). Asian modernity and the post human future: Some reflections. In S. S. Lim & C. Soriano (Eds.), *Asian perspectives on digital culture: Emerging phenomena, enduring concepts* (pp. 171–190). New York, NY: Routledge.

Thussu, D. (Ed.) (2009). *Internationalizing media studies.* London and New York, NY: Routledge.

Wang, G. (Ed.) (2011). *De-westernizing communication research: Altering questions and changing frameworks.* London and New York, NY: Routledge.

Glossary

Bayanihan   Taken from the word *bayan*, referring to a nation, town, or community, and connected to the concept of *pakikipagkapwa* (relating to the other), this term underscores a spirit of communal unity or effort to achieve a particular objective. *Bayanihan* pertains to a traditional Filipino practice in which a community of Filipinos helps a neighbor (literally) move a house (then a nipa hut) from one place to another. Although *bayanihan* practiced in the original form has become rare in modern times, the word has come to mean any manifestation of the powerful spirit of communal unity that can make seemingly impossible feats possible through the cooperation of many people working toward a common goal.

The *Bhagavad Gita*   also termed the *Gita*, is a seminal text in Sanskrit of the Hindu ethico-religious system, incorporated in the ancient Indian epic, The *Mahabarata*. It provides a summary of the core beliefs of Brahmanical Hinduism, presenting a synthesis and critique of the varied philosophical concepts and schools of thought. Strongly alleged as an interpolation, it is criticized for its legitimation of the Indian caste system.

Confucianism   is an ancient Chinese philosophy that influences societies in Taiwan, Hong Kong, Macau, Singapore, Vietnam, Korea, and Japan. Confucianism states that if every individual knows his/her role in society, social and political order will prevail. Five principal relationships are at its center: husband and wife, parent and child, older sibling and younger sibling, older friend and younger friend, and ruler and subject. These relationships are regarded as reciprocal, where the former should show benevolence and the latter should show respect. However, Confucianism's strong division between husband and wife (and more generally between male and female members of society) has often been blamed for rigid gender role divisions and male dominance in Confucian societies.

Face   the image of an individual or entity in the eyes of others. 'Face' has particular traction in East Asia, with various iterations noted in countries such as China, Japan, Korea, and Vietnam. Face encompasses three dimensions: (i) self-face: concern for one's own image, where a person gains face by attaining status that is conferred by one's social group or by earning the status through competition and individual effort; (ii) other-face: concern for another individual's image, where you uphold other people's images by displaying affirmation and acquiescent behavior; and (iii) mutual face: concern for the images of both parties and of their relationship, where interested parties collectively give face to one another, so that every member of the social group is subjected to mutual restrictions and possibly coercion. Face can therefore be gained but also lost. Individuals who lose face acquire a bad reputation and loss of respect or prestige and suffer embarrassment or humiliation among the peer group. Loss of face also occurs when people expect group mates to respond to them or their requests in particular ways, but do not find these expectations realized.

Guanxi (关系) a basic but key concept involved in the intricate social ties constituting Chinese culture. *Guan* signifies 'to connect' or 'to close up,' while *xi* denotes 'to tie up' or 'to link.' The combination, *guanxi*, connotes social ties among parties that make up a social network in Chinese society. *Guanxi* has three key characteristics: (i) *guanxi* takes root in familiarity or intimacy and thereby includes not only a utilitarian view of relationship but also *ganqing* (affection, attachment), the rapport of an emotional interpersonal relationship. (ii) *guanxi* involves various degrees of reliability of personal relations and social supports, according to the degree of *guanxi* between people. The sense of reliability, the idea that individuals appeal to and draw strength from others within their *guanxi,* leads to the fact that the individual in society is always considered an entity within a network of *guanxi*, the social ecology of relational interdependence. (iii) *guanxi* carries a norm of reciprocity. It is a mutual obligation for both sides in *guanxi* to respond to requests for assistance. Like 'face,' *guanxi* has particular traction in East Asia, with similar concepts in countries such as Japan (*Aidagara*) and Korea (*In-maek* or *Yeon-jul*).

Harmony notion understood to be at the core of Eastern philosophy, particularly Confucianism. This notion emphasizes the importance of knowing one's place and being attuned to one's surroundings, whether natural or social.

Jeong (also written as *chŏng or cheong*) means a particular state of mind that arises from, and/or facilitates, close emotional links between people closely bonded. In *jeong* relationships, I and You remain inseparable and are integrated into *uri* (we) (See Choi & Choi, 2001).

Kapwa representing one of the core values of Filipino personhood, *kapwa* implies other people connected to a person by virtue of one's awareness of a shared identity. Although *kapwa* is often translated as 'other,' *kapwa* regards other people as closely connected to oneself or even extensions of oneself, while the English term 'other' implies difference and separation from oneself. *Kapwa* therefore implies a moral obligation to treat one another as fellow human beings and therefore equal. Developed from the root word, *kapwa*, the term *pakikipagkapwa* is a verb referring to a collectivistic logic that runs through Philippine society, implying that one's actions (i.e., use of the mobile phone) are conducted in consideration of one's *kapwa*, or in the process of acknowledging someone as *kapwa*.

Lokah samastah sukhino bhavanthu   a popular Sanskrit *sloka* or prayer, whose origin is still debated, that wishes all beings in all worlds live in a state of peaceful happy existence.

Loob   literally, inside. In Filipino cultural psychology, *loob* refers to the person's innermost self. Philosophical perspectives allude to *loob* in characterizing individual agency and volition, which connotes independence from external influence and control. As a ground of moral action in the world, however, *loob* appeals to common humanity and predisposes the individual to relationship and community. In everyday usage the state of one's *loob* bespeaks of the person's over-all character as a person.

Maŭm   (also written as *maeum*) can be translated as 'mind' or 'heart.' In comparison to the English term mind, *maŭm* refers more to an emotional process rather than the rational or cognitive process of consciousness (See Choi & Kim, 2007).

People Power   In Philippine culture, this concept implies bringing down abusive power (i.e., colonizers, dictatorships, corrupt leaders) through the collective effort or power of the masses. This term is salient in the Filipinos' collective memory given important socio-political events in history: the revolutions of the masses during the Spanish, American, and Japanese occupations and during mass mobilizations against Philippine presidents. The term became popular in 1986, when hundreds of thousands of Filipinos gathered on Epifanio delos Santos Avenue (EDSA) to protest the dictatorship of then President Ferdinant Marcos and eventually led to his ouster. Since then, the term 'People Power' has symbolized the reclaiming of Philippine democracy. The role of the mobile phone in the exercise of 'People Power' revolutions was salient in pushing for the resignation of another President, Joseph Estrada, wherein political mobilization was catalyzed by the spread of text messages stating 'Go 2EDSA, Wear Black.' The viral exchange of this text message mobilized tens of thousands to troop again to EDSA, which eventually led to the overthrow of President Estrada.

Sarva loka hitam   A Sanskrit phrase derived from ancient Vedic literatures in India, *sarva* means 'all,' *loka* can mean 'world' or 'all beings,' and *hitam* means 'well-being.' Put together, this concept refers to the well-being of all (stakeholders).

Uri   (also written as *woori*) means the collective of 'we-ness.' In Korean language, *uri* tends to be used as a foundational unit of agency. Thus, in conversations, Koreans tend to say 'our house' to refer to 'my house' (See Han & Choi, 2011).

Ying hun   (影魂) literally 'shadow and soul.' In Chinese expressions, this word conveys the more abstract notion of 'apparition,' in contrast to haunting encounters with ghosts or *gui hun* (鬼魂). *Ying hun* can be used metaphorically and figuratively to refer to the benign essence of the dearly departed. It is also associated with traditional Chinese shadow theater or *Piying* (皮影) 'Skin theater' in China.

Yeonjul   (also written *yŏnjul*) refers to affective linkage, which can be compared to social networks in English. As a relative term, *yeongyeol* is used more neutrally to mean the connections between people, which may thus be more comparable to the English term social network (See Yee, 2000). However, *yeongjul* rather than *yeongyeol* is a culturally specific term, and it is used relatively often in everyday conversation.

Notes on Contributors

Iccha Basnyat is an Assistant Professor of Communication at the National University of Singapore. Her research examines the cultural context of health, structural limitations to health care, health inequalities, and women's experiences at the margins, along with interrogating public health campaigns that aimed at individual behavior change. Her research also examines the use of technology among hard-to-reach, at-risk, and marginalized populations. Her research is rooted in culture and community-based participatory approach. Her work has been published in the journals *Health Communication*, *Health Education & Behavior*, and *Computers in Human Behavior* among others.

Ganga S. Dhanesh is Assistant Professor in Communication Management at the Department of Communications and New Media, National University of Singapore, where she completed her Ph.D. in 2011. She holds a Master's degree in Business Administration from the Cochin University of Science and Technology, India, and has had experience in corporate and non-profit organizations in the fields of employee relations and corporate communication. She has presented her research work at international public relations conferences and has published in the areas of corporate social responsibility and relationship management in journals such as *Public Relations Review* and *Journal of Communication Management*.

Gerard Goggin is Professor of Media and Communications and ARC Future Fellow at the University of Sydney. His books include, with Mark McLelland, the *Routledge Companion to Global Internet Histories* (2016) and *Internationalizing Internet Studies* (2009), and the *Routledge Companion to Mobile Media* (2014, with Larissa Hjorth) and, with Rowan Wilken, *Locative Media* (2015) and *Mobile Technology and Place* (2012). Gerard is currently finishing a collaborative book, provisionally entitled *Asia Pacific Internets*.

Liew Kai Khiun is an Assistant Professor at the Wee Kim Wee School of Information and Communication at the Nanyang Technological University in Singapore. He obtained his B.A. (Hons 2nd Upper) and M.A. at the National University of Singapore and was awarded his doctorate from the Wellcome Trust Centre for the History of Medicine at University College London in 2007. Upon completing his doctorate, he served at the National University of Singapore between 2007 and 2009 as a Post-doctoral Fellow at the Cultural Studies Cluster of the Asia Research Institute and a Visiting Fellow teaching Popular Culture at the Department of Sociology.

Yeon-Ok (Yenn) Lee holds a PhD in Politics from Royal Holloway, University of London. Her research interests centre on digitally mediated politics and activism, with expertise in the Asia–Pacific region. She is Doctoral Training Advisor at the School of Oriental and African Studies (SOAS), University of London, and a member of the Centre of Korean Studies at the same institution. She is also an adjunct faculty member of the Research School of Social Sciences at the Australian National University and serves as an associate editor for the *Journal of Contemporary Eastern Asia.*

Sun Sun Lim holds a Ph.D. in Media and Communications from the London School of Economics. She is an Associate Professor at the Department of Communications and New Media and Assistant Dean for Research at the Faculty of Arts and Social Sciences, National University of Singapore. She studies technology domestication by young people and families, charting the ethnographies of their internet and mobile phone use, publishing more than 50 monographs, journal articles, and book chapters. Her recent research has focused attention on understudied and marginalized populations including juvenile delinquents, youths-at-risk, and migrant workers. Her latest book *Mobile Communication and the Family: Asian Experiences in Technology Domestication* (Springer, 2016) focuses on the social implications of mobile communication for familial relationships. She serves on the editorial boards of the *Journal of Computer Mediated Communication, Journal of Children and Media, Communication, Culture & Critique,* and *Mobile Media & Communication.*

Jun Liu is an Assistant Professor at the Department of Media, Cognition and Communication at the University of Copenhagen, Denmark. His research covers the interrelationships among media, culture, and politics with particular attention to the importance of new media in China. He has articles published in *Modern Asian Studies, Television & New Media,* and *China Perspectives.*

Michael Prieler is an Associate Professor at the School of Communication at Hallym University, South Korea. He has worked and studied for more than 10 years in Japan and South Korea. His research focuses on media representations of gender, race/ethnicity, and age in Japan, South Korea, China, the Philippines, and the United States. He has published on these areas in books and in a variety of international journals.

Manuel Victor J. Sapitula obtained his Ph.D. in Sociology at the National University of Singapore (NUS) and is currently Associate Professor and Chair at the Department of Sociology, University of the Philippines Diliman (UPD). His research interests are in the field of religion and society in the Philippines and Southeast Asia. He has published on Christian churches and organizations, Marian piety, religious pluralism, and traditionalist Catholicism in the Philippines.

Cheryll Ruth R. Soriano is an Associate Professor of Communication at the De La Salle University, Philippines. She is interested in the social and political implications of new media, and much of her research has explored the politics and dialectical tensions involved in new technology mediations of activists and users from the margins. She also conducted research on mediatization of rituals, mobile advertisements and gender ideologies, technology and consumer culture, and ICTs and rural livelihoods. Her recent works appear in the journals *Media, Culture & Society*; *Communication, Culture & Critique*; *Telematics and Information; and Journal of Creative Communications,* among others, as well as in edited volumes. Cheryll obtained her Ph.D. in Communications and New Media from the National University of Singapore.

T. T. Sreekumar is Professor and Chair of Digital Communication at MICA, The School of Ideas, India. He is the author of the book *ICTs & Development in India: Perspectives on the Rural Network Society* (Anthem Books, London, 2011). His work has been published in the journals *Information Society, Media Culture and Society, Science Technology and Society, Third World Quarterly, Journal of Contemporary Asia* and *International Journal of Technology Management* among others. His research interests include new media and technoculture, the impact of the Internet in developing countries, mobile communications, civil society in South Asia, religion and new media, and global civil society and new social movements. He is the editor of the *Journal of Creative Communications (Sage)* and serves as member on the board of editors of several other publications.

Kyong Yoon is an Assistant Professor in Cultural Studies at the University of British Columbia Okanagan, Canada. His research interests are transnational mobility, digital mobile communication, and transnational media audience. His recent research project concerns Korean immigrants' use of new media in Canada.

Index